THIS HOUSE WILL DIVIDE

A History of the
Northern Ireland Parliament
1921-1972

Copyright © 2018 Emmet Doyle

All rights reserved.

ISBN: 1973850133

ISBN-13: 97819738501370

All images used under creative commons licensing or from public records.

CONTENTS

Preface	5
Context	9
1920-1928: Commencement	22
1928-1938: Consolidation	92
1938-1965: Fragmentation	128
1965-1972: Endgame	191
Conclusions	229
NI Parliamentary election results	231
Endnotes	237
Bibliography	242

Acknowledgements

This book is dedicated to Mr Shaun McLaughlin and Ms Anne Hutton, both former teachers at St Joseph's Boys' School in Derry without whom I would never have had the opportunities I have enjoyed. They continue to inspire me and I know that their dedication and ethos of support and hard work has had an impact on others' lives, they are owed a huge debt by many generations in Derry.

I would like to acknowledge the Deputy Keeper of Records at the Public Records Office, and both the staff at PRONI and at Parliament Buildings for lending their time and expertise to this book. I would also like to acknowledge my friends and family for allowing me the time to research and complete the work.

I especially want to thank Mr Pat Ramsey, former Social Democratic and Labour Party Assembly Member for Foyle without whom I could not have fostered such a deep interest in the legislature Mr Sammy Morrison for his gracious assistance with photos.

Preface

The basis for the idea of writing this book was twofold. Primarily, as a Nationalist born in the 1980's and being from Derry, 'Stormont' was a focus as to why the conflict had begun in Northern Ireland. For generations before me, it was a manifestation of inequality, misrule and hatred.

The legacy of housing and employment neglect in my own city is apparent in our local history, yet many of my own generation have forgotten the story of the Stormont Parliament, its decisions and the physical and political chaos left in its wake.

Secondly, I found myself with a unique opportunity several years ago when I began work as a Parliamentary Adviser in the very building at which so much ire was directed. I always felt personally that I was there to serve the people in my own city and across the North, yet cognisant of the fact that the trappings of the old, discredited Parliament surrounded me.

The utilisation of an old Parliament building for a new political Assembly posed a unique mix. It had the opportunity to create change outside its hallowed halls yet could never escape the perceptions that the shell in which it lived brought with it.

I wanted to explore the history of the old Parliament from birth to death, analyse its successes, its failures and the ethnopolitical construct it became. A Parliament with so little checks and balances yet a functioning Executive. An Executive whose main opposition lived in the hearts of minds of thousands of its own citizens and a judiciary appointed from amongst the ranks of its own Parliamentarians.

At the very heart of my personal focus in writing this book is to manifest a bastion against revisionism. For far too long the story of the beginning of our conflict and its constituent parts has been mired in opportunistic revisionism. This can only ever be a negative and may make difficult the reading of this work for those who seek to engage in the practice.

Our collective history is full of narratives relevant to different sections of the community, however what must never become part of those narratives is unfounded caricature of an institution, its outworking's and those leading it. Our history will only become owned by us all if we can be confident of the facts, for good or ill.

It was nigh on impossible to complete this book without addressing the obvious key tenets of our commentary on this time in our history – violence, gerrymandering, housing and employment.

I had not envisaged that these issues would encroach on the overall nature of the book, at least outside of commentary on legislation. All of these and more are included, but also those things which, because of the key issues focussed on as part of our political history – do not get a fair hearing such as transport reform, achievements on unemployment insurance and the ability of those behind the stone pillars to win concessions for Ulster on the back of either British or Irish government détente.

When we also look on discrimination in the Northern state underpinned by the Stormont Parliament, we, Nationalists at least, imagine Derry or Caledon, and that the discrimination was directed solely at those in our community. That was not the case, yet it has become an accepted feature of our past.

Strangely, one of the manifestations of the old Parliament is the not very sexy realm of transport reform. When one thinks of Stormont, public transport is not usually the first thing that comes to mind, yet for all the changes resulting from the last twenty years, that work undertaken in Parliament Buildings lives on today, and so it stood out, at least to me.

What this book is not, is a social commentary nor is it an attempt to revisit the fantastic works of Bew, Arthur and those eminent academics on the mechanics of our politics. What it is, is an opportunity to indulge in the profile of a legislature, its practices and its personalities. The work undertaken inside the marbled walls of Parliament Buildings, or in the Library of the Union Theological College had implications for many sections of our society, little of which becomes part of the story we recognise today. It is an opportunity to learn more about the forgotten parliament and perhaps fill gaps in its role in our history.
It is evident in looking at the phases of the Northern Ireland state and its leaders that we too, now, have repeated some of the mistakes that characterised it.

In Craig, we have the state builder, the Unionist strongman that will stand firm against the Sinn Fein threat to the South and enhance the relationship with London to secure Northern Ireland's place within the Empire. In building the apparatus of the state and forming its characteristics as a Protestant enclave, he abandoned the principles set out in the vision of the

King in his first speech to Parliament. There would be no reconciliation, there was no security in that, only in solidifying the loyal against the disloyal.

Andrews held on only to the principle of the loyal and the disloyal, without any semblance of progress. Maintenance was the order of the day and without his talented cabinet colleagues particularly in Finance, his tenure would have been without accomplishment.

Brookeborough brought to his office the same penchant as Craig. An aristocrat with strong links to those in the know in London, he was the creator of the policy of seeking subvention without intervention. At home, he oversaw a part-time cabinet that merely reacted to many social issues and adopted a stance of watching the Imperial Parliament for direction. Unable to even countenance what it meant to be unemployed or faced with crushing poverty, it was the age of the aloof.

His downfall came because of his inability to recognise the end of the something for nothing attitude at Westminster, and in humiliating fashion because of the dismissive attitude of his aristocratic colleague Glentoran, and the Hall Report.

His loss was O'Neill's gain. At times naïve, the country gentleman should be credited with being able to create a balance in the province like none of his predecessors – of economics and cohesion. However, having ploughed this furrow, he forgot the staple of the government which he led, the ability to secure the loyalty of one's own.

Chichester-Clark became the man without a chair at the end of the game of Unionist musical chairs and became Prime Minister to rekindle the warm feeling felt by some Unionist MPs about the 'good old days' of hegemony and safety in Stormont.

Faulkner became the Prime Minister with the memory lapse. He seemingly forgot the attitude of the Government in London from the time of O'Neill in demanding serious reform of the state and sought to engage antiquated methods underpinned by antiquated views. His inability, if not disregard for the new dispensation in London, Dublin and in the hearts and minds of those who rebuked his rule led to him fulfilling the biggest fear Unionist had, the loss of their power and status in a state created for them.

Of course, it would be remiss of me to neglect the slowly simmering power of the Labour movement throughout the period covered in this book. It swept aside Unionists and triumphed in Belfast when working class communities refused to eat the cake being offered by Stormont's tired monoliths. It is in this record we truly put the mistakes we have all made since 1972 into perspective. Unity, liberalism and idealism were the challenges set by many voters across the community spectrum in this state, and yet left both Nationalists and Unionist parties bereft in many ways.

Far from being a rallying call to the support of labour values, it is however important to acknowledge that when speaking about the 'old Stormont' we remember that some stood alone for the betterment of all, and perhaps if we tried harder to espouse that principle today, we might all be closer to the vision of a place worthy of our children.

All life is a transaction, we trade the can for the cannot and vice versa, but one thing that should always remain true is our history, for good or ill.

Context

On three occasions the issue of 'Home Rule' – the maintenance of Irish affairs in a local legislature with control over Irish affairs under the Imperial Parliament, had plagued Westminster and the loyal Unionists not just in Ulster, but throughout the Union.

The first two attempts to legislate for Home Rule in Ireland in 1886 and 1893, had failed with the House of Lords' refusal to pass the Bills.

The constitutional crisis brought about by a Tory-led House of Lords' failure to pass Lloyd George's 'People's Budget' in 1909 gave Home Rule an opportunity and energy other legislative concerns could only dream of. The People's Budget as it was coined by the Liberals, sought to raise taxes on the rich to pay for welfare services and was vehemently opposed by the Tories.

A threat from Liberal Prime Minister H.H. Asquith to petition the King into creating hundreds of Liberal peers, dismantling the Tory majority and its veto, brought the issue to a head with two general elections held in January and December. The poll in January returned a two-seat Liberal victory over the Tories.

The December result left the Liberals one seat behind the Tories and increasingly reliant on the Irish Parliamentary Party to command a majority in the House of Commons and administer a Government.

The passing of the Parliament Act in 1911 removed the power of the Lords to reject outright money bills and other public bills sent to it from the Commons following a third attempt in one Parliament.

The bill proposed a Home Rule Parliament in Dublin, whilst still sending Irish MPs to Westminster, albeit a drastically reduced number. The Dublin Castle machinery would be dismantled, to be replaced by a Lord Lieutenant who would represent the Crown in Ireland.

1904

Opposition to the idea of Home Rule had naturally attracted the leadership of the Unionists in Ulster who would be affected most by its implementation. In September 1904, Sir Anthony MacDonnell, the most senior civil servant in Ireland proposed a 'middle way' – effectively a devolved parliament that would improve the administration of the country – it was completely rejected by Unionists.

Following this interjection, Unionist MPs met in October 22nd, 1904 in the Central Hall, Belfast to place unionism on a 'war footing'. It was at this meeting that the idea of a co-ordinating body to oversee opposition to Home Rule was formulated, and a second meeting was to be held in March 1905.

1905

The Ulster Unionist Council was formed on March 3, 1905 in the Ulster Minor Hall presided over by Colonel James McCalmont. A motion proposed by Sir Daniel Dixon was passed:

"That an Ulster Unionist Council be formed, and that its objects shall be to form an Ulster union for bringing into line all local unionist associations in the province of Ulster with a view to consistent and continuous political action…"

The Duke of Abercorn served as the body's President. He was a well-known political Unionist and was Grand Master of the Orange Order from 1886 until his death in 1913. In order to solidify and give strategic direction to the unionist masses, it was agreed at the first meeting of the Council that members would 'subordinate all minor differences to the all-important question of the maintenance of the Union'.

1910

The UUC was bolstered by the input of the Orange Order. The Grand Lodge of Ireland, of which Cols McCalmont and Saunderson were Deputy

Grand Masters pledged on December 7th, 1910 'that the Grand Lodge of Ireland give every assistance to the subcommittee for practical purposes, recently formed by the Ulster Unionist Council'.

The Order also had fifty members on the Council and continued to play a key role in its machinations until recent times.

"The extent to which the Order had been built into the Unionist Party structure from the earliest times effectively ensured that it remained ultimately loyal to the government."[1]

1912

Protestant Churches also gave their input into the Home Rule debacle. A Special General Synod of the Church of Ireland on 16th April 1912 was summoned 'for the purpose of taking counsel as to the present crisis in its relation to the welfare and responsibilities of the Church'. The Church's Primate stated that "over one million Protestants regard the prospect of Home Rule as disastrous to Ireland".

The Church also passed resolutions at the Synod against Home Rule and went as far as to prepare for a petition proposed by Col C. G. Tottenham. Both the input of the Orange institution and the churches further strengthened the hand of political unionism and awakened public anger towards the proposals which London could not ignore.

As a means of showing the Government the scale of opposition in Ulster to Home Rule, a mass march was held in April 1912 attended by over 200,000 people.

This was to be followed by the signing of a 'covenant' inspired by the Scottish Covenanters that would give the public the opportunity to define their anger and force the Government into abiding by the will of the people who did not want Home Rule in Ulster.

A public 'Solemn League and Covenant' was produced by Sir Edward Carson, a Dublin barrister and leader of the anti-Home Rule lobby in Parliament as Leader of the Irish Unionist Parliamentary Party and James Craig, appealing to all Ulster unionists to reject the provisions of Home Rule in opposition to the Government.

Almost half a million men and women signed the Covenant on 'Ulster Day', 28th September 1912, setting Ulster Protestants on a collision course with not only the British Government, but with most of the Catholic population in Ireland. The UUC had pledged itself to the Covenant on the 23rd September.

The Covenant read;

BEING CONVINCED in our consciences that Home Rule would be disastrous to the material well-being of Ulster as well as of the whole of Ireland, subversive of our civil and religious freedom, destructive of our citizenship, and perilous to the unity of the Empire, we, whose names are underwritten, men of Ulster, loyal subjects of His Gracious Majesty King George V., humbly relying on the God whom our fathers in days of stress and trial confidently trusted, do hereby pledge ourselves in solemn Covenant, throughout this our time of threatened calamity, to stand by one another in defending, for ourselves and our children, our cherished position of equal citizenship in the United Kingdom, and in using all means which may be found necessary to defeat the present conspiracy to set up a Home Rule Parliament in Ireland. And in the event of such a Parliament being forced upon us, we further solemnly and mutually pledge ourselves to refuse to recognise its authority. In sure confidence that God will defend the right, we hereto subscribe our names.
And further, we individually declare that we have not already signed this Covenant.

1913

Throughout the painstaking process, the potential of Home – or 'Rome' Rule was watched by a Unionist people in Ulster in horror.

In 1885 the Grand Lodge of Ireland sought volunteers to defend against the first Home Rule Bill, which ebbed away following its defeat, only to be revived again during November 1910 to defend against the second Bill.

The political ramifications for Home Rule, if it was not already transparent, became clear on 9th April 1912, when political leaders including Tory leader Bonar Law took the salute of thousands of loyalist volunteers who marched from Belfast to Balmoral.

It was not until January 1913 that the Ulster Unionist Council formally organised the volunteers into the Ulster Volunteer Force, comprising a maximum of 100,000 members all of whom had to have signed the Solemn League and Covenant. Lieutenant General Sir George Richardson was appointed Officer Commanding in August 1913.

The Royal Irish Constabulary had reported by January 1914 that the force numbered 80,000.

On 6th December 1913 the Government took the drastic step of banning the import of arms to Ireland, such was their concern about the potential for civil war over the issue of Home Rule. This angered many Nationalists, given that the Irish Volunteers had been formed the only weeks previously at a meeting of the Rotunda in Dublin with the aim of securing and defending Home Rule.

1914

June 1914 saw the beginning of a split that would decimate the Irish Volunteers. Irish Parliamentary Party leader John Redmond, unable to countenance a force of such numbers in Ireland that he could not control, demanded appointment of members to the provisional committee to seize power over the Volunteers.

By July 1914 it had 180,000 members whose aim was to 'secure and maintain the rights and liberties common to all the people of Ireland'. Its members were drawn from the Gaelic League, the Ancient Order of Hibernians and Sinn Fein.

In August of that year, Redmond again pushed the leadership of the Volunteers to a split by promising Westminster that she could pull troops from Ireland and that the Volunteers would defend Ireland for the Empire during the war, such was his ambition to see the Home Rule Bill become law.

The impasse in Parliament over Home Rule gave rise to several novel ideas out of the quandary – for example a letter that appeared in a prominent newspaper in February 1914 by Sir Horace Plunkett raised the idea that Ulster would be part of a Home Rule Parliament, but that they could leave if "after a fair trial, they find it impracticable".

The Government seized on this as a real practical idea that might defuse the ever-growing crisis.

Edward Carson made a speech on 11th Feb 1914 outlining the outright resistance of Ulster to the provisions of Home Rule, and the fact that Ulster was prepared to resist.

"If these men are not morally justified when they are attempted to be driven out of one Government with which they are satisfied, and put under one which they loathe, I do not see how resistance ever can be justified in history at all".

Five days later, David Lloyd George proposed a paper to the British Cabinet that would allow for every county in Ireland to hold a referendum on whether to be ruled from a Home Rule Parliament.

If a county was to vote against the proposal, they would be excluded from Home Rule for a period that would run until the next election – the outworking being, if Liberals won the next election, they would be able to fully implement the Home Rule project, and if not, the twenty-eight counties he believed would vote to be ruled by Dublin, would have already established a Home Rule system that could not be easily dismantled.

Monday 20th February 1914 saw a letter written by John Redmond to the Prime Minister outlining support for a form of the Plunkett and Lloyd George proposals – a major departure from a long-standing principle that would reject any form of Home Rule that did not extend the length and breadth of the island.

At the Second Reading of the Bill on 9th March, the Prime Minister delivered a change to the terms agreed by Redmond – rather than an exclusion period for any county that voted to remain outside Home Rule lasting only until the next election; this was now to be for six years. Unionists led by Carson sensed that the resolve of the Government on exclusion for Ulster was weakening, and Carson continued to push for permanent exclusion.

On 20th March of 1914, the crisis reached the very corridors of Downing Street when officers at the Curragh Barracks in County Kildare resigned their commissions rather than acknowledge using force to subdue the Ulster Volunteer Force in order to implement Home Rule. The orders from Irish Command were preventative, to secure munitions in areas across the North to stop UVF weapons raids but it was felt by those officers that this was a precursor to active engagement – many of them had some connection to Ulster, and were supporters of the Conservative Party, who took full advantage of the event.

General Sir Arthur Paget, Commander of Crown Forces in Ireland at the time, communicated the resignations to the War Office in London, ending his telegram with 'Fear men will not move'.

Known as the 'Curragh Mutiny', this event was a watershed moment and convinced the British Government of the need for a re-think of Home Rule legislation in Ireland.

Little rest was to come, as on the night of 24th April, the Ulster Volunteer Force sealed off the town of Larne without resistance. Their aim – to land arms that would demonstrate to the Government Ulster's determination to fight if necessary to preserve Ulster and destroy Home Rule.

A total of three million rounds of ammunition and many thousands of rifles were landed, much to the dismay of the Government in London – all endorsed by Edward Carson months before.

Under pressure from Nationalists, the Prime Minister told the House of Commons that the 1914 Bill would be passed unblemished, but that an amending Bill would be passed alongside, granting Ulster's six-year exclusion from Home Rule. The Home Rule Bill finally passed the Lords on 15 May 1914 with the exclusion Bill introduced six weeks later.

Following the decisive mutiny at the Curragh and the Larne gun-running operation, the King became increasingly concerned that civil war in Ireland was a real possibility, and pressed Asquith for a solution. On 21st July, a conference of all Irish leaders took place in Buckingham Palace to avert war and seek to finally resolve the Irish question.

In attendance were the Prime Minister, John Redmond, John Dillon, Edward Carson, Bonar Law, James Craig and Lord Lansdowne.

The conference failed to address key questions, such as the areas to exclude and the timeframe for exclusion, and the counties of Tyrone and Fermanagh being treated inside or outside of an exclusion zone became a major sticking point, with neither Carson nor Redmond willing to concede.

Carson was of the belief that a gesture of this magnitude by allowing Tyrone and Fermanagh to be part of any excluded zone would increase trust and make it more acceptable for Ulster to come under Home Rule in a 'reasonable time'. When this was rejected, it solidified his view that a 'clean cut' of six counties of Ulster must be permanently excluded from Home Rule.

The Irish Volunteers attempted to mirror the success of their counterparts in Ulster by landing weapons in Howth, county Dublin in July. This event was to be more of a propaganda victory than that of the UVF's – happening in plain sight during the day.

Former diplomat Roger Casement and other senior members of the Irish Volunteers arranged to land ammunition and arms in Howth to counter the Larne landing. Bought from Germany, had this been only a short time later, it would have constituted assisting the enemy.

Casement's yacht, the Asgard, brought 45,000 rounds of ammunition and 1,500 rifles ashore on 26th July, which was then transported into Dublin by road. Unlike in Larne, where the authorities were either caught off guard or colluded with the UVF in the operation depending on your point of view, the Howth landing was set upon by the Dublin Metropolitan Police, with backup from troops sent from Dublin.

When unrest broke out between supporters of the Volunteers and the army, the latter opened fire killing three and wounding others, souring the engagement at Buckingham Palace.

The significance the action compared to Larne and the treatment of the UVF was not lost on Nationalists. The ranks of the Volunteers swelled and the parliamentary debacle over Home Rule now had to partner it the sight of two well-armed opposing forces in Ireland whose actions depended on the resolution of the Irish question.

On 4th August, Britain declared war on Germany who had invaded Belgium, Britain being sworn to protect the neutrality of the northern European state.

Little over a month later on 20th September 1914, Redmond gave a speech at Woodenbridge, Co Wicklow that would further test the resolve of Nationalists who wanted Home Rule.

Precipitating a final split in the Irish Volunteers, Redmond called for them to join the British Army and fight on the Western Front – he believed this would heal the division between Nationalists and Unionists in Ireland. Instead, it would begin a catalogue of events that would lead to the demise of Redmond and his Party.

Most of the Volunteers heeded Redmond's call and became the National Volunteers, the remaining 13,500 stayed under the leadership of Eoin MacNeill and secret members of the IRB, keeping the name Irish Volunteers, ready to play their part in the 1916 Easter Rising.

1915

In May 1915, Prime Minister Asquith was forced to form a wartime coalition government with the Unionists and Labour following the Shell Crisis and the slaughter at Gallipoli. The Cabinet consisted on 12 Liberals, 8 Unionists and 1 Labour Minister.

The Government only lasted until December 1916, when Asquith was replaced as Liberal Prime Minister by the 'Welsh Wizard', David Lloyd George who was only too aware of the Irish situation.

1916

In Ireland, the Irish Republican Brotherhood had sought to capitalise on their mantra that 'England's difficulty is Ireland's opportunity' and began a rebellion in Dublin at Easter in 1916 alongside James Connolly's Irish Citizens Army.

Key sites in Dublin such as the General Post Office and Boland's Mill would be seized by the rebels, who were unable to capture Dublin Castle, the centre of British Administration in Ireland.

Whilst this event captured the imagination of many Nationalists in Ireland, it caused great anger in Britain who saw the action as a distraction from the war effort.

It was only when the rebellion was crushed, and the ringleaders were executed, did sentiment across Ireland turn against the British, who had used a gunship in the Liffey to pound rebel positions in the city centre, which now lay in ruins.

The rebellion did not spread as the leaders had hoped, and was situated largely in Dublin, which some minor skirmishes elsewhere. Whilst much has been written of the importance of the Rising, it is important to document here as the moment when the long-held demand for Home Rule began to change to full independence from Britain.

In Europe, the men of Ulster and the rest of Ireland fought side by side in the British Expeditionary Force at the Somme. The 36th Ulster Division was formed from the UVF and the 16th Irish Division created from Redmond's National Volunteers following his Woodenbridge speech.

The 16th Irish Division became prominent in the capture of Guillemont and Ginchy in September 1916, suffering over 4,000 casualties. At the Battle of the Somme, 1st July 1916, the 36th Ulster Division were to capture a German redoubt but in a single day, lost nearly 5,000 men. Both divisions fought side by side at the Battle of Messines, and suffered heavy casualties and by mid-August, both divisions had lost almost 50% of their number.

The sacrifice made particularly by the Ulster division was widely regarded at home as a show of commitment to the Union and remains a key piece of Ulster's heritage – with their anniversary at the Somme falling on the same day as the Battle of the Boyne. However, when the Irish division veterans returned home, to an Ireland turned upside down, they were reviled and treated as untouchables.

1917

The death of Irish Parliamentary Party MP James Joseph O'Kelly on 20th December 1916 triggered a by-election for his North-Roscommon seat. Standing against the IPP candidate Thomas Devine was Sinn Fein's George Noble Plunkett, father of Joseph who was executed for his role in the Easter rebellion – it was the first time that Sinn Fein had successfully challenged the IPP electorally, winning a majority of 1,314 and setting the scene for the 1918 General Election.

In June 1917, the Government called the Irish Convention, an assembly of Irish politicians and stakeholders to agree a form of government for Ireland in a dramatically changed political environment.

Asquith informed the House of Commons on 25th May 1916:

"At the unanimous request of his colleagues my right hon. Friend who sits beside me, the Minister of Munitions (Mr. Lloyd George), has undertaken to devote his time and his energies and his power to the promotion of that result. He has already put himself in communication with the authorised representatives and exponents of the views of the different Irish parties. And if there be, as I believe there is—I do not underrate the difficulties in the least degree—if there be, as I believe there is, among Irishmen, no less than among the people of Great Britain, an honest and resolute desire to take advantage of this opportunity for the obtainment of that which, to us as a nation and an Empire I do not hesitate to say is the greatest boon that could possibly be achieved, I cannot but hope that my right hon. Friend in his mission of peace and reconciliation and of possible unity will not only carry with it the good wishes, the ardent hopes, of all Members in every quarter of this House, but something more—I believe that such a result can and ought to be attained."

In June, the Ulster Unionist Council approved Unionist participation in the Convention. During the convention, issues such as customs and excise were discussed, and representatives of Unionism in the other three Irish provinces were present – and who refused any semblance of partition.

The Third Home Rule Act was still on the statute books, with a temporary exclusion for Ulster agreed with Nationalists. However, as was his way, Lloyd George had secretly promised Carson permanent exclusion to conclude the talks and set the parties on a road to agreement.

A document entitled 'Headings of a Settlement as to the Government of Ireland' was circulated by the cabinet and exposed the duality of Lloyd George's negotiations. It fatally wounded the IPP and John Redmond's credibility at home, which led to the rise of Sinn Fein.

1918

On 6th March, John Redmond died in London, to be replaced as leader of Nationalism at the Convention by Stephen Gwynn. The issue of Unionist safeguards in a future Irish Parliament, fiscal powers and federal government in Ireland were the main sticking points but were all but agreed in the final report sent to Downing Street.

However, events in Europe overtook the discussion as on 21st March, the German's Spring Offensive had created a massive manpower shortage in the British Army. To redress this, Lloyd George created a 'dual policy' – he would grant Home Rule but also introduce conscription – a highly controversial issue in Ireland.

Irish politicians echoed the view of the Irish people that conscription could not be implemented in Ireland and Home Rule supporters and Sinn Fein members alike joined together to vehemently oppose it, calling a general strike on 23rd April.

The 'Conscription Crisis' as it became known, also affected the electoral fortunes of the IPP further, when Arthur Griffith, founder of Sinn Fein, defeated the IPP candidate in East Cavan.

In April, a committee was created by the cabinet under the leadership of Walter Long, a well-established Unionist, to draft provisions for Home Rule after the Convention.

In November, the war ended with the Armistice signed on the 11th. This precipitated the focus of the Government on the Peace Conference rather than on Ireland, leaving this instead to Long's Committee.

The general election of December 1918 was the final nail in the coffin for the Irish Parliamentary Party, having lost 61 seats to Sinn Fein, a total wipe-out winning only 6 seats to its previous 67.

This electoral rout changed the dynamics again in Ireland, with the Unionists in Ulster seeing a more radical Sinn Fein now speak for most of the Irish people, and a clear Unionist electoral victory in Ulster's seats.

1919

Sinn Fein's abstentionist policy meant the Irish Nationalist voice in Westminster fell silent, and their focus turned to establishing the First Dáil which first met on 21 January 1919. The gathering in the Mansion House by Sinn Fein MP's adopted a Declaration of Independence from Britain and on the same day, the Soloheadbeg ambush took place which began the Irish War of Independence and cost the lives of two RIC policemen.

1920

Walter Long's committee had created what was now a Fourth Home Rule Bill, which would create two unicameral parliaments in Ireland, and partition the country, with Northern Ireland to comprise of all Ulster counties excluding Donegal, Monaghan and Cavan, and the rest called Southern Ireland.

The Bill was opposed by Nationalists and Southern Unionists in the House of Commons and some Ulster Unionists who wanted all of Ulster to be excluded. It became law on 23 December 1920 as the Government of Ireland Act.

Thomas Harbison, MP for Tyrone North East summed up the position of Nationalists;

"In supporting the rejection of this Bill, I would like to say that so far as I can understand from the speeches on the Government side of the House, that there has been nothing of reality about the whole performance. It is a case of make-believe. The right hon. Gentleman, the Chief Secretary, introduced the Bill, the title of which is "A Bill for the Better Government of Ireland." I could change that title and make it more appropriate by altering one letter, when it would read, "A Bill for the Bitter Government of Ireland." For the last 40 years the party to which I belong has come here to try to find a way of knitting together in one solid bond of friendship the two peoples. Up to the present we have failed, for reasons that I need not now go into. The Bill, however, which is produced here to-day, is a Bill not to create friendship but to create discord, and that not only between England and Ireland but between Irishmen and Irishmen."[2]

A Lord Lieutenant would be shared by both Parliaments, and a Council of Ireland would be created to co-ordinate matters of mutual concern.

1

1920-1928: Commencement

A fragile mix of economic depression, intercommunal mistrust and political fervour gave rise to a bitter element of strife amongst the Catholics and Protestants in the new Northern Ireland even before Long's Committee had reported and a new Home Rule Bill passed.

One of the first and arguably the primary litmus tests for the programme of partition was the splitting of the Irish civil service to serve the new states.

"The 1920 Government of Ireland Act divided the Irish administration in ways never previously proposed. Originally the legislation proposed that the Irish departments would be divided north and south with sections that could not be partitioned allocated to the Council of Ireland, thus being shared between north and south. By the final stages of the Bill, under pressure from the Ulster Unionists, a 'clean cut' between north and south was envisaged with the Council of Ireland acting as a potential vehicle for future unity."[3]

Because of the political machinations, the Irish administration would have to be totally divided north and south. Civil servants operating in Northern Ireland and managing northern public services when the Act came into force remained with that new administration, as was the same in the new Southern Ireland.

Any civil servants outside of this cohort were put under the jurisdiction of the Civil Service Committee created by the Act which would determine which area they would work in.

Primarily, civil servants were asked to determine which jurisdiction they wished to serve in. Many civil servants in the South were from or had family connections in Ulster, and so transferred North, and vice versa.

This was also true of English officers in Ireland and Irish officers in England. Both were given the opportunity of transferring. Senior officials wished as much as possible to fill the ranks of the two respective civil services with those who had opted to work in the jurisdiction.

Ernest Clark, an evangelical Protestant and former preacher and senior official in the Irish office that would oversee the creation of Northern Ireland was a close confidant of James Craig and despite being a civil servant who should naturally take his orders from Dublin Castle, he deferred to Craig on many issues.

Clark had started in the civil service at age 17. He was posted to Cape Town in 1904 to establish new income tax system by the Colonial Service and luckily for his future employers, had worked with Lord Colwyn in 1919.

He became Assistant Under Secretary for Ireland in September 1920 following lobbying for the creation of a position in Belfast by Northern Ireland Parliamentarians.

"Months before the elections under the 1920 Act to establish the new Irish governments, Craig and Clark worked together to create an administrative apparatus for Belfast that would have written across it, as Craig urged Clark to write across his own chest, ULSTER!"[4]

Both men set about establishing Ministries and then formulating their required civil service support. Adam Duffin of the Belfast Chamber of Commerce leant his input to the number and responsibilities of Ministries, and even discussed possible Ministers – far from the planned evolution in the mind of the Dublin Castle officials.

He had suggested eight Ministries, but Clark and Craig settled on seven.

Whitley Councils, known in modern times as Joint Consultative Groups where management and staff met together to determine pay and conditions were utilised by the Castle in sticking to the plan under the 1920 Act to allocate those officials to the administration they wished to be transferred to.

However, Craig and Clark believed despite the clear roadmap set out in the Act, and the longstanding processes of the civil service for transferring staff, managing pay and conditions and following the letter of the law, that they should act in the best interests of the new administration and move ahead at pace with recruiting officials.

"The determination of Craig and Clark to push ahead with staffing the Belfast departments in advance of elections and the creation of the Civil Service Committee fatally undermined Anderson's [Under-Secretary] strategy. In this determination Craig and Clark had the support of the Lloyd George cabinet."[5]

Indeed, both men started to look outside the processes envisaged by the Act to fill positions almost immediately, as there was a suspicion, mutual it turned out, that the southern administration would seek to retain the cream of the service.

Sir John Anderson gave Clark the opportunity to hire from within the Irish administration men to act as principals for the new Belfast departments, believing that this would become redundant when the Civil Service Committee met and made their legally binding decisions as to allocations.

"In fact, Craig and Clark were already filling the key posts with Ulstermen such as Sam Watt with his well-known anti-Catholic views, Gordon from

DATI, Dale and Litchfield from the British service, Magill and Duggan from Dublin and W.D. Scott from the Treasury."[6]

It is at this juncture that we can see the political ramifications of allowing both men to hand pick officials for the new state. The senior officials in Dublin insisted that such recruitment would follow the same processes as the trawl throughout the service.

"Clark staffed his own office first, recruiting officers from London such as Scott from the Treasury, but also choosing men of Ulster Protestant background like Captain Petherick, a war veteran who had served in the Inniskilling Fusiliers. In this initial recruitment to the senior ranks of the nascent northern civil service preference was given to firstly, men of Ulster Protestant background, secondly Englishmen who were presumed to be sympathetic to an Ulster Protestant state, and lastly, other Protestant Irishmen. The northern state-builders saw Northern Ireland primarily in sectarian rather than territorial terms' 'Ulster' meant 'Protestant'."[7]

This would inevitably create an inextricable link between the political ideology of those leading and those serving, resulting in the corruption of the civil service and creating a state that would have no interest in acting equitably for the benefit of all its inhabitants, and more importantly, in civil service speak – it set a precedent that would then go unchallenged.

In April the organisation representing executive officers in the civil service wrote to Craig seeking assurances that standard processes for recruitment and remuneration would be followed as outlined in the overall partition strategy for the administration – they received no such assurances.

The debacle over the establishment of an administration fit for purpose rumbled on until after the inaugural election.

In July 1920, following an incendiary speech by Edward Carson on the Twelfth celebrations and bitter editorials in papers such as the Orange News expressing the fear of some impending Sinn Fein takeover, Loyalists met during their dinner hour at the Harland and Wolff shipyard and following this, forced Catholics and some liberal Protestants from work, motivated undoubtedly by sectarian hatred, but also by an increasingly precarious labour market which put pressure on working class loyalist communities.

"Immediately after the meeting a violent onslaught was made upon the Catholic employees as well as on a dozen or two of Protestants who refused to bend the knee to Carson. They were peremptorily ordered to clear out. Being in a majority of less than one to six, they could not put up a fight with any hope of success."[8]

"...it is also impossible to disentangle the workplace expulsions and subsequent violence from the post-war recession in linen and engineering, unemployment among demobilized Protestants, and the employment of Catholics at Harland and Wolff."[9]

The shipyards were not the only establishments affected by the expulsions, as Sirocco engineering works employees made clear as they excluded Catholic workers:

"We decline to work with these men who have been expelled recently until the Sinn Fein assassinations in Ireland cease."[10]

On the same night, a group of Loyalists gathered at the entrance to the Falls district of Belfast, prompting the intervention of troops. Three Catholic men were killed and seven injured. Loyalists also attacked houses in the Ballymacarett district of South Belfast and looted shops. This riotous behaviour carried on for a second day and night, culminating in the attack by Loyalists on St Matthew's Church on the Newtownards Road, prompting, perhaps for the first time, shots being fired at loyalist mobs by troops.

The military fired rounds at the Redemptorist monastery in Clonard, killing Brother Michael Morgan. Officials said troops were returning fire, but a later inquest determined that the firing was unprovoked and that Brother Morgan had been killed by a sniper. The finding of the Coroner's Court was that that 'the firing by the military was entirely unnecessary for the purpose of suppressing riot, and was unprovoked by any person at Clonard Monastery'.

The 23rd July continued with the torching of Catholic homes in predominantly Protestant areas of Belfast.

The Daily Mail wrote on 1st September 1920 that "Belfast is in its present plight and is faced with future trouble simply and solely because there has been an organised attempt to deprive Catholic men of their work, and to drive Catholic families from their homes."

By the end of the month, whilst widespread violence had ceased, approximately 8,000 Catholic workers had been forced from their workplaces across Belfast – and according to G.B Kenna's work, 1,225 of these were ex-servicemen.

Clark, not long in his post, sought to address directly the expulsions. Ulster workers had formed Vigilance committees and demanded that expelled men sign a declaration that they were not associated with Sinn Fein or the IRA. The Expelled Workers Union naturally refused this and Clark himself negotiated that the men swearing on their honour that they were not in the IRA could return to work.

A second wave of attacks began on 24th August when a mob again attacked St Matthew's, this time defended by the local community. Homes, businesses and evictions of Catholics were widespread throughout this latest outrage.

The military declared a curfew on the whole of Belfast on 30th August, and the disturbances ceased for a time, at least on a large scale. However, on 26th September, two RIC policemen were shot dead in the Broadway area, followed by the RIC killing of three innocent Catholic men.

The same month, a petition was presented to the Dáil in Dublin seeking a boycott of goods from Belfast in solidarity with the expelled workers.

A motion by Sean McEntee of Monaghan South introduced the motion which was amended to declare any religious tests for employment illegal in Ireland. This initiated a trade blockade on goods from Belfast, and local committees ensured that local businesses enforced the boycott.

In the early months of the boycott, little co-ordination existed, and only local IRA units carried out any boycott of goods as the Director of the Central Belfast Boycott Committee, Leon Henderson, had been imprisoned.

However, on 17th December in the Dáil, the Acting President informed the House that the boycott was being 'stringently felt, especially by the banks. In order that the boycott might be properly carried out it was essential to place a man in charge of operations in Dublin.'

A committee was established in Dublin to oversee the maintenance of the boycott and local committees were set up to liaise with it. Donohue's work shows that the boycott was particularly enforced in Cavan and Monaghan.

When local unionists refused to uphold the boycott 'the local branch of the ITGWU picketed Protestant shops and prevented Catholics from entering these premises.'

The availability of bread was particularly hard hit by the boycott, with most of the more affordable bread coming from Belfast rather than Dublin.

Local IRA units operating throughout the country particularly in the border region upheld the boycott vociferously - even firing on vehicles that refused to stop for searches. They also conducted organised searches of premises, trains and trucks and destroyed goods originating in Belfast and its environs.

Testimony from Christopher Fitzsimmons, a member of 2nd Battalion, Dublin Brigade of the IRA made to the Irish Bureau of Military History gives an account of how he and his colleagues arrested a man working for a Northern company and dunked his head in the 'canal at Charlesville Mall and then handcuffed him to the railings at St. Agatha's Church'. He was later set free by the Black and Tans.

His unit also took goods from shops and destroyed them such as cigarettes, tobacco, snuff and linen that had been made in Belfast, issuing warnings to shopkeepers to refrain from stocking them.[11]

Joseph MacDonagh, on his appointment as substitute Minister for Labour wanted to 'set up a boycott committee in every town in Ireland.' Fines appropriated by local committees were sent to Dublin's central committee and onto the Ministry of Finance, even throughout the period of the Truce.

Blacklisting firms was another tactic used throughout the country, isolating firms from 1921 in Scotland, England and throughout Ireland that did business with Belfast firms.

The effects of the boycott were felt widely in Belfast and connected towns as outlined by the Inspector General of the RIC in May 1921:
"The Belfast Boycott is spreading. It is useless to pretend that this is not extremely serious, and it is significant to note that some large English firms are now yielding to it and promising to obey the orders of Dáil Eireann."[12]

The original focus of the boycott was the banking and insurance industries, though it had been widened to include all goods.

Nevertheless, northern based banks were affected by the boycott. By 1922 all sub-branches of the Belfast Bank were closed, which was met by a surge in opening of southern-based banks around the border, such as Hibernian and Munster and Leinster, which opened 15 new border sub-branches.

The Ulster Traders Defence Association estimated the cost of the boycott to be between £5 million and £10 million.[13]

The boycott played a significant part of the lead up to the Irish Civil War. On 26th June, Leo Henderson was arrested by pro-Treaty forces in Dublin after seizing 16 cars from Ferguson's garage in enforcement of the boycott. In return, the Deputy Chief of Staff J. J. O'Connell was taken hostage. The next day, as will be later referred to, the Four Courts were attacked.

A key tenet of Carson's 12th July speech that had whipped up the Belfast frenzy was the desire of the Ulster leadership to revive the Ulster Volunteers.

"We will re-organise, as we feel bound to do in our own defence, throughout the province the Ulster Volunteers who sent you such splendid help to maintain our Empire during the war. But one thing we will not submit to is that we should be left helpless and hopeless in the face of our enemies, and we tell you [the Government] that, come what will, in the last resort, we will rely upon ourselves, and, under God, we will defend ourselves."[2]

It is worth remembering at this point that the transition taking place in the civil administration following the passing of the Government of Ireland Act meant the RIC was still technically the police force across Ireland, but it was deeply mistrusted by the Ulster Unionist leadership. Woven through Carson's speech, and indeed through the actions of the mobs who attacked Catholic homes and business that summer, was a demand that the Government give the Ulster Volunteers control over the security of the Northern state in readiness for the new administration in Ulster.

On 1st November 1920, the Ulster Special Constabulary was formed from the membership of the UVF, led by Wilfrid Spender. It would be characterised by an 'A' full-time force of officers numbering 3,000, a 'B' force comprised mainly of UVF militiamen 10,000 strong and a 'C' force of 16,000.

1921

On 25th January 1921 Carson made clear to a UUC delegation who had met him in London that he did not want a role in the new Northern Ireland government and so couldn't serve as UUP leader. On 3rd Feb Craig was elected his successor in preparation for receiving the reins of power in Ulster.

Speaking at the Ulster Unionist Council after having been elected as Carson's successor, he said;

"It will be you and I together who will make a success of this that has been entrusted to us."

The day later, Craig reported to the Cabinet that following a conversation with Lord Balcarres, it was expected that the site of the new Parliament in Stormont would be considerably more expensive at the top of the Estate but in the interests of 'dignity and grandeur', Craig insisted.

Indeed, Craig commented to the Cabinet that if the local administration were asked to pay even for part of the labour to level the upper Stormont site, he would take the money from the Unemployment Fund 'which he was expecting to get from the British Government to help his arrangement in regard to the shipyard workers'.

Craig returned to Ulster 5 April 1921 accompanied by Charles Blackmore who would later serve as his Private Secretary.

Private correspondence from Sir Ernest Clark on 14th April revealed that he believed the Ministry of Home Affairs was too small, and Labour too big, and so suggested that certain functions be added to both creating the Ministry of Labour and Health Insurance and the Ministry of Home Affairs and Local Government.

As part of the preparations for the creation of Parliament, Craig issued a list to Buckingham Palace to ascertain the King's approval for honours for a large number of those involved in the recent work and in the anti-Home Rule movement.

Correspondence from the King's private secretary to Craig complained that the list was too big, and that he should furnish the King with a list of the achievements of those listed. Eventually a small number of appointments were made.

The new Northern Ireland Parliament had been created by the King on 3rd May and an election for the new Northern Ireland Parliament via Proportional Representation was held on 24 May.

On 5th May, a truly historic meeting took place between Eamon De Valera and Craig in Dublin. The Ulster leader had been asked to meet the Lord Lieutenant before he returned to England and received word from Mr De Valera that he wanted to meet whilst he was in Dublin.

A meeting took place between the two men for the first time informally, where Craig sought to ensure that Mr De Valera understood that Ulster would not now submit to any situation whereby it would lie outside the British Empire. With no clear outcome or achievement arising from the meeting, Craig went home to Belfast and set about ensuring as many Loyalists as possible were elected to the new Parliament.

It was created as a bicameral legislature, with a House of Commons and a Senate, despite originally being proposed as a unicameral House before the legislation was amended by the House of Lords. A Parliament not borne out of the determination on behalf of whom it would enact legislation, rather borne out of a technicality, manifested out of thin air without much fervour.

Union Theological College served as the home of the Northern Ireland Parliament after its creation and short stay in Belfast City Hall. The Chapel of the College housed the Senate, and the Gamble Library held the House of Commons until Parliament Buildings at Stormont was finished in 1932 where it decanted back to City Hall for a short time before moving to its permanent residence.

Fifty-two members were to be elected from nine constituencies, five county boroughs such as Antrim, four Borough constituencies, relevant to the four constituencies of Belfast, and one University constituency, Queen's University.

In the first election as was to be expected, the Unionists won 40 of the 52 seats, including all but one in Antrim, half of those in Armagh, all but one in Belfast and all but one in the University constituency.

Only in Fermanagh and Tyrone constituency did Nationalists make any impact, with Nationalists taking two and Sinn Fein taking two of the eight.

An anomaly of the 1921 election was the usefulness to the Ulster Unionists of the UULA (Ulster Unionist Labour Association) which was created in 1918 by Carson to stop any seepage of working-class unionist support to the mainstream Labour movement. It worked – six members of the UULA, who sat as Ulster Unionists, were returned to serve in Parliament.

"In return for Protestant workers' votes the Unionist government subsidized the shipbuilding industry to maintain high levels of employment."[14]

Joseph Devlin, the Northern Nationalist leader won two seats in Antrim and West Belfast but did not take up either seat.

Heavy hitters from the newly partitioned south were elected to Northern seats. Michael Collins was elected in Armagh, de Valera became a Down MP and Arthur Griffith became a Fermanagh and Tyrone MP, though all refused to take their seats, alongside all Nationalist members.

Nationalists and Sinn Fein had aligned on an anti-partition ticket. The election to the Southern Ireland legislature was held on the same day, returning members unopposed and allowing Sinn Fein to focus its energies on the Northern poll.

Craig was declared Northern Ireland's first Prime Minister by the Lord Lieutenant and a declaration by the Speaker of the House of Commons at Westminster in March 1922 that banned discussions of Irish affairs which pushed Ulster and any oversight of governance out of the purview of the Mother Parliament.

He wasted no time in appointing his inaugural Cabinet.

In Finance, Hugh Pollock of Belfast South was appointed. He had proven himself adept in the complex financial affairs between Britain and Ireland at the Irish Convention and had been a former president of the Belfast Chamber of Commerce.

(L-R: Archdale, Bates, Londonderry, Craig, Pollock, JM Andrews, PRONI: INF/7/A/5/9)

In Home Affairs, effectively the Home Office, Craig named Richard Dawson Bates who sat for Belfast East. Dawson Bates was known for his loyalty in the Party and dedication to the mantra that Catholics were disloyal and untrustworthy. He had served as Secretary of the Ulster Unionist Council since 1905.

"The Home Affairs Minister Dawson Bates, at perhaps the most sensitive department in terms of national security, had a young typist sacked when it was revealed in the press that she was Catholic. He declared afterwards that he did not want even his most junior employee to be a Papist."[15]

Lord Londonderry was appointed as the first Education Minister and Leader in the Senate. As a respected war veteran and having served in the post-war coalition government in London as Under-Secretary of State for Air from 1919, he was well versed in the politics of the empire and friendly with figures such as Winston Churchill.

A farmer and landowner in Fermanagh, Edward Archdale MP for Enniskillen was tasked with the Agriculture Ministry. He had previously been a Tory Westminster MP and was a retired member of the Royal Navy. He also served as Commerce Minister.

County Down MP John Miller Andrews became Minister of Labour. A founder of the UULA, he was also a successful landowner and businessman. He was also known as extremely partisan and a confirmed practitioner of sectarianism in his public office.

"After the public came to know of the fact in 1926, two Southern Catholics employed in the Ministry of Labour after transferring from Dublin Castle, were forced to leave by the Minister, John Andrews."[16]

He had family connections to Lord Pirrie of Harland and Wolff and his brother had been managing director but had perished when the RMS Titanic sank in the North Atlantic.

Milne Barbour would join the Cabinet in 1925 as Minister of Commerce. He had family connections to Andrews, as his sister had married Thomas Andrews who was lost at the sinking of the Titanic. He had previously served as a Parliamentary Secretary to the Ministry of Finance.

Each Ministry would also have a Parliamentary Secretary, particularly useful for the Education Minister who, as a Senator, did not have speaking rights in the House of Commons.

The Northern Ireland Parliament first sat on 7th June to elect a Speaker. Meeting at 11:30am, the Lord Lieutenant chaired the event. In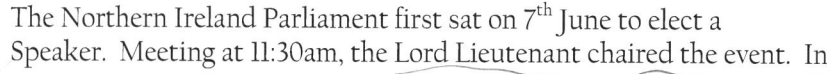

accordance with Craig's plans, Sir Hugh O'Neill of Antrim was submitted to the will of the House and elected unanimously as Speaker.

As part of the ceremony and without precedent, the Speaker addressed the Lord Lieutenant offering himself to the King as the Speaker of the Commons;

"My Lord Lieutenant,
I have to acquaint you that in obedience to His Majesty's Commands, His Majesty's faithful Commons of Northern Ireland, in the exercise of their undoubted right and privilege, has proceeded to the election of a Speaker, and as the object of their choice I now present myself to you, and submit myself with all humility to His Majesty's gracious approbation".[17]

Following this, the Lord Lieutenant suspended the House for half an hour the new Speaker then returning in formal dress, and takes the Oath, followed by all MPs.

On that first sitting, an indication of the unique position of a Parliament within the United Kingdom under the Westminster Parliament became clear in one motion moved by the Prime Minister:

"That this House do adopt the Standing Orders relating to Public Business in use in the House of Commons of the United Kingdom, with such modifications as appear in manuscript in the volume now in the custody of the Clerk of the House; and do further adopt the rules of Parliamentary practice and procedure set forth in the twelfth edition of Sir Erskine May's treatise on the law, privileges, proceedings, and usages of Parliament."[3]

Arthur Irwin Dasent was appointed the first Clerk of the Parliaments in Belfast. He was a senior Clerk in the House of Commons and was transferred to oversee the smooth running of the new Parliament.

With one motion, the Prime Minister effectively created the Standing Orders and conventions of the House, without one amendment from the Members and without seeking to carve out a purely Ulsterised profile for the new Parliament.

Such practices as the Outlawries Bill were carried directly over from London. This Bill was symbolically read directly after the King's/Queen's Speech in the House of Commons to signify that the House set its own business and did not rush to debate the Address.

The election of the 24 members of the Senate was also put in motion on this day, for members of the House of Commons to vote by post, the poll closing at 3pm on 16 June.

Two ladies were elected, Julie McMordie in South Belfast and Dehra Chichester (later Parker) in Londonderry, both Unionists. Chichester would go on to become the longest serving female MP in Ulster and serve as a Minister.

Thomas Moles, MP for South Belfast was elected the Deputy Speaker and Chairman of Ways and Means.

His role in Ways and Means brought great importance. The Committee was responsible for making recommendations on and reviewing the Government's budget.

All 24 elected members of the Senate were male Ulster Unionist members, supplemented by ex-officio members the Lord Mayor of Belfast, who throughout the life of the Senate, was a Unionist and the Mayor of Derry. The Nationalist Mayor of Derry in 1921, Hugh O'Doherty, did not take the Oath and therefore relinquished his seat in the House.

Senators were to serve an eight-year term with half of the House up for re-elected every four years using Proportional Representation.

The Senate was unlike the House of Lords in that it never lost its government majority, and did not in the clear majority of cases, revise in any grand way, legislation sent to it from the Lower House. It was to have its own Speaker, two Deputies, a Leader of the House and one Deputy.

Lord Dufferin was elected the Senate Speaker. Overseeing the ceremony acting as Black Rod was Sir Frederick Moneypenny, the City Chamberlain.

Craig's standing order motion further bolstered the image of the Northern Ireland Parliament as a legislature styled in no small way to that of Westminster. It had the same Principal Officers in the Gentleman Usher of the Black Road and the Sergeant-at-Arms. The former is a principal officer of the Upper House usually, and in Westminster is the Monarch's representative in the Houses of Parliament responsible for the royal parts of the Palace of Westminster.

The Sergeant-at-Arms is responsible for security in the House of Commons and those areas under its control, at least in the Palace of Westminster. The office holder is also part of the Speaker's Procession, a picture of which is included in this book.

Such ceremonial roles with their historic background linked the Parliament in Belfast to Westminster but their presence did mean the opportunity to put in place a typically Ulster Parliament with its own distinct identity was lost.

Returning to the upheaval in the civil service, the Civil Service Committee outlined in the 1920 Act had to be convened when both new governments allocated members to it. Craig was clear that he did not want an administration staffed exclusively from Dublin and he received support from his new cabinet for this policy.

The northern government, such as it was, began undertaking its own recruitment processes via selection boards it established, and by head hunting acceptable officials from Dublin it believed it could trust, much to the dismay of senior officials and junior civil servants alike.

The first cabinet meeting was held on 15th June in Cabin Hill, an extensive residence in Knock that had previously been home to the Lord Mayor of Belfast, Robert James McMordie QC who served 1910-1914. After his death in 1914, his widow, Julia (nee Gray) offered the residence to Sir James Craig for use in establishing the first Northern Ireland Government.

Notably, she would go on to become one of two women elected to Parliament in 1921.

Rent was agreed at £80 per month after two other options, Tyrone House and Danesfort fell through. Interestingly, the Treasury refused to pay for the residence, and even Stormont Castle when the Prime Minister entered, as the 1920 Act had only provided that the UK Government would pay for an official residence of the Speaker of the House of Commons, not the Prime Minister.

In correspondence, a point was made to Sir James that both maids in the residence were Catholic.

Extensive preparations had been made for the visit of Their Majesties to Belfast on 22nd June to open the first Parliament. The Royal Yacht 'Victoria and Albert' guided the King and Queen across the Irish Sea to Donegall Quay where they were met by the Royal Carriage that would take them to the Albert Memorial, through Hugh Street and Castle Place to Donegall Place and finally Donegall Square North.

The route was lined by thousands of troops from 1st Batt. Norfolk Regiment, 1st Batt. Somersetshire Light Infantry, 2nd Batt King's Own Yorkshire Light Infantry, the Royal Ulster Rifles, Royal Irish Fusiliers and 2nd Batt. Royal Iniskilling Fusiliers.

Prior to the Royal Address, prayers were said by leaders of the churches in Ulster – notably no representative of the Roman Catholic Church was present.

The King delivered his first speech to members of the Northern Ireland Parliament, calling on members to promote reconciliation:

"I speak from a full heart when I pray that my coming to Ireland to-day may prove to be the first step towards the end of strife amongst her people, whatever their race or creed. In that hope I appeal to all Irishmen to pause, to stretch out the hand of forbearance and conciliation, to forgive and forget, and to join in making for the land they love a new era of peace, contentment and goodwill."

At the end of his speech, a 21-gun salute was fired from the Naval Escort and by the 3rd Battery of the RFA. Their Majesties were then treated to a lunch by the new Government in the Great Hall before travelling the short distance to Ulster Hall where they were met with a guard of honour consisting of the RIC and Ulster Special Constabulary.

After receiving loyal addresses from Ministers and numerous civil organisations, the couple returned to the Royal Yacht escorted by RIC and USC officers lining the streets.

It was not all without controversy. Some members of the Imperial House took issue with the King opening a Parliament in the United Kingdom outside of Westminster.

On 23 June 1921 the Departments of the Prime Minister and of the Ministers of Finance, Home Affairs, Labour, Education, Agriculture and Commerce were created as outlined in the King's Speech.

Under Section 2 of the Government of Ireland Act that created the Council of Ireland, both the Parliaments of Northern and Southern Ireland were to elect members to sit on the body. The Northern Ireland Parliament duly elected the following:

J.M. Andrews	Milne Barbour
Dawson Bates	William Coote
James Craig	Herbert Dixon
William Grant	Robert Johnstone
Crawford McCullagh	Samuel McGuffin
Robert McKeown	David Shillington
Robert Anderson	

With Senators Lord Londonderry, Rt Hon Samuel Cunningham, Adam Duffin, T Greer, J Hill-Dickson, J Porter-Porter and J.A. Woods.

The Southern Ireland Parliament having never met did not appoint members to the Council.

Speeches were made by members following the address by the Lord Lieutenant, and espousing the spirit of friendship and good relations as invited by the King, Major David Shillington (UU, Armagh) stated:

"We will be careful in all our acts, to inspire confidence amongst all classes of the community, and by the help of Almighty God to always keep before us the vision of what we would like not only our own province, but our whole country to eventually attain."

Following this, Captain Harry Mulholland (UU, Down) first brought the idea of educational reform to the attention of the Parliament, which would become a major issue in the coming years. The House adjourned until 20th September when it would consider estimates.

The UK Prime Minister continued to push for a resolution in Ireland. On 24th June, he wrote to both Eamon de Valera and Sir James Craig inviting them to a conference in London.

De Valera replied to the Prime Minister four days later informing him that he would ask the Dáil to appoint representatives, but importantly that he wanted to seek talks firstly with the unionist minority. To that effect, he wrote to Sir James Craig, the Earl of Midleton, Sir Maurice Dowerell, Sir Robert H. Woods and Mr Andrew Jameson inviting them to Dublin for talks.

On 29th, Sir James telegrammed to refuse the invitation, prompting a reply from de Valera calling on him to allow the Irish question to now be solved by those on the island of Ireland.

In early July, two meetings took place with both sides of the debate in Ireland. At the end of the talks, a statement was issued calling for all hostilities in Ireland to end. The same day, 8th July, de Valera agrees to Lloyd George's invitation to London. A letter from the Prime Minister to Lord Midleton agrees with the conference sentiment and outlines the British willingness to a cessation of violence.

Possibly the most significant event in the early life of the Parliament occurred on 11 July 1921, the truce between the British Government and the IRA in the South to end the Irish War of Independence.

The spiralling cost to the British and the pressure put on the IRA by the Black and Tans and the resulting shortage of manpower created breathing space for both sides.

To many Nationalists, the truce and the resulting talks posed an opportunity to undo partition and justify their refusal to sit in the Northern Ireland Parliament.

On 14th, 15th. 18th and 21st July, both men met for long periods to discuss the current impasse in Ireland, violence and the future of the country. The British Government issued a written position to Dublin offering full Dominion status for Ireland, though allowing for the recognition of the Parliament of Northern Ireland.

This was far short of the position of Dublin following the 1918 election and was unpalatable to Republican leaders who did not buy the premise set out by Lloyd George that Ireland was being given the highest level of freedom to determine its destiny within the realms under the Crown.

In correspondence leading into September, Dublin and London fought forward and back on the issue of Ireland's status. Dublin would send plenipotentiaries to any conference, but London could not recognise them as speaking for a 'foreign power'.

A delegation on behalf of the Provisional Government led by Michael Collins met a British delegation headed by Lloyd George to discuss the future arrangements in Ireland following the conflict.

The Government of Ireland Act had already granted a devolved status to both Northern and Southern Parliaments, and naturally the aim of Republican leaders was full independence and a withdrawal of the British from Ireland.

During the talks, Lloyd George repeated his tactic from the Irish Convention of plurality – forcing the hand of Collins and the Irish delegation by promising 'terrible and immediate war' if the Treaty as agreed in early December was not signed immediately, removing the ability of the delegation to seek approval from the Executive in Dublin.

The impact of the Treaty not only in the South, but also to Northern Nationalists, cannot be overstated. It included two significant provisions – primarily that under section 12, Northern Ireland could withdraw from the newly created Irish Free State within one month of the Treaty becoming law and secondly that if the Northern Ireland Government did decide to opt out, that a Boundary Commission would be established to draw the boundaries of the new state.

"If before the expiration of the said month, an address is presented to His Majesty by both Houses of the Parliament of Northern Ireland to that effect, the powers of the Parliament and the Government of the Irish Free State shall no longer extend to Northern Ireland, and the provisions of the Government of Ireland Act, 1920, (including those relating to the Council of Ireland) shall so far as they relate to Northern Ireland, continue to be of full force and effect, and this instrument shall have effect subject to the necessary modifications.

Provided that if such an address is so presented a Commission consisting of three persons, one to be appointed by the Government of the Irish Free State, one to be appointed by the Government of Northern Ireland, and one who shall be Chairman to be appointed by the British Government shall determine in accordance with the wishes of the inhabitants, so far as may be compatible with economic and geographic conditions, the boundaries between Northern Ireland and the rest of Ireland, and for the purposes of the Government of Ireland Act, 1920, and of this instrument, the boundary of Northern Ireland shall be such as may be determined by such Commission."

At the first sitting following the summer recess, James Craig gave a statement to the Northern Ireland Parliament on events that had occurred regarding the Truce.

He stressed in the House that whilst members of his Government had been invited to an earlier conference to bring about the truce, they had not been party to the negotiations resulting in it, and had indeed pressed Ulster's case in a letter to the Prime Minister on 29th July stating;

"Our acceptance of your original invitation to meet in conference in London still holds good, and if at any time our assistance is again desired we are available, but I feel bound to acquaint you that no meeting is possible between Mr. De Valera and myself until he recognises that Northern Ireland will not submit to any authority other than His Majesty the King and the Parliament of the United Kingdom, and admits the sanctity of the existing powers and privileges of the Parliament and Government of Northern Ireland."

This was followed by a telegram to the Prime Minister agreeing to a meeting proposed by De Valera in Castle Bellingham, but only when he received in writing from him an acceptance of the above, agreed at a Cabinet meeting on 4th August.[18]

Instead, Craig called for sections 69 and 72 of the 1920 Act to be activated immediately, to give the Northern Ireland administration full legislative powers over its affairs. It had already moved to establish essential services and appointed to key posts, such as the appointment of Denis Henry as Lord Chief Justice.
The Truce had now added to the uncertainty of the future of the transfers in the civil service and had now effectively opened the floodgates, undermining the processes put in place by senior officials.

The new Minister of Finance in the North, Hugh Pollock had sought to undertake the recruitment via their own selection boards of the civil servants for Belfast, however even his own colleagues sought to undermine that process and recruited their own officials.

It was around this time that allegations of religious discrimination began to seep out of the selection boards and back to Dublin. Officials expressed outrage that a sectarian dimension had been injected into the process.

"The pattern of Ulster Unionist Party and civil service relations was established in the short period of 1920-21 as intensely parochial, nepotistic and anti-Catholic."[19]

Indeed, at the NI cabinet meeting on 4th August, a letter was read from the Ulster Ex-Services Association objecting to the appointment of a Mr Coyle, a Catholic, as Permanent Secretary at the Department of Agriculture. In fact, Mr Coyle had been appointed as head of a branch within the Department.

However, the cabinet were clear in their reply to the letter;

"It was decided he (the Prime Minister) should reply stating that the Government intended to enrol members of all creeds in their staff provided their loyalty was unquestioned and it was hoped Southern Ireland would be equally broad-minded".[20]

"Suitable huts" were thought to be appropriate and had been secured by Craig until provisions for a new Parliament Building could be secured. The Ministers of Finance and Home Affairs were given the task of making private enquiries as to the most suitable site for the permanent Parliament.[21]

At another Cabinet meeting not long after being given the task, the Ministers reported to the Prime Minister that the Presbyterian Assembly College Building had been rented by the Board of Works. They were not yet able to find a suitable site for the permanent Parliament and were asked by Craig to seek a fair offer for Belvoir Park, an offer having already been received for Orangefield.

Cabinet then ratified the purchase of the Stormont Estate in East Belfast in August and so the roots of the loyal Ulster administration began to seep into the soil. The new site would be mere feet from Cabin Hill, Craig's residence. The Ulster Unionist Party met on 25th August following an inspection of the site by Lords Crawford and Balcarres to approve the purchase of the site and of Stormont Castle.

On 20th August, it was resolved in the House;
"'That this House approves of Stormont Castle Demesne as the place where the new Parliament Houses and Ministerial Buildings shall be erected, and as the place to be determined as the seat of the Government of Northern Ireland as and when suitable provision has been made therefor."

The Truce, in fact gave Craig and Clark, who now headed the new Belfast civil service the opportunity to push on with securing the state in their own image through the security apparatus in the Ulster Special Constabulary. Negotiations between the British Government and the Sinn Fein leadership that would lead to the truce meant both sides took their eye off the ball in terms of administration.

On 24st August the Government formally purchased the Stormont Estate for £20,000.

On 31st August Mr Cope, Assistant Under Secretary in Dublin attended a meeting and undertook to give instructions in writing which would clear any confusion on behalf of the military regarding their powers under the Restoration of Order in Ireland legislation – however, no such instructions were given, arising in a feeling by Loyalists that the authorities had abandoned them.

"It is quite clear to me that if the Government of Northern Ireland is to retain the confidence of the people they cannot stand on one side and allow the present policy of drifting to continue".[22]

In a memo to the Cabinet on 12th September, the Minister of Home Affairs produced a memo for his colleagues outlining the chaos ensuing throughout the country due to mixed messages and confusion about security.

Colonel Carter-Campbell was forced to admit that a misunderstanding between him and the Police Commissioner was the reason for not utilising troops. The Colonel was prepared if needs be to bring artillery into Belfast to quell any widespread violence.

The issue of educational reform was again raised very early in the tenure of the new Parliament by Mr William Coote (UU, Fermanagh and Tyrone) on 21st September 1921, commenting on the hardship some teachers were experiencing in the climate of that time.

In replying to his points, the Parliamentary Secretary to the Ministry of Education, Mr Robert McKeown (UU, North Belfast) informed the House that three sets of Commissioners had been created under the Ministry, for National Education, Secondary Education and for Endowed Schools owing to the three separate education systems, primary, intermediate and technical.

At this point, the proportion of civil servants owing to the North and South had not yet been implemented, and the Parliamentary Secretary was forced to admit that they did not have full control over the Ministry's affairs.

Mr McKeown informed the House that a Commission of Inquiry would be set up on education to look at issues such as housing for schools, amalgamation and teacher's pensions. He admitted that the state of intermediary education in the Province was 'deplorable' and that teachers in that medium were being poorly paid and many had indeed left for England and Scotland.

Money from the Imperial Parliament to remedy the problems faced by the new Northern education system was not forthcoming, but the ambition of the new Government was clear;

"I can only assure the House that it is the wish and the desire of the Ministry of Education to see that every child throughout the Northern Province receives the same encouragement and has the same facilities for education as children have in other parts of the United Kingdom. And it will be our desire to forge and fashion a measure of reform which I believe will bring that about, and, perhaps, too, taking into account what has been done in other schemes, we may be able to produce a measure of reform which will put this province somewhat ahead of any other kingdom or province in the world."

Dublin only transferred the control of education services in the North on 1st February 1922.

On 4 October 1921 the Minister for Labour, J. M. Andrews (UU, Down) informed the House that the total number of unemployed in Northern Ireland at time was 78,000.

Finance, too, was neglected, forcing Craig to write to Sir Hamar Greenwood in Dublin asking for £130,000 in addition to £20,000 which had already been advanced to his Government 'in order to prevent a complete breakdown of the financial machinery'.[23]

Control of the judiciary was transferred to the Northern Ireland administration on 1st October by Order in Council and the High Court for the time being would sit at the Antrim Courthouse. The relationship the

Parliament had with the judiciary throughout its tenure had the capacity to make other legislatures uneasy.

Nine MP's – 8 of whom were Ulster Unionists, were appointed to the bench at varying levels throughout the life of the Parliament. Five Attorneys General were appointed to the judiciary from levels of High Court Judge to Lord Chief Justice. In other democratic systems, the judiciary would remain completely independent of the legislature and executive, but not necessarily in Northern Ireland.

On 1st November the Prime Minister accepted on behalf of the Cabinet the plans for the new Parliament buildings.

Into the hands of a shocked Craig was handed the reins of power on 9th November when he got his wish and the British government transferred functions of departments to Belfast without warning, with the Civil Service Committee to allocate staff in a fair way having never met. In a cabinet memo on 12 September, the Dublin authorities had indicated that all members of the civil service allocated to Dublin outside of their wishes had refused to report, and as such some offices would be double staffed, the cost of which being borne by the UK Government.

Correspondence from Mr Blackmore in the Ministry of Finance to Mr Petherwick in Dublin on 11th November regarding the 'Ulster way' being undertaken in terms of recruitment effectively killed the Civil Service Committee allocations;

"The statement that the Selection Board should exercise full and undivided responsibility for the appointment of the subordinate clerical grades does not, in my opinion, imply that full weight will not be given to any recommendations made by Ministers for appointments in their Departments. On the contrary, the recommendations of the departments must be a very important factor".[24]

The transfer of services came at the right time, as cabinet records clearly demonstrate the fears of ministers in late September that the Northern Ireland Government would 'be prove to be a farce and the Northern Parliament will be nothing more than a debating society' should the delay go on any longer.[25]

To sidestep the blockage of the governments appointing members to give life to the Civil Service Committee, the Lord Lieutenant made appointments. Civil servant representatives were horrified and even attempted a legal challenge to the appointments and any transfers required by the committee's deliberations.

The saga came to an end on 16th January 1922 when the new Provisional Government formally banned any officials from moving north without express permission, leaving itself with the bulk of the established Irish administration of Dublin castle, and the northern establishment with a loyal rump of handpicked men who would acquiesce in the sectarian management of the state. It was not unforeseen, as Craig had made representations to the Prime Minister that any civil servant transferring who had Sinn Fein sympathies could not count on the Northern Ireland Government for protection.

On the following day's sitting following Craig's speech, Robert Lynn (West Belfast, UUP) made a speech further emphasising that Ulster had been loyal and even by accepting its own Parliament, had done its part for peace. He also made a comment that sums up the feeling of members of the Parliament about the negotiations in London;

"We are told, of course, by Mr. De Valera, when he is in a cooing mood, that Ulster can have far more from a Sinn Fein Parliament in Dublin than it has ever got from the Imperial Parliament. There are two comments I wish to make on that. The first is that we do not recognise this Sinn Fein rebel organisation in Dublin. We want nothing from it, and we are certainly not going to place our liberties and our rights under the control of the men who have brought disgrace on Ireland during the last few years."

Craig made a statement to the House on 12 December on the Truce, recognising not only the apparent betrayal of Ulster by the British Prime Minister by agreeing to provisions that could affect Northern Ireland without the input of the Northern Government, but also commenting on the impact the Treaty will have on Northern Ireland;

"To characterise the position as anything short of grave, serious, would be a great mistake. I have faced many a difficult problem. I have faced, we have all faced, times of grave crisis. Sometimes it has been possible to make up our minds in a moment as to the right attitude to observe, and on other occasions it has taken us a considerable time to thresh out the proper course to pursue; but never before has the situation been so complicated as that which has been created by the signatures attached to what is called a Treaty between the British representatives on the one hand and the Sinn Fein representatives on the other."

Craig wrote to Lloyd George on 14th expressing his outrage at the agreement to establish the boundary commission;

"At our meeting on the 9th December you explained that it was only intended to make a slight re-adjustment of our boundary line so as to bring into Northern Ireland Loyalists who are now just outside our area and to transfer correspondingly an equivalent number of those having Sinn Fein sympathies to the area of the Irish Free State.

...As I intimated to Mr Austin Chamberlain by telephone before leaving London, I reserved to my Government the right of dissenting from the appointment of any Boundary Commission".[26]

During this turbulent period, a significant piece of legislation was rushed through the House in one day, the Local Government (Emergency Powers) Bill. This Bill effectively gave the Northern Parliament the power to dissolve a local government entity and replace it with a Commissioner should it refuse to carry out its duties in the new state.

The Minister of Home Affairs, Richard Dawson Bates informed the House on 6th December that following a letter sent to all councils in the six counties, the County Council of County Tyrone informed the Ministry that they refused to recognise the Northern Ireland state and intended to seek governance from Dáil Eireann.

Mr W Coote (UU, Fermanagh and Tyrone) who was also a member of the Council gave an overview of the perils it found itself in given what he called Sinn Fein's 'unwritten law of the revolver'. The Minister was able to confirm that day that the Council would not meet any further, and that a Commissioner would be appointed to undertake the day-to-day responsibilities of the authority.

"Following the passing of the controversial bill through Parliament, Dawson Bates set up a government body to deal with trouble areas, with John Leech, K.C. as Commissioner."[27]

The House was adjourned on 12 December 1921 following a speech by the Lord Lieutenant who recognised the financial situation Ulster found itself in and informed members of his hope that Government Departments would be fully established in early 1922.

"Financial responsibility has been transferred to the Government at a time of unprecedented depression; it now appears impossible to realize the expectations of a large surplus, foreshadowed in the white paper on which the financial Clauses of the Government of Ireland Act, 1920, were based. It, therefore, becomes imperative that expenditure in many departments should be restricted to the bare necessities of the case. I confidently rely upon the people, in their own best interests, loyally to support the Ministers of the Crown in their endeavours to promote economy".

1922

On 7th January 1922, Dáil Eireann approved the Treaty, prompting the resignation of Eamon De Valera and a split in opinion along agreement and opposition lines. Several days of blistering debate had taken place from 19th December on the articles within the Treaty.

The establishment of the Irish Free State within the Empire with the same Dominion status as Canada, rather than full independence, angered many TDs. Article 11 of the Treaty effectively copper fastened the partition of the country, a fact unacceptable to many who had fought in the War of Independence. The Oath of Allegiance to the King would remain intact.

On 10th January, Arthur Griffith was elected President by Dáil Eireann, leading De Valera and his supporters to withdraw from the House. Sectarian violence continued to dog the communities of Ulster, with a growing number of both Catholics and Protestants murdered in cold blood. In order to attempt to address the general political situation that was fanning the flames of discontent, Michael Collins and James Craig met in London on 23rd January and again in Dublin on 28th January and agreed what became known as the first section of the Craig-Collins Pact.

In the optimistic document, it was agreed that the Northern, Southern and British Governments would send a representative to sit on the Boundary Commission and significantly, Craig agreed to 'facilitate in every way possible the return of Catholic workmen – without tests – to the shipyards as and when trade revival enables the firms concerned to absorb the present unemployed.'

For Collins' part, he agreed to end the Belfast goods boycott immediately. Collins revealed in his discussions that it was being used by some tradesmen in the south to undermine their competitors and was causing strife within the ranks of Sinn Fein.

Both men agreed to meet again to discuss, amongst other things, the fate of post-Truce prisoners.

At a meeting of the Cabinet in Belfast on 26th January on the talks, Craig briefed colleagues on his meeting with Collins and his deliberations in London.

"for three hours he (Craig) was alone with Mr Micheal Collins and made it clear to him that at present an All-Ireland Parliament was out of the question, possibly in years to come – 10, 20 or 50 years Ulster might be tempted to join with the South, but the Prime Minister had felt that Mr Collins should know his exact position which was that he would do nothing to prevent an All-Ireland Parliament, and that if he were convinced it was in the interests of the people of Ulster, he would frankly tell them of his views, but should such an eventuality arise, he would not feel justified himself in taking part in an All-Ireland Parliament but that he would erect no barriers around Parliament, but in no case would he pass through them himself.

He asked Mr Collins straight out whether it was his intention to have peace in Ireland, or whether we were to go on with murder and strife, rivalry and boycott and unrest in Northern Ireland. Mr Micheal Collins made it clear he wanted a real peace and had so many troubles in Southern Ireland, that he was prepared to establish cordial relations with Northern Ireland, to abandon coercion, but hoping to coax her into a union later".[28]

The obvious panic in Belfast over the Treaty culminated in a letter from James Craig to the Prime Minister in London on 6th February 1922;

"Since correspondence began on the subject of an Irish Settlement we have relied on a sentence in your letter of 20th July 1921 to Mr De Valera which runs as follows;

"It (the Settlement) must allow for recognition of the existing powers and privileges of the Parliament and Government of Northern Ireland which cannot be abrogated except by their own consent".

Although the necessity for giving a final decision on behalf of the Government of Northern Ireland does not arise until after our Parliament has voted itself out of the Free State, as a result of our deliberations today. I have to inform you that we adhere throughout this principle laid down by yourself, and cannot consent to any alteration of our boundary except by mutual agreement, failing which in respect of any territory in dispute the Boundary to stand as defined in the Government of Ireland Act 1920."[29]

Only a few days before, on 11th February, events conspired to create one of the most serious security situations for both administrations since partition.

The Ulster Football Final was to be held in Derry that night, and a group of Monaghan players, some of whom were members of the IRA led by Dan Hogan, were stopped by 'B' Specials on their way to the match at Dromore and arrested.

The Border had been a hive of activity prior to this event, but the retaliation for the arrest of the IRA members was to become known as the 'Clones affray'. A small group of armed 'B' Specials were travelling to Enniskillen to reinforce the garrison there. As the railway had passed out of Northern Ireland and into the South at Clones, the officers were seen as a threat to southern security and as an opportunity for action by the local IRA that could not be missed.

Matt Fitzpatrick, commandant of the local IRA unit sought to arrest the Specials, and approached the train carrying the officers. He was shot and killed by an officer after giving a warning to the men to surrender.
The shooting which followed killed five members of the Specials, the remainder who could not flee across the border having been arrested.

The attack at Clones was part of a seemingly never-ending cycle of IRA activity on the border, met with attacks on Catholics in Derry and Belfast.

On 30th January, enraged at the Pact, the workers of Workman and Clark shipyard met and declared they would "not work with Papists" – seriously hindering Craig's ability, if exercised, to return Catholics to work.

"Mr Collins honoured his signature immediately by removing the boycott. On the other hand no serious attempt seems to have been made to make the Pact effective in Belfast. Sir James Craig may have intended to fulfil his obligations, but probably found himself helpless before the threats and operations of the shipyard dictators."[30]

Between 6th and 25th February, intense violence shook Belfast, with 43 people killed and 85 in total wounded, the majority of both were Catholics. A bomb had been thrown at children playing in Weaver Street, a Catholic enclave. Two children were killed outright with four more to die later in hospital.

The violence had prompted Craig to ask Churchill to despatch thousands of troops into the South to rescue those officers and other border loyalists who had been captured by the IRA. Of course, Churchill refused, but there was a stay placed on the evacuation of troops from the South whilst a resolution was found to the on-going issues.

On 21st February in an attempt to find a solution, the British Government released the IRA men from Monaghan, prompting the IRA to release their loyalist prisoners, allowing the evacuation of troops to resume on 28th - the same day the interim report of the Committee on Police Organisation ordered by Dawson Bates, Minister for Home Affairs (UU, East Belfast) reported on, recommending the establish of a new police force for Ulster.

Craig was furious and agreed with his colleagues at the 13th March cabinet meeting that the Lord Lieutenant be informed that further interference with the administration of justice in Ulster would mean they would reconsider their positions.

Further atrocities took place, notably what became known as the 'McMahon Killings' in Belfast. On 23rd March, two USC officers were killed by the IRA in Great Victoria Street. In the early hours of the next day, five suspected 'B' Specials set off to the house of respected Nationalist, Owen McMahon.

Five of the McMahon family were shot dead in their home. No official investigation was undertaken by the Northern authorities, though it was widely believed District Inspector John Nixon operating from the Shankill was responsible for the murders.

Michael Collins speaking on behalf of the Provisional Government, released a statement on 27th March aimed at Craig in readiness for his meeting with him a few days ahead. In it, he pulled no punches – 'Sir James Craig has not kept his honourable undertaking with me.'

He went on:
"On Tuesday last, a Deputation, seven in number, representing the expelled workers, met Sir James Craig, but got nothing from him but a bare statement to the effect that he could not keep his undertaking with

me owing to the difference existing from the Boundaries question and the tense feeling created by other causes.

Feeling over the Boundaries question and over the horrible Belfast atrocities, which have revolted the civilized world, is just as keen and just as tense in all parts of Ireland, inside and outside the Six Counties, as it is in the portion of the Six Counties which supports Sir James Craig, but still that did not prevent our part of the agreement being honoured.

If this is the way Sir James Craig intends to honour any obligations he may incur with us, meetings will, I am afraid, serve no good purpose, as he obviously looks upon such agreements as mere scraps of paper.

His accusation that we were promoting trouble in Belfast is an indication of his defined attitude of hostility towards our people and his disregard for the simple truth of the situation. 'Southern Ireland' he declared in a speech in the Belfast Parliament on the 15th instant 'desires to coerce Ulster citizens and stir up strife here by bombing our citizens and sniping at them, and carrying on their warfare to the best of their ability.' This is, of course, an absolute fabrication, but I must say that I consider it an outrageous statement for any man in Sir James Craig's position to make at any time, but especially at the present tense moment.

Sir Dawson Bates, Sir James Craig's Home Minister, told the Belfast Parliament on the same occasion that as soon as he took up office he ordered their constabulary to refuse to continue the liaison arrangements under the Truce. This was another clear indication of his attitude.

Our position with regard to the North-East corner, as I have stated earlier, has been consistently one of willingness to do all we can to effect peace in that portion of the country and to meet the objections and difficulties of Sir James Craig's party as far as we possibly can. We are always ready to attend every meeting where there is any likelihood of this object being attained, and in this spirit we have accepted the present invitation from the British Government.

But whilst hoping for the best, I can only say that I see no way out of the Northern impasse until Sir James Craig radically alters his present inimical attitude towards the Government of Ireland and towards the helpless minority in Belfast."[31]

Prior to the second Craig-Collins meeting on 30th March, Craig made a statement to the NI Parliament on the progress of issues agreed at the first meeting, and took aim at Southern Republicans who blamed the Northern administration for the lack of protection for Catholics and the constant attacks on them;

"Underlying the thought behind certain leaders in the South, and certainly frequently expressed in the Press across the Channel, we have the charge reiterated over and over again that there is a desire amongst the Protestants in the North and especially in Belfast, to carry out a pogrom against Catholics as Catholics. That is a very malicious statement and, in my opinion, is made of malice afore thought for the purpose of creating the very thing that we are all here so anxious to avoid.

I repudiate it with all the language at my command, and I can point, for positive proof that no such thing has ever been the policy of the Protestants here, to one or two significant facts. The Orange Institution is directly charged with being at the bottom of this pog-rom.

I am an Orangeman myself. I am proud more of being an Orangeman than of anything else. There is no secrecy about the Orange Institution. It is open for anyone to hear and learn what our tenets and beliefs are.

The whole organisation is built up and founded upon one simple statement, and that is civil and religious freedom for all. There is not a single member of this House all Protestants, nearly all Orangemen-who will deny that civil and religious liberty, for all."

This lengthy repudiation of responsibility for the violence against Catholics in the North, and its ferocious language is surprising for two reasons. Primarily, the insertion by Craig about the Orange Order, a Protestant-only fraternity that forbade the admission of Catholics and his belief that he organisation is built upon religious freedom for all. From the records of Parliament, no specific reference is made to hold the Prime Minister to account on his promise to secure the re-instatement of Catholic workers.

Secondly, the tone of the comments made by Craig comes in stark contrast to the progressive and optimistic he reached with Collins in London only days later.

The agreement reached between the Northern and Southern Governments, overseen by the British Government, entitled 'Heads of Agreement between the Provisional Government and the Government of Northern Ireland' can only be seen in hindsight as one of the most progressive documents constructed in the history of relations between the North and South.

Article one gleefully declares: Peace is today declared.

This remarkable statement is made even more so by the remainder of the agreement.

Both Governments undertook to co-operate 'in every way' to restore peaceful conditions in 'unsettled areas'. Collins gained significant reform of USC operations – in mixed areas a force half of Catholics and Protestants would be used, and all those officers 'not required for this force to be withdrawn to their homes and their arms handed in'. This was a significant concession from Craig who, backed by his Government, wholeheartedly supported the USC.

Further police reforms included the provision that Catholic recruits to the USC were to be assisted by an all-Catholic committee, that all police are to be uniformed on duty, and that when officers are not on duty, their arms are secured in a military barracks or under the charge of a competent officer. Any searches for arms were to be comprised of a balanced complement of officers.

Anyone charged with a serious offence that lead to a sentence of more than six month up to death, was to be given the opportunity to avail of a special court established to hear their cases.

A committee was to be established in Belfast comprising an equal number of Catholics and Protestants to investigate outrages which would have direct access to the Government, and that the press would only report outrages of a nature derived by this committee to be factual.

Craig also secured equally important concessions. Article six is blunt and to the point; 'IRA activity to cease in the Six Counties'. He and his supporters had always held firm on their conviction that the Northern state was under attack by the IRA at the direction of people like Collins and De Valera.

Article seven sought to sidestep the issue of the issue of the North opting out of a united Ireland under Dublin, and the issue of the Boundary Commission by committing both sides to a further meeting on these issues.

Both Governments were to secure the return of the homes of anyone both North or South who lost it as a result of expulsion and in an intervention by the British signatories, a fund of £500,000 would be allocated to the Northern Ministry of Labour to be spent exclusively on relief work, split down the lines of one third for Catholics and two-third for Protestants.

Any excluded workers who could not return for example to the shipyards due to the economic depression could avail of this relief work scheme, and Craig gained the inclusion that ex-servicemen would receive preference from the two-third share set aside for Protestants.

A small prisoner release scheme for all political prisoners held before March 31st, 1922 was agreed and both Governments agree to temper their words 'in the interests of peace'.

On 4th April Craig made a statement to the Northern Parliament, touting his victories in securing the legitimacy of the judicial system in Ulster by virtue of the agreement that from 31st onwards, the normal legal procedures would apply to all.

He also made no secret of the victory in securing article six. In his mind, this surrendered anyone in the North charged with atrocities on behalf of the IRA to the Northern courts, with the Southern state having officially relinquished responsibility for them.

Not one to miss on a political opportunity, Craig also used his speech to call on the political leaders of Nationalism to take their seats in Parliament, to avoid 'deals being done behind their backs';
"Moreover, I am not without hope that before the year is out their representatives in this Parliament will come and take their seats and relieve us of the awkward position of having, as it were, to deal behind their backs, which is to me a very unfortunate way of doing business, and one which I most heartily detest."

On the same day, Craig sent Collins a progress report on his implementation of the agreement. He briefed him that the Labour Minister had met the Belfast Corporation regarding unemployment, that a

Bill would be introduced to the House of Commons to give effect to article four and that he was awaiting names from Collins for the Catholic Police Committee.

He also raised issues such as the occupation of the Loyal Orange Institution in Ireland headquarters in Dublin and the continued boycott of Northern goods in Donegal.

The next day in the House came debate on an issue that would affect the future of Northern Ireland unbeknownst to many who spoke – the future of the policing arrangements following from the publication of the report from the committee of investigation in February.

The report recommended that a new police force be established for Northern Ireland, comprising two thirds of current members of the Royal Irish Constabulary, and one third from the Special Constabulary.

One third of the new force should be recruited from Catholics, a third from Protestant RIC members and the rest from the USC. The Royal Irish Constabulary would be disbanded by the 31st May following passage of the Constabulary Bill which would be laid before the House and the new force, pending agreement from the King, would be styled 'The Royal Ulster Constabulary' which was approved on 29th April.

During the debate, Craig made an announcement that legislation would be laid before the House to indemnify members of the new force and officers of the Crown when acting in the defence of Northern Ireland. He referred to papers he had laid before the Cabinet.

However, such legislation was never brought forward.

Craig had met with senior Cabinet members in London in the weeks previously on security and had been assured by the Chancellor of the Exchequer and the Colonies Secretary that in the event of any incursion by the South over the border, Britain would stand by Ulster, indeed five more battalions were being brought to Ulster, bringing the total to twenty-two.

The precarious economic situation Northern Ireland found itself in as previously outlined in the King's Speech was laid bare in the House on 24th May 1922. At the beginning of the year nearly 68,000 or 25% of the North's insured population was unemployed.[32]

As part of the Government of Ireland Act and its Finance Memorandum, the Northern Ireland Government expected, based on estimates of 1919-20, to operate with a surplus of £1,903,500 in 1920-21, equivalent to around £59.5m in today's climate.

However, high unemployment and the post-war depression had hit local and Imperial finances hard. The House was duly informed by the Minister of Finance Hugh Pollock (UU, South Belfast) that in reality the surplus in 1921-22 would be £64,730 and was estimated to yield a surplus of only £69,000 the following year. The unemployment fund alone was in deficit by £490,000 and would be in the red to the tune of £700,000 for the following year.

This balance was merely to run the services transferred to the Northern Ireland Government, excluding any new initiatives such as educational reform.

Unemployment across Britain had risen to 10% after 1919-20 and remained high well into the 1930's, with Northern Ireland's rate at 22.9% in 1922 and despite a sound financial position in terms of fiscal performance, the UK National Debt rose to 180% of Gross Domestic Product in 1923.

At the Cabinet on 1st April, the Prime Minister made good on his promise on the £500,000 unemployment relief fund. It was to be managed by the Minister of Labour and a committee representing ex-servicemen, the White Cross, British Legion and a representative nominated by Mr Collins alongside the Loyalist Relief Fund and Expelled Workers Union.

However, the fund was to be used only in Belfast and its surrounding area, and Craig suggested to the Minister that Catholics should as far as possible carry out work in their own areas.

T.J Campbell was to be appointed to the committee outlined in article five of the pact alongside other prominent Catholics in Belfast and Mr Frank McArdle of Rosemary Street was to act alongside Minister Andrews on the allocation of the unemployment grant.

Collins had serious concerns about the implementation of the article dealing with the northern legal system and the imprisonment of those who had committed crimes due to the political situation.

He wrote to Craig;

"I have consulted my colleagues and many prominent Catholic citizens of Belfast and there are all at one in the opinion that if peace is to be maintained and confidence restored an impartial investigation into all the occurrences must be held at once".[33]

Craig himself wanted to secure the primacy of the courts in all cases. On 11th, Collins sent a list of names of prisoners in Derry, Belfast and Peterhead prisons that he believed should be released, Craig refused, saying only those convicted of 'technical' crimes would be considered for release.

By June 1922, 46 relief schemes had been approved by the Unemployment Grant Advisory Committee and 469 Protestant and 277 Catholic workmen were being employed in Belfast.[34]

It would seem that by 27th April, cordial relations between the two had broken down, as demonstrated in correspondence from Collins to Craig;

"Now with regard to your letter of 25th inst. It is such an astonishing accumulation of evasions and charges supported by little or no data that I can only conclude its raison d'etre was for purely propaganda purposes – to be used by the various journals of British Press combine, which is playing such an important part in the game of disunion and internal conflict in our common country".[35]

He complained to Craig that he had only appointed one person to the Boundary Commission and that that person had no authority to act on behalf of the Northern Ireland Government.

The economic provisions on the 1920 Act left the new Governments in the North and South in somewhat less control of their destinies than what some may have imagined. All excise duties, income tax, corporation tax and even revenue from postage were to be reserved matters, with a Joint Exchequer Board established to allocate how much of this revenue was to be given back to the respective administrations.

An Imperial contribution was to be made to the Imperial Parliament annually, £18 million in the first year, and 44% of this was borne by Northern Ireland.

The Government sought to utilise other forms of economic stimulation such as via the Loans Guarantee Act which was first passed in 1922 and annually re-imaged until 1934 would give a lifeline to the linen and shipbuilding industries by guaranteeing loans of up to £2,000,000, extended to £14,500,000 by the end of its tenure on the statute books.

"The state employed several measures to support the Belfast shipyard. It enacted the Loans Guarantee Act in 1922, backing loans to the shipyards, allowing the yard to borrow capital and gain advantage over its competitors in securing orders."[36]

The Loans Guarantee Act 1922 gave opportunity to safeguard shipyards and as such the Protestant working class. Viscount Pirrie supported the Act and in return for its passage, he kept Pollock up to date with the progress of the return of expelled workers.

The Second Reading of the Constabulary Bill took place on 24th May 1922, the Parliamentary Secretary to the Ministry of Home Affairs, Mr Megaw (UU, Antrim) reporting to the House that the new Bill embodied all the recommendations of the report compiled by the investigatory committee.

However, during his speech, Mr Megaw also informed the House that the Special Constabulary would remain in place;

"This is no time to disband or to lose any opportunities we have of using the services of the Special Constabulary."

Indeed, in October of that year the Government reduced the number of 'A' Specials significantly and safeguarded the number of 'B' Specials. Despite the creation of this force arising from the ranks of the pre-war UVF, comments had been made in the House expressing the willingness of the Government that Catholics join the USC, albeit highly unlikely.

On 21st March 1922 a piece of legislation was given its Second Reading that still rings in the mind of many older Nationalists to this day – the Civil Authorities of Northern Ireland (Special Powers) Bill – known to many in its many manifestations as the Special Powers Act.

The Act sought to provide the civil government the same power as the military under the Restoration of Order in Ireland Act 1920 which effectively suspended the civil liberties of some who were suspected of being nationalist rebels. It replaced the right to be tried in a civil court with that of a court martial.

The short Bill of only 13 articles introduced the power of flogging to authorities for certain offences, such as arson and the death penalty for explosive offences. The Minister of Home Affairs had the power to create further Regulations under the Act at his disposal.

"Thirty-five regulations incorporated into the schedule of the 1922 SPA were drawn directly from the ROIA. They included the power to impose curfew, close licensed premises, prohibit public meetings and processions, ban military drilling, military uniforms and uniforms indicating membership of proscribed organisations, and to establish stringent requirements for the possession of firearms, explosives, or petrol."[37]

A special court of summary jurisdiction comprising one or two magistrates would sit in the trials of any suspected of offences under the Act. The Act was to be in place for one year only unless extended by Parliament.

The Minister wanted it to go further, but the cabinet decided to postpone any provisions that would effectively abolish trial by jury for some offences.

Days after the Bill received Royal Assent one of the first regulations was put in place – a curfew in Belfast from 28th April. The violence in the North had reached a climax in the month preceding the Second Reading of the Bill. Sixty-one including the McMahon family were killed in Belfast that month alone.

In May, the toll was yet higher at 67, and included the killing of W. J. Twaddell, the Ulster Unionist MP for West Belfast who was shot dead outside his business premises in the city centre of Belfast on 22nd. The Prime Minister gave a heartfelt speech in the House following Mr Twaddell's assassination and the Parliament voted a sum of money to arrange 'what would be tantamount to a State funeral';

"It is true that the first horror of this dastardly outrage may have passed way, but the memories of Ulster people are long, and I am sure there is not a Member of this first House of Parliament of Ulster who will ever forget the tragic end that met our dear friend who has departed."

According to Cusack, almost 500 people had lost their lives between July 1920 and July 1922.

The Special Powers Act had already been utilised by this time to close roads across three counties.

On 23rd May, General Solly-Flood updated ministers on the strength of the military in Ulster. Eight battalions were in Belfast alone, and five in reserve to move to the frontier if needed. Significantly, Craig showed no problem in giving the G.O.C. a carte blanche in dealing with any unrest.

"The Prime Minister pointed out that if a sudden emergency arose in consequence of the present trouble it may be necessary for the G.O.C. or General Solly-Flood to take some drastic action that would not be strictly covered from a legal point of view. He said he thought it would be very unfair to make either of these officers responsible and he considered that the Cabinet should give a written undertaking that the Government of Northern Ireland would be prepared to stand over any such action. This was unanimously approved and the Minister of Home Affairs and the Attorney-General were asked to draw up the necessary instrument."

A decision made by the Prime Minister months previous on the utilisation of the Unemployment Relief Grant money only in Belfast came back to haunt the Cabinet after severe criticism and they were forced to vote £50,000 to be used outside Belfast – a small amount, to placate those in Derry in particular.

In relation to the continuing delays on the Stormont site, the Labour Minister wrote to Craig on 4 April informing him that he had met with a delegation of employers from the building trade who were complaining about lack of movement on the site.

In the South, the Free State Government had been met with the anti-Treaty forces of the IRA who on 14th April had occupied the Four Courts in Dublin. At any rate, this provided a distraction and turned significant attention from the Northern state. A political stalemate ensued, with Michael Collins forced to confront his former comrades in arms.
A vicious and calculated attack on a small village outside Newry on 17th June 1922 struck at the very core of the new state and further solidified the fear, mistrust and anger directed at its southern counterpart and those in positions of power.

A group of up to thirty IRA volunteers were despatched from Dundalk in County Louth to Altnaveigh with orders to retaliate for the murder of two IRA men in Newry shortly before and because, according to James Marron, one of the men involved, it was a 'stronghold of the B force murder gang'.

Newly released files from the Bureau of Military Archives in Dublin on military service pensions during that period show that Mr Marron, who was appealing a decision by the Board in 1941 not to award him a pension for a particular period of service, alluded to a cover-up of the operation by its commander, Mick Fearon.

"We had a talk over it and we came to the conclusion, that if it was ever known, that our lives would be in danger. And we had no guarantee that it would not be known," wrote Marron.

"We knew the people and saw them every day. We were well disguised on the job and are not known as yet to have been on it, that was the main reason why we gave as little information as we could."[38]

Eight people were killed in total in the attack, 7 men and one woman, and dozens of houses were burned to the ground. Marron's evidence makes reference to being ordered to 'burn every house and kill every male'.

It was one of the worst atrocities of the time and struck fear into Protestant communities close to the frontier.

Days later on June 22nd, the Northern and British Governments were shocked to learn of the murder of Sir Henry Wilson. Wilson had played a major role in Ireland and was lately the Chief of the Imperial General Staff of the British Army. He had played a background role in the Curragh mutiny, and was a lifelong Unionist, serving voluntarily as Military Adviser to the Ulster Government. His two attackers were apprehended and in August and hanged.
Two IRA members, Joe O'Sullivan and Reginald Dunne shot and killed Sir Henry in London after having unveiled a memorial. Michael Collins had branded Wilson "a violent Orange partisan", likely because of his role in

Northern Ireland in advising the Craig Government on security matters, including increasing numbers of the 'B' Specials.

The next day Craig reported the assassination to the House of Commons in Belfast – "Sir Henry Wilson has laid down his life for Ulster." Craig informed members that following the murder of W. Twaddell, he had asked Sir Henry to allow his name to go forward to replace him. He used the opportunity to rally the loyal inhabitants of Ulster to the realisation that Ulster remained under sustained attack.

"I do hope and trust that there will be no further doubt in the mind of any man that what Ulster is engaged in is a battle not for Ulster alone, but for the Empire, and if anything is needed to steel the nerves and hearts of Ulster people it is the fact that they are battling not for a selfish cause but for one which affects the whole of the people of the great Empire to which they are proud to belong."

Recently released Military Service Pension files from the Republic's Military Archives show that records of a Mary Egan of London who had kept her home as a safe house for volunteers included evidence from Mr Mick Murphy, formerly OC of 2nd Battalion of the Cork 1st Brigade, IRA, who testified that her Kingsbury Park residence was used for a meeting to arrange for the murder of Sir Henry but was not carried out due to another murder in the vicinity of his residence. His evidence also reveals that Mrs Egan's daughter Nellie was to assist the men in the operation.[39]

Yet another potential calamity met the Belfast Government in July over their Local Government Bill. The Bill sought to replace proportional representation as the method of electing councillors in the province. In moving the Bill, Lord Londonderry referred only to the excessive cost of conducting elections by PR.

Churchill had refused to allow the Bill to be given Royal Assent of grounds that the change of electoral system could affect all of Ireland. Craig pulled no punches and informed the Prime Minister that this was a 'grave step on the part of the Imperial Government and that to allow this precedent to be created would warrant the interference by the Imperial Government in almost every Act introduced in Northern Ireland'. Churchill was persuaded to allow the Act to be given Assent.[40]

A week following this incident, the order was given by Arthur Griffith in Dublin to end the occupation of the Four Courts, with the Irish Free State forces bombarding the building with artillery, a watershed moment in the Irish Civil War and Ireland's history.

In August, only months after meeting Craig a second time to secure the Craig-Collins Pact, Michael Collins was shot at killed in Cork by anti-Treaty rebels. He was pre-deceased by his friend of long standing and founder of Sinn Fein, Arthur Griffith who had died suddenly on 12th August.

In September, the Third Dáil began passage of the Irish Free State Constitution Act, which gave force of law to the Anglo-Irish Treaty. The process had begun under the late Collins on entering Dublin Castle.

The slightly amended plans for the new Parliament and Administration Buildings in Belfast were approved by His Majesty's Office of Works on Halloween and were approved by the Cabinet.

Returning to the ongoing work on educational reform, schools in Ireland at this time were largely denominational, though funded by the State. The Committee Mr McKeown alluded to in his September 1921 speech was appointed a year later, to be headed by Sir Robert Lynn (UU, West Belfast).

"The Chairperson of the Commission on Education, set up in 1922 (Sir R Lynn) to determine the education system for the new state, set out his principles – 'there are two people in Ireland, one industrious, law abiding and God fearing, the other slothful, murderous and disloyal."[41]

It had sought representation from a wide range of stakeholders across the education system, but the Catholic Church refused to send representatives, fearing that a non-denominational system was the aim of the new Education Minister, Lord Londonderry.

Cardinal Michael Logue had refused to sit in the Committee and indeed even refused to recognise the new Northern state, as did the Church. Londonderry wrote to him on 29th August and received a frosty reply;

"judging by the public utterances of some members of the Belfast Parliament and their sympathisers, I have little doubt that an attack is being organised against our Catholic schools. I fear the Commission proposed of your Lordship, I am sure with the best of intentions, will be used as a foundation and pretext for that attack".[42]

Lord Londonderry was deeply shocked by the Cardinals refusal, and even sought assistance from the Lord Lieutenant, writing to him on 4th September;

"it is naturally very disappointing to me at the outset to meet with this refusal to co-operate on the part of so important a section, and I regret that I fail to understand the objection raised...I do not know whether I am right in ask you to give me your assistance in the matter, I would do anything to raise this committee above all political and sectional prejudices, and when I tell you how all the leading educationalists here have pressed me to have a strong and influential Catholic representation I cannot feel there is any justice in Cardinal Logue's accusations."[43]

Around a third of Catholic schools in the North refused to come under the new Education Ministry and instead continued to take direction – and salaries in the case of teachers, from Dublin until October 1922.

Those involved in the compilation of the report believed that the secondary school system would not be radically changed, and those representing technical education wanted a continuation of the status quo.

Both the Presbyterian and Church of Ireland representatives on Lynn's Committee pushed for a scheme of local grant aid through local government. In the interim report, Lynn accepted a form of local aid that would link the local funding to the amount of control a local authority had, the rest remaining with the Ministry.

Each local council was tasked with establishing local committees for the oversight of primary schools. Each committee would have a relationship with their local schools depending on which class it fell into.

The report suggested three 'classes' of primary education to frame the governance. Class I would be entirely funded by the local committee and the Ministry, Class II would be run by special committees and Class III would be entirely independent of local government. All teachers would be paid by the Ministry.

Catholic schools rejected any semblance of local committee control despite input from the committee.

"..it is clear from the minute book of the Lynn committee that committee members realised early in their deliberations that the Catholics would have nothing to do with the local primary school committees; any contemporary familiar with the Catholic reaction to the education bills of 1919 and 1920 or, aware of the policy statement of the Catholic school managers opposing all reforms in Ulster primary education, could hardly have thought otherwise."[44]

Derry and Belfast had subcommittees of their councils to manage the finances and running of local primary schools, whilst other regional committees possessed authority over other areas.

Mr Coote, on rising to speak during the debate on the King's Speech on the return of Parliament, expressed his anger about the seemingly segregated system that would now seem to become reality with the opt-out of the Catholic Church;

"The little tots dare not sit beside each other to be taught the rudiments of education as little neighbours together. If they cannot be taught and brought up in the same schools sitting at the same seats together, how will they be good citizens together?"

At an adjournment debate on 25th October 1923 following the summer recess, again Mr Coote expressed his anger that the Bill fell far short of a democratic system and the role of denominations. The Education Bill became law on 16th October having received Royal assent over the summer period.

Indeed, records from the discussion of religious instruction at cabinet on 15th December shows that Minister of Finance expressed the view that 'the province demanded religious education' whilst concern was expressed by some that an amendment to the Bill would come rendering education purely secular.[45]

The House passed the Local Government Act on 10th October, abolishing proportional representation for local elections, followed by, in 1923, redrawing the boundaries of some local government areas which would later become a source of real consternation for Nationalists.

The Northern Ireland Government had decided to retain the system of local government franchise that was in place in Britain at the time, that is, that businesses, primary tenants and their spouses have the vote – and in the cases of businesses, several votes.

The 1898 Local Government (Ireland) Act had given the franchise to householders but also significantly, those who lived in part of a dwelling.

As reflected in the Treaty, The Lord-Lieutenant would be replaced by a Governor General in Dublin and a Governor of Northern Ireland, and Northern Ireland would be given one month to secede from the South, and did so the day after the Act was assented to, by making the following declaration in the Northern Ireland Parliament:

MOST GRACIOUS SOVEREIGN, We, your Majesty's most dutiful and loyal subjects, the Senators and Commons of Northern Ireland in Parliament assembled, having learnt of the passing of the Irish Free State Constitution Act, 1922, being the Act of Parliament for the ratification of the Articles of Agreement for a Treaty between Great Britain and Ireland, do, by this humble Address, pray your Majesty that the powers of the Parliament and Government of the Irish Free State shall no longer extend to Northern Ireland.

In no small irony, the first Governor of Northern Ireland was the Duke of Abercorn, son of the Duke who had been Grand Master of the Orange Order and first President of the Ulster Unionist Council.

On 7th December when moving the declaration in Parliament, Craig played to the House.

"The moment there is any question of going under a Dublin Parliament I refuse to stand here, I cannot conceive that it is for the good of the people or for the good of Ireland as a whole to attempt anything of the kind, and therefore we may go ahead in our own way for the betterment and well-being of our own people here, trusting that the South may settle its affairs and get settled down to good government."

1923

In assenting to the declaration and the Senate doing the same, the legislative partition of Ireland was complete; Ulster would remain outside the Dublin Parliament's remit and continue to self-govern within the

Empire and within the United Kingdom. A week later the Northern Parliament was prorogued until 27th February 1923. The Treasury had approved the plans for the new Parliament House in November and Unionists began to feel that the turmoil and growing pains of the new state were beginning to calm.

Correspondence from the Office of Works on 7th March indicated that land clearance at the Stormont site should be completed by May, with excavation and road laying in October followed by the laying of foundations and the construction of the lower part of the building by October 1924.

A further significant event came on 24 May 1923 with the end of the Civil War in the South, giving the authorities more of an opportunity to seek resolutions to internal disputes and governance, giving the Northern government freedom to progress with its legislative mandate.

By October 1923, the relief scheme initiated by Craig-Collins continued to show promise with 1,195 Catholic and 2,332 Protestant men were employed on relief schemes in Belfast. It was also however, a barometer of the growing unemployment problem.

On 17th October the Ulster Unionist Council held an event in the YMCA at Wellington Place, Belfast welcoming Lord and Lady Carson back to Belfast. At the event which was covered by the Belfast Newsletter, an outline map of the new Stormont Parliament and adjoining buildings was unveiled which included plans to erect a statue in honour of Sir Edward at the entrance to the central thoroughfare outside the new Parliament Building.

The proposed Law Courts and Administrative Building would sit in opposing 'L' shapes at right angles.

At the UK general election held in December, the threat of Labour to the hegemony of Unionism again was demonstrated when Harry Midgely came very close to unseating Sir Robert Lynn who was previously elected unopposed. Midgely cut Lynn's majority to only 2,720.

This year also saw the passing of the Promissory Oaths Act that sought to underpin further the zero-sum view that Northern Ireland's leaders had on 'loyalty'. The Act required all civil servants and teachers in the state to swear an oath to the King and to the Northern Ireland Government.

On November 1923, the Minister for Home Affairs, Mr Dawson Bates, moved the Second Stage of the new Housing Bill, stating;

"I do not think anyone in this House will disagree with me when I say that perhaps next to the unemployment problem the housing question is one that presents the greatest difficulty to the Government at the present time."

In his opening speech the Minister referred to the lack of affordable good quality houses in the province, despite there being between 8-10,000 empty properties in Belfast alone. Houses built under a previous 1919 Bill from Westminster erected dwellings that no worker could afford to rent.

The Bill would provide a small subsidy for private enterprise to build more houses, based on a policy used by the Belfast Corporation at the time, though at the consternation of urban workers both Catholics and Protestants who lived outside the city centre.

A committee to be set up in the coming years would expose this policy as mismanagement on the part of the Corporation and as such undermined the overall regional housing policy into the 1930's.

Given the unique problems and their economic consequences in Northern Ireland of policing, security and unemployment insurance, the Northern Government had sought for a considerable period to persuade the Imperial Government to reform how it paid its Imperial contribution, which was set and due to be deducted from NI's consolidated funds even before services were paid for.

This resulted in a desire within the Unionist government to maintain the level of services with those in Britain, but given the financial formula of the 1920 Act, this meant following that policy would lead to virtual bankruptcy.

The Treasury this year had decided to send the Northern government's financial policies and formulae to arbitration and it established the Northern Ireland Arbitration Committee or Colwyn Committee headed by Lord Colwyn. Its role was to examine the case put forward by the Northern Ireland Government on whether the imperial contribution should be based on taxable capacity after essential services were paid for, rather than before.

The committee comprised Lord Colwyn, Sir Laming Worthington-Evans – the Postmaster General and Sir Josiah Stamp, a respected economist.

"The kernel of the argument presented by the Northern Ireland government was that it should make an imperial contribution according to taxable capacity based upon a capacity to raise revenue on the same basis as Great Britain and after having met local expenditure. Any balance in the Northern Ireland budget should be handed over under agreed conditions, one of which was a surplus of a definite amount".[46]

Following its first report to the Chancellor in September, £400,000 was granted to the Belfast Government towards new teacher training college, police depot and increased expenditure for prisons and asylums.[47]

Seeing an opportunity, the Belfast Government wrote to the Colwyn committee on 23rd September asking it to consider the financial results 'arising from the division of the UK Unemployment Insurance Fund' – it initially refused.

Craig suggested amalgamating both UK and NI unemployment funds and a committee was established by Lord Cave, Lord Chancellor. It recommended that the NI fund should remain separate but that there should be a 'partial amalgamation of responsibility for the deficit'.[48]

This reflected the relief of a significant economic stressor.

1924

1924 saw a relative lull in any major political events that affected the Northern state. The Southern state began to recover from the Civil War and the difficulties that presented, largely keeping its focus on internal issues.

A potential hangover from the disturbances that marked the birth of the state was that one of those interned during the trouble of 1921-22 was Cahir Healy, a Westminster MP. At the cabinet meeting on 25th January the Minister of Home Affairs briefed his colleagues on his case.

It was clear that Ministers did not want to release him, and it was eventually agreed that the Minister would arrange to hand him over to

Black Rod in the Imperial Parliament, but in doing so he was banned from re-entering Northern Ireland.

Another legacy of the violence took the attention of Ministers. District Inspector Nixon, long rumoured to have played a role in the McMahon murders, had been dismissed by Craig for making a political speech at an Orange Order gathering. However, the matter was now in court and Dawson-Bates had received word from the Secretary of the Supreme Court of Judicature of Northern Ireland that the Lords Commissioners did not feel they could sign the warrant for his dismissal, and that the Governor must now become involved.[49]

In February, a rare glimmer of Unionist internal maladministration was laid bare. Lord Londonderry had complained at cabinet on 24th February that Unionist Members of Parliament in Westminster were taking it upon themselves to have private negotiation sessions with senior Ministers, which undermined him acting on behalf of Craig.

Following the end of the Irish Civil War, the Irish Free State and British Government moved ahead with appointing their representatives to the Irish Boundary Commission, though Craig refused to appoint a Northern Ireland Government representative.

His view was clear;

"If the Boundary Commission were to sit, and if when it sits it were to grant to the Free State less territory than it hoped for and expected, what is to prevent the Free State applying the screw once more on the British Government, or any British Government by entering; such protests that it might be forced into another Treaty and take away from Ulster so much of her territory that the Northern Government would find it impossible to carry on, and the Northern Parliament would be nothing but a laughing stock."

He threatened to resign as Prime Minister should the Commission recommend removing land from Northern Ireland.

He had discussions with the Chairman, Justice Feetham in July and reported to the cabinet that he had told him that Catholics did not want to be transferred to the Free State, and only expressed that view due to intimidation according to 'their information'. This was clearly untrue and a further tactic to dampen any moves by the Commission to extract areas from Northern Ireland.

In October 1924 the British Government appointed Mr Joseph Fisher, former foreign editor of the 'Daily Chronicle' and then editor of the Unionist 'Northern Whig' to represent the Northern Ireland Government on the triumvirate.

The same month saw complaints by the Cabinet that stone masons were being used to undertake manual labour on the Stormont site, adding to the lengthy delay in completion. All this in the face of high unemployment amongst the masses who might undertake such work.

The Southern bogeyman, Eamon De Valera, it was mooted, might visit Northern Ireland in the next few weeks, and Sir James made it clear that should he enter the territory, he should be served an order to leave immediately, and that should he refuse, he would be arrested and trialled.[50]

1925

The Free State Government under the auspices of its North-Eastern Boundary Bureau had completed since its inception in 1922 a significant amount of research and cartography based on district electoral divisions, which clearly identified areas of National majority for use in arguing the case at the newly convened Boundary Commission.

The Commission was chaired by a South African judge, Justice Richard Feetham, representing the British Government, Eoin MacNeill, a republican and literary scholar of long standing representing the Irish Free State, and Mr Fisher to represent the Northern state.

The Unemployment Insurance Act received Royal Assent and the House was informed on 13th March. It had ended a potentially dangerous situation for the Unionist government. In Britain, the Conservatives had introduced the means test as part of safeguarding the insurance fund from abuse. However, Labour when it took power sought to increase rates whilst also assuring the Tories that abuse would not be tolerated and the test became more stringent. However, on the fall of Labour from power in November 1924 the Tories were rigorous in establishing that claimants were 'genuinely seeking work'. This had created chaos across the UK and in Northern Ireland where high numbers of people were being disallowed assistance.

This then fuelled the outdoor relief scandals that would unite Catholic and Protestant.

The Colwyn Committee published its second report on the issue of Northern Ireland's finances, and as Bogdanor states;

"the Colwyn Committee proposed a drastic modification to the initial financial settlement."[51]

Effectively, the report argued that Northern Ireland's necessary spending should be at the same per capita level as in Great Britain and that the Imperial contribution should not be paid until these services had been paid for. It is unsurprising that the Government sought to address the issue, given its deficit at the beginning of 1925 was half of its entire budget, approximately £3.6 million.

In a period of continuing financial uncertainty for the Northern Ireland Government, this represented a major coup, however with any increase it wanted to make to its own transferred services, it would pay in the imperial contribution.

It is clear both from the financial threat and the issue of the lingering Boundary Commission, the future of Northern Ireland had not been under threat to this level since 1922. This made for a nervous Ulster Unionist Party going into the 1925 election which was called on 3rd April especially with unemployment having only dropped 1% since 1921.

Sir James Craig was right to be nervous. His aim right throughout the Home Rule crisis and the first mandate of the Parliament was to maintain absolute control over Unionism in the form of the Ulster Unionist Party. He was not as clever as Carson in foreseeing potential threats for example within labour when Carson created the UULA.

When the ballots had been counted, Craig had lost eight seats. Sinn Fein had been reduced by four, given to its focus being in the South following the Cumann na Gaedheal election outcome in August 1923.

Nationalists gained four seats bringing their tally to ten, but the most significant outcome was that four independent Unionists had taken seats. These were all at the expense of UUP candidates.

The Northern Ireland Labour Party had gained three seats, largely at the expense of Republicans, this complemented their victory in the Poor Law elections of June 1924 when five LPNI candidates were elected to the Belfast Board of Guardians - and Unbought Tenants Association, which represented tenant farmers, took one seat in Antrim, defeating Ulster Unionist R. D. Megaw, a significant loss to Craig and his confidant Dawson Bates, who Megaw served as Parliamentary Secretary to the Ministry of Home Affairs.

The leader of Northern Nationalism, Joe Devlin had fought the election and had pledged to take his seat as opposed to the united abstentionism of 1921. On 28 April 1925 Devlin, MP for West Belfast and Thomas McAllister, MP for Antrim took their seats.

Three days previous, a deputation met both MP's following a conference the previous Tuesday in both constituencies that had decided the practice of abstention should end. Addressing the deputation, Mr Devlin had commented that;

"since his election, he had had pressing and repeated appeals from all sections. It had been pointed out to him that there was no chance of the Boundary Commission coming to a conclusion for some considerable time. He had made inquiries and had been informed that the deliberations of the Commission might go on for twelve months and probably longer. In view of that fact, and also because he had been returned to Parliament, not only by the votes of his own people, but by thousands of tolerant, generous-minded Protestants, he felt compelled to review his position".[52]

As was process, MPs were to elect new senators after the General Election, and whilst the Nationalist Mayor of Derry would not take his seat as an ex-officio member after the 1921 election, the Nationalists proposed two members of the senate one of these being Thomas Campbell who later withdrew, but in an unexplained anomaly, the postal papers those Nationalist MPs were required to use to nominate and vote did not reach the returning officer until after the allotted time which both MP's bitterly disputed, resulting in a motion to the House on 2 September 1925 by Mr McAllister (Nat, Antrim) as follows;

"That in the opinion of this House the decision of the Returning Officer at the recent election for the Senate not to count the ballot papers which reached him after the close of the poll should be reviewed, because such papers, though posted in ample time, were subjected to an unreasonable delay; and in view of these special circumstances this House directs the Returning Officer to undertake a recount of the votes, such recount to include the ballot papers which were not received in time."

McAllister informed the House that the letters of himself, Devlin, and Mr George Henderson (Antrim, UT) had been sent on Saturday in time for the ballot to close but were not received by the House until Tuesday following, the explanation of the Postmaster being that no-one was there to sign for the registered papers.

Mr Vincent Devoto, the nominated candidate, would have received high enough preferences from the three members to have him elected, but given the inadmissibility of their votes, an Ulster Unionist was elected instead. Sir James Craig confirmed that if the votes were counted, the seat would have been confirmed to Mr Devoto.

From the Hansard of the day, it is clear Sir James Craig was irked by the attack on the Parliamentary processes, replying to Mr Devlin that;

"If the hon. Members were really sincere in their anxiety to support this Constitution they might have been in this House itself three years ago."

Breaking ranks, Sir Robert Lynn (UU, Belfast West) urged the Prime Minister to allow for a recount on having concern for the status of minorities.

"I would appeal to the Government even now, for the strengthening of the good feeling that is growing to reconsider the question. No great harm surely can be done to the majority, but an act of justice would be done to the minority by having a recount, and I do hope that the House will vote in favour of a recount. At any rate I, for one, will, though I vote alone."

The motion amended to reflect that the result was correct, and all procedures carried out correctly was carried by a majority of the House.

Sir George Clark, Grand Master of the Orange Order, was elected to the Senate to bolster his brethren who made up every other member. Robert Dornan became the first non-Unionist member of the Senate, sitting for the NI Labour Party.

The period from May 'til August of 1925 saw a flurry of activity in the completion of the new Parliament House. It is often said that the new building was to be a monolith of unionist rule, but so involved was Craig in the intricacies of the construction that it was reported at Cabinet meetings during that period that he had sought changes to where specific rooms would be situated on the site, and where staff would work.

On 12th November Craig reported to the Cabinet that he and the Finance Minister had been asked to attend a meeting with the Office of Works about the new Parliament. He reported to colleagues that Lord Peel explained that 'the cost of the creation of the buildings under the present plans had risen enormously and now aggregated over £3,000,000, and it was in order to see what could be done to effect saving that the conference was called'.

At the meeting Lord Peel and his officials proposed that the dome on the roof of the building be eliminated and two additional floors be added to house staff which would negate the need for an administrative building, saving around half a million pounds.[53]

It was proposed to house up to 930 civil servants in the building as well as the Parliamentary apparatus. As such, the Commons chamber was reduced by cutting in half the Strangers Gallery.

Craig was so keen to move forward with the plans, that minutes of the meeting disclose;

"Sir James Craig said definitely that he was prepared to take a strictly utilitarian building, considering primarily the interests of the civil service; that, in his opinion rapidity in execution was of primary importance and that he was prepared to sacrifice almost anything to achieve that end".[54]

In return, Sir Francis Baines guaranteed that the buildings would be completed in three and a half years and the Office of Works would build the main thoroughfare, the Processional Way as part of the construction process. At the next cabinet meeting when presented with the amended plans, Ministers agreed to proceed but Parliament was not informed until the Prime Minister made an informal comment in the House on 8 December.

The Law Courts building would now be situated in central Belfast and Parliament would contribute £185,000 to the cost to accommodate approximately 250 staff of the Ministry of Commerce, Stamp Office and

Estate Duty Office in the new building whose location was chosen for convenience.

(An artist's impression of an earlier design of Parliament Buildings)

The new House, 'instead of having a large building lying empty a great part of the year, the enlarged building will be a busy hive of industry throughout the whole time' according to Craig.

His enthusiasm was not always shared by colleagues. In a letter from JM Andrews on 10th November, Craig was informed;

> "I am really afraid that in view of the fact that so much work has been uselessly done, so much material ordered, some of which has been delivered on the site which may prove to be unsuitable, there may be something approaching a scandal, which will not only blacken the Imperial Government, but will also blacken ourselves to a lesser degree".[55]

In an unprecedented move in early August, the Cabinet released a statement outlining their request that the House should be immediately reconvened 'in consequence of the continued prevalence of unemployment and the necessity for authorising further borrowing powers to the Unemployment Fund'.

The House was requested to meet on 1st September where the Resolution about the Unemployment Fund was read, to be debated the following day. The Cabinet was asking the House to advance £750,000 owing to the pressure on the fund and the continued deficit of work in the textile industry.

A Bill was passed in October which waived the 30 contributions claimants must have before being able to access assistance, and reduced employer's contributions by tuppence.

The Bill was given an all-day sitting, much to the annoyance of some members, but passed.

In moving to set the frontier, Section 12 of the Anglo-Irish Treaty in setting up the Commission referred to the border being set "so far as may be compatible with economic and geographic conditions".

As far as Nationalists were concerned, a transfer of areas like Derry, Newry and South Armagh to the Irish Free State was the only logical outcome of the work of the three-man panel. Unionists however felt an obvious threat to the Northern state's viability if it became too small to support itself and wanted the border left the way it had been set.

However, on 7th November 1925 the Commission's fate was sealed when the Morning Post, a pro-Tory paper published notes of the negotiations of the Commission, with cartography. The sources showed that rather than territory being taken from Northern Ireland, it was to gain territory from the Free State in the form of parts of East Donegal.

The leak caused a major political crisis in Dublin who were shocked by the contents of the reports. On 21st November, the Free State Government representative, Dr Eoin MacNeill, issued a statement to the Executive Council outlining his views on the situation, and resigning from the Commission and offering his resignation from the Government. In his statement, he made clear;

"Dr. MacNeill continued that he had been in touch with representative persons of all kinds in Ireland and that the unanimous opinion of all classes was that the fixing of a boundary line such as that indicated as in the Morning Post would be a violation of the Treaty.

He himself would not go so far as to say that such a line would endanger the Treaty, but it would certainly endanger the common objects of the Treaty, that it would seriously injure the friendly and existing sound relations between the two countries.

Dr. MacNeill developed his argument on these lines and finished by stating that under the circumstances he had come to the conclusion that it was his duty to withdraw from the Commission and to place his resignation immediately in the hands of his Government."[56]

Four days later, the Free State Government sent a telegram to the Secretary of State for Dominions in London seeking an urgent meeting regarding the Boundary crisis;

"We are convinced that the situation calls for a conference between the two governments with a view to seeing how far it is possible to arrive at some settlement of this matter less likely to afford grounds for serious discontent and possible disorder."[57]

It was agreed at this meeting that the Prime Minister would speak to Sir James Craig on the issues raised and suggested that the President of the Executive Council and he should meet, and the British Government would not coerce Ulster to any deal outside the realms of the Boundary Commission, which Ulster had forced upon it.

A flurry of meetings and diplomatic cables followed, and at a meeting with Kevin O'Higgins and the Prime Minister on 28th November, three options were set forward, as if the Commission being bound by law reported, then the recommendations would become legally enforceable.

"There are three courses open and trouble, in the nature of the case, attends any of them. The first alternative - Let the Boundary Commission deliver judgment. The second alternative - Accept the existing boundary. The third alternative - The delimitation of a boundary to be agreed between the two Governments."[58]

The next day, all representatives met with the inclusion of Sir James Craig. On 2nd December following discussions between the Irish Free State and the British Government at the Treasury, a magnanimous agreement was reached that would benefit all three parties, though would frankly leave Nationalist hopes in Ulster in ruins.

The Boundary would remain at the 1920 format, whilst Article 5 of the Treaty which required the Irish Free State to pay towards the public debt of the UK would be waived, effectively reducing Irish debts to Britain to a nominal £5m.

This was finally agreed on 3rd December in an amendment to the Treaty hastily named 'Agreement Amending and Supplementing the Articles of Agreement for a Treaty between Great Britain and Ireland to which the force of law was given by the Irish Free State (Agreement) Act, 1922, and by the Constitution of the Irish Free State (Saorstát Éireann) Act, 1922.'

As part of the earlier discussions, Kevin O'Higgins agreed he would seek the agreement of Nationalist MPs to take their seats in the Northern Ireland Parliament.

The agreement to maintain the Northern Ireland border decimated the views of Northern nationalists that either they would soon be under the control of a friendly government in Dublin, or that the entire partition arrangement would fall and bring about a united Ireland. Instead, Joe Devlin was forced to recognise that the future of Nationalism in the North must have a voice in the new Parliament and called on the public to recognise it.

On 9th December Sir James Craig presented the Agreement to the Northern Parliament and declared;

"Ulster rejoices, and rightly rejoices, at the termination of this long-drawn struggle, and Ulster individually and collectively is kind enough to overwhelm me - and I hope my colleagues at the same time - with compliments for having got the ship safely steered to port."

It was also during this period that following the Agreement, the Northern Government moved to dispose of the 'A' and 'C' Specials, following discussions about the costs of these services which were largely met by the Imperial Parliament. The 'B' Specials would remain as a special reserve force.

1926

In the new session of Parliament beginning March 1926, Mr Joe Devlin's call for Nationalist members to take their seats was heeded and he and his colleagues were joined by the two Nationalist members for Derry, Mr George Leeke and Mr Basil McGuckin and by Mr Patrick O'Neill from Down.

During the years leading to 1926, the Northern Ireland Cabinet had been in contact with the Treasury regarding the problem with Unemployment Insurance in the province – that is, that the financial burden on the state arising from the insurance fund was unsustainable and foisted upon Ulster as part of the 1920 Act.

In February 1926, Winston Churchill appraised the Imperial Parliament of an agreement reached with the Northern Ireland Government on the future provision for unemployment insurance. He outlined to members that 51% of the income of Northern Ireland came from only shipbuilding and linen industries, which was not sustainable in terms of providing for insurance. In 1926 the unemployment rate in Northern Ireland hovered at around 25% and should this agreement not have been met, the NI fund would register a deficit of around £2 million in a single year.

The agreement reached meant that 75% of any deficit in the Ulster fund would be met by the Imperial Parliament and resulted in what the NI Finance Minister referred to as equal contributions for equal benefit.

This negated the need for any cut in the benefit available in Northern Ireland.

On 16th March 1926, Mr Andrews moved the Second Reading of the Unemployment Insurance (Agreement) Bill, proclaiming it to be 'in my opinion one of the most important measures which this House has ever been asked to consider. After all, it is a Bill to ratify an Agreement entered into between His Majesty's Imperial Government and our Government for the purposes of establishing a mutual re-insurance scheme in order to ensure that insured persons throughout Great Britain and Northern Ireland shall receive for equal contributions equal benefits.'

This, coupled with the Loans Guarantee Act which facilitated the employment of some 7,658 men in the Harland and Wolff shipyard by March was a significant achievement, this at a time when the total number of insured men working in the shipyards was 17,591 - acting as the main buffers to unemployment in the North going forward.

March 1926 brought was is perhaps seen as one of the most divisive of public policy issues in Northern Ireland at that time for the minority – the abolition of proportional representation for Parliamentary elections. This is progressed in 1927.

In May 1926, a General Strike crippled England's heavy industry, transport and fuel industries. This gave rise to the fear in Northern Ireland that such an event would render the state paralysed. Considering this, the Minister of Commerce, Mr J. M. Barbour (UUP, Antrim) alongside the Minister for Home Affairs introduced the Emergency Powers Bill.

Whilst endorsing the right to strike, the legislation provided strict penalties on those who may seek to interrupt the supply of 'the essentials of life' by giving the Governor of Northern Ireland the power to instigate a State of Emergency and allowed Ministers to lay regulations before the House to give them powers to adapt to any situation arising under the Act.

Crucially, whilst no industrial strife manifested itself in Northern Ireland during this period, the Act remained on the statute books and could in theory, and indeed later in practice, be used to give the Government powers when political strife became apparent in a state with a history of sectarian violence. It was amended in 1964 but largely remained on the statute books until 2004.

An Imperial Conference was held in London in October bringing together all the dominions of the British Empire to discuss future arrangements for the governance and status of the constituent nations. Ireland had long pushed for legislative freedom it believed was already granted under the Treaty, but other countries could not agree, and a further conference was scheduled for 1930 to examine further those proposals.

It is notable for the Balfour Declaration, named after Lord President of the Council and former Prime Minister Arthur Balfour. It was agreed at the Inter-Imperial Relations Committee of the Conference in November and recognised dominions of the Empire as 'autonomous Communities within the British Empire, equal in status, in no way subordinate one to another in any aspect of their domestic or external affairs, though united by a common allegiance to the Crown, and freely associated as members of the British Commonwealth of Nations.'

1927

Two highly controversial Bills saw passage in 1927. Firstly, the Trade Disputes and Trade Union Bill which following from the strike in England in 1926, shook the Unionist Party into action against any possible organised labour distress in Ulster, and so it copied the English legislation and effectively banned a general strike by workers.

Sam Kyle, the Labour member for Belfast North opposed the Bill, describing it as 'the most obvious declaration of class war that has ever been made in this country'. He was supported by the Amalgamated Engineering Union and the Amalgamated Transport and General Workers Union, and he was convinced this legislation was solely aimed at the growth of the labour movement in the Province.

It also targeted specifically Labour's funding by establishing that political contributions from union members would now require an opt-in.

As referred to in March of 1926, the Ulster Government confirmed on 13th October 1927 that it intended to abolish Proportional Representation for Parliamentary elections and to introduce single member constituencies for the Northern Ireland Parliament.

Mr Kyle (Belfast North, NILP) put a motion to the House that the Government did not have the authority to change the system even under the 1920 Act, and that if it did, a select committee of the House should draw up the new constituencies.

During the debate, the Prime Minister, now Viscount Craigavon, branded those using later preferences under PR to elect non-UUP candidates as not knowing what they were doing.

"I hold, and hold strongly, that Proportional Representation submerges and clouds the issue so that at election time the electors do not really understand what danger may take place if they make a mistake in voting when it gets to the third, fourth, fifth, or sixth preference. By an actual mistake they did not intend to commit, Ulster may one day wake up to find itself in the perilous position from our point of view of being submerged in a Dublin Parliament."

Continuing Craig's duplexity regarding the minority Nationalist community, he stated in the same debate;

"What I want to get in this House, and what I believe we will get very much better in this House under the old-fashioned plain and simple system, are men who are for the Union on the one hand or who are against it and want to go into a Dublin Parliament on the other."

In defending the Government's plans, he referred to constituencies being too large so that voters were not able to avail of the service of their elected representatives, and again stated that voters seem not to know what they are voting for under Proportional Representation.

Whilst Nationalists saw this change as an attack on their representation and solidifying the Unionist stranglehold on power, it should be remembered that Craig had taken to the celebrations on 12th July to warn about the threat to unionism from independents and splits in the Unionist ranks.

Mr Devlin in responding attacked the Government's plans as being solely to protect the Ulster Unionist Party's majority. He gave numerous accounts of issues whereby Nationalists being co-opted onto local government were blocked by Unionist members and where representation on school boards running predominantly Catholic schools were in some cases majority Unionist.

Throughout the 1920's Unionists represented over 65% of the population of Northern Ireland and yet controlled 85% of its local authorities, leaving Nationalists to manage only Strabane and Newry authorities.

Thomas Harbison (Fermanagh and Tyrone, Nat) swore the Oath and took his seat in the House on 26th October, to be followed by Collins of Armagh, and Donnelly, Healy and McHugh the following week following Fianna Fáil's entrance to the Dáil, leaving only two non-Nationalists as abstentionists in Belfast.

Bogdanor states of the abolition of PR:

"It is just possible that the retention of proportional representation could have prevented the congealing of Northern Ireland politics into a sectarian mode and assisted in the formation of a more inclusive state in which the Catholic minority would have gained legitimacy."[59]

1928

On 29th January, Nationalist leaders organised a rally in Belfast to protest the abolition of Proportional Representation. Newry Urban Council passed a motion referring to it as a 'great blow to the working classes'.

Hostility at the highest level of government remained focussed on the South despite Nationalists being coaxed into the Belfast Parliament. It was manifested this time when in February, Fianna Fáil leader Eamon De Valera was arrested in Newry and sentenced to one month in prison under the Special Powers Act. He had been under an exclusion order for some time and had been previously arrested in 1924 when campaigning in Newry and Derry for Republican candidates.

Discussions at the cabinet on 1st February focussed on the looming crisis because of the Board of Guardians refusing to grant outdoor relief competently in Belfast.

Outdoor Relief was effectively work allocated to married men to work on roads and the like for a period of a few days a week for six months. The pay was very low, standing at between 8 and 24 shillings depending on the size of his family.

This was the only relief offered by the Board of Guardians under the Poor Laws for those who could not get any money at all due to the means test. The amount of money under the outdoor schemes was much lower than its counterparts in the rest of the United Kingdom

The rate of relief stood at 12 shillings for a man, wife and one child.

The Minister of Home Affairs informed his colleagues that the Board were meeting on the 2nd to consider a letter he had sent proposing that the Government would be willing to consider any application for a loan in order to meet the difficulty and also asking them to formulate a scheme by which the labour test could be applied to road work for which a grant could be made from the Road Fund.[60]

It was the first of a flurry of meetings held by the Government to exert pressure on the Guardians.

On 27th March 1929 the House of Commons (Method of Voting and Redistribution of Seats) Bill passed the legislative hurdles and became law, abolishing PR for parliamentary elections.

On 19th May the foundation stone for the new Parliament and Administrative Building was laid by the Governor on the Stormont Estate, East Belfast.

It was to be a red-letter day for the Unionists and their supporters. Extravagant plans were laid, and high-profile speakers and politicians were to attend.

The Home Secretary and his wife were to attend alongside the Chancellor of the Duchy of Lancaster. Viscount Peel, First Commissioner of Works and Lady Peel alongside Sir Lionel Earle, Secretary to His Majesty's Office of Works, Sir John Anderson and Lord and Lady Carson were all invited.

On arrival, the Governor was greeted by the band of the 1st battalion, West Yorkshire Regiment playing the National Anthem. Flanked by his guard of honour comprised of the Royal Iniskilling Fusiliers he was received by military and RUC leaders.

Overhead flew the No. 502 (Ulster) bomber squadron.

Lord Peel presided over the event, with the Governor laying a casket underneath the foundation stone containing local papers, coins, copies of Hansard, a message from His Grace on parchment and a matching message signed by the Prime Minister and Cabinet.

The casket was 15" long and 12" wide to fit underneath the huge foundation stone which remains today.

The Governor's message read;

"Saturday 19th May 1928

I hereby certify that on this day in the presence of a representative gathering of the people of Northern Ireland, I, laid the Foundation Stone of this the Parliament and Administrative Buildings of Northern Ireland. Abercorn"

(Image of the casket with its contents before being placed under the Foundation Stone. Belfast Telegraph 19th May 1928 (PRONI, GOV/3/6))

Once the Governor laid the stone, the troops of HMS Caroline fired a twenty-one-gun salute, with the 60,000 attendees watching on.

Speeches were given by the Prime Minister and the Leader of the Opposition, Labour's Sam Kyle MP. 'Land of Hope and Glory' accompanied the Governor from the platform and to a lavish luncheon provided for all special guests.

A telegram was then dispatched to the King informing him of the ceremony.

Nationalist members issued a statement on boycotting the ceremony, reported in the Belfast Newsletter on 4th May;

"The Nationalist members of the Northern House of Commons met in their room and considered the question of their attendance at the laying of the foundation stone of the new Parliament House at Stormont, to which they had been invited.

Apart from the National Issue, the treatment to which the large minority in the Six Counties is subjected would render it impossible for the Nationalists to participate in such a function.

Their people are rigorously excluded from their rightful share in all offices and appointments under the control of the Northern Administration. The boycott of Nationalists and Catholics in such places is indeed almost complete.

They are gerrymandered in two counties where they possess large majorities into the position of helpless minorities upon the public Boards. For these reasons and others, which they have endeavoured to voice in the Parliament, the Nationalists cannot attend the ceremony on 19th May"[61]

Sam Kyle, leader of the Labour Party and Leader of the Opposition was also keen to ensure his position was clear and wrote to the Northern Whig the next day;

"I have often said, and I say again, that I disagree with the Government in the choice of a site for the Parliament House, and further that the monies to be spent, whether by the Parliament of Northern Ireland or the Imperial Parliament, could be used much better if spent on erecting workers dwellings.

However, this is not the point I want to make clear, which is that Labour has decided to take its place at the ceremony as, for the time being, Labour is the Official Opposition in the Northern Parliament."

Not everyone was pleased with the plans for the new Parliament Building. In Westminster, MPs expressed their concerns about the price of the new building, and it was described as:

"a towering edifice out of all proportion to the business it was housed to transact."[62]

The designs of the building were lavish. It would have six pillars – one for each county of Northern Ireland at its entrance and throughout the building and was adorned with palmette or shell acroterion on all sides of the exterior.

Originally, a clock would have sat in the centre of the main pediment, but this was replaced by a Greek-inspired depiction – seemingly two tribes sending warriors away and sharing gifts. A pointedly calm scene. Like much of the Stormont Parliament, however, it is open to interpretation, and has been said to depict Northern Ireland presenting the flame of loyalty to Great Britain.

In the same month, the House saw bitter debate on the passage of the Civil Authority (Special Powers) Act for a further five years. Nationalist members, not in the House at the original passage, informed the House of the failings in the community of the Act and how given the Minister of Home Affairs stated there is relative peace, why the Act should be extended. Sam Kyle, the Labour member for North Belfast was equally scathing in his opposition;

"I do not know that any argument would be of any avail to convince the right hon. Gentleman of the great harm he is doing to the fair name of the Six Counties by proposing to make this Act a permanent feature of our legislation. According to the Bill he himself is the Civil Authority. He may be an excellent gentleman in his private life, but I am not going to say that I would trust him to have the right to say whether a meeting I was at was treasonable or not treasonable, because a person who has been associated with people who have made use of treasonable utterances in the past would be no judge of what was treasonable and what was not treasonable."

Parliament was prorogued on 16th April 1929 to facilitate the election of the new House in May under the new first past the post system in the new single member constituencies.

However, there was to be no rest for the Cabinet who met on 31st July to discuss the ongoing saga of outdoor relief.

"The Minister of Labour referred to the letter sent by the Ministry of Home Affairs to the Belfast Board of Guardians and pointed out that there was a possibility of their refusing to apply for an extension of the special order permitting them to give outdoor relief.

He viewed this position with grave anxiety as if the Board of Guardians persisted in their refusal, a serious condition of affairs would be created. He also gave instances which had come to his notice of cases where families were in direst straits. The time had probably arrived when the Board of Guardians must be made aware of their responsibilities."[63]

This persisted throughout the summer. At the next cabinet meeting on 2nd August, Ministers' fears were realised when the Board of Guardians had decided not to make an application for an extension of the order permitting them to provide outdoor relief.

In fact, the Guardians had made clear they believed the fate of the destitute was for the Government to consider, and they had the power to do so under the Unemployment Insurance Acts.

Ministers, stunned, now considered that legislation may be needed to force the Guardians into action by amending the Poor Law which was brought forward after the cabinet meeting held on 28th September.

It would seek to amend section 13 of the Poor Law Act 1898 to enable any Board of Guardians in Northern Ireland to grant special outdoor relief in cases where the Minister of Home Affairs is satisfied that exceptional distress prevails in the Union concerned.[64]

2

1929-1939: Consolidation

The 1929 election was yet another watershed moment in the development of Northern Ireland.

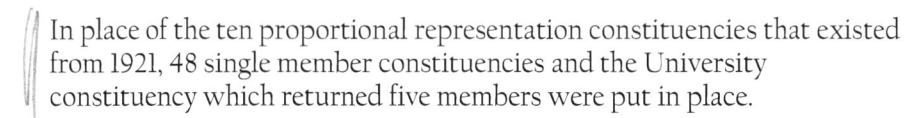

In place of the ten proportional representation constituencies that existed from 1921, 48 single member constituencies and the University constituency which returned five members were put in place.

"The Representation of the Peoples Act (NI) 1929 abolished the system of proportional representation as had obtained in the Six Counties between 1920-1929 and replaced it by a system which effectively limited to ten the number of seats which Nationalists could win at elections to Stormont."[65]

The Ulster Unionist Party had 16 members returned unopposed and took 37 seats in total. It held all the seats in county Antrim, 3 of 4 in Armagh, 11 of 16 in Belfast, 6 of 8 in Down, 2 of 3 in Fermanagh, 3 of 5 in Derry and 3 of 5 in Queen's.

The only county to have more Nationalist MP's than Unionists was Tyrone, where the UUP took 2 of 5 seats.

Nationalists returned 6 seats unopposed and took all eleven they had aimed for. Despite the Labour jump in vote share, they returned only one member, Jack Beattie in Belfast Pottinger. Three Independent Unionists were returned; Henderson in Shankill, Nixon, who had been believed to have been involved in the McMahon killings in Belfast Woodvale and R.J. McNeill in QUB.

The Unbought Tenants Association candidate, George Henderson ran under the banner of the Ulster Liberal Party but lost his seat. The first Speaker of the House, Hugh O'Neill, did not run and was replaced as Speaker by Henry Mulholland.

Craig's aim of consolidating the Unionist vote with the UUP and wiping out the threat of Labour was largely achieved. The state of the parties in the new House would largely be replicated until the abolition of Parliament in 1972.

Given the result for Nationalism, it remains hard to determine if the move to proportional representation was directly aimed at weakening Nationalist representation in the House, as had been feared.

The Senate retained its matching Unionist majority and saw Nationalist members elected for the first time. Thomas Campbell, Thomas McAllister and John McHugh. McAllister would go on to be the first Nationalist office holder in the Senate when he was elected Deputy Speaker, a role he would hold until 1932.

Arthur O'Neill Chichester took over as Clerk of the Parliaments.

1930

The continuing reform of education in the province was further progressed in early 1930 with the passing of a new education act, which rather than continuing to press for a secular system as Londonderry's original provisions had catered for, actually regressed and instilled religious education in the future of the system, at the expense of any integrated system.

The Education Act of 1930 spelled the end of Londonderry's vision for an integrated education system as envisaged in the 1923 legislation. In wanting to coax Catholic authorities into co-operating by restoring most of the grant that was withdrawn in 1923 and by granting a 50% grant for building in voluntary schools as well as granting a non-denominational bible study provision for Protestant schools which Londonderry had vetoed in 1923, the government had overseen the creation of two separate systems for education based largely on religion.

"They were now invited to agree to Bible teaching (which was subversive of their faith) and to legislation that could compel a Catholic teacher either to give such teaching if ten Protestant children joined his school or to suffer the consequences of refusal."[66]

The saga of the construction of Parliament Buildings rumbled on, and at the cabinet meeting on 4th June final decisions were made about the design of the senate, namely the idea by the Minister of Commerce that Irish linen should adorn the wall panels which Ministers had hoped would come from a wealthy benefactor. The damask was installed and was rubbed by members entering the senate. The worn fibres remain in the chamber today.

Members were briefed about the current state of affairs relating to the new Parliament's construction. The government had already spent £13,600 in acquiring the land around the new site and a further £1,000 for the planting of new trees and shrubbery along the Processional Way and across the estate, but many problems remained unresolved.

"In consequence of the dumping in this vicinity of an enormous quantity of material which was excavated from the new Processional Road, this particular area has become waterlogged, and in the winter period of the year is now converted into a large lake. In the Spring and Summer periods of the year when this stagnant water has evaporated or dried up, a highly objectionable condition of things obtains, as the place, in addition to producing unpleasant odours, becomes a breeding centre for mosquitoes and other obnoxious pests. To apply an effective remedy by a fairly extensive scheme of levelling and draining will necessitate the expenditure of, probably, several hundreds of pounds."[67]

In October, a further Imperial Conference was held in London to discuss the status of dominions and their legislative freedom. The Balfour Declaration had laid the groundwork for this new modus of operation for colonies and dependents.

W.T. Cosgrave represented the Irish Free State, flanked by Ministers. It was at this conference following the 1926 Balfour declaration that dominions should not be governed directly from Westminster that the Statute of Westminster was agreed.

1931

In October the Oireachtas acted against the IRA by passing the Constitution (Amendment No 17) Act. It inserted Article 2A, allowing the Executive to constitute a State of Emergency, and establishing the Special Powers Tribunal to try civilians for political crimes, overseen by officers of the Defence Forces.

It also brought the Free State in line with Northern Ireland in terms of prohibition of some armed groups such as the IRA and gave Gardaí the right of stop and search. As soon as the Act was passed W.T. Cosgrave initiated the State of Emergency and proscribed groups such as the IRA, Cumann na mBan, Saor Eire and Fianna Eireann.

In London, the Statute of Westminster was passed, giving legislative freedom to Britain's dominions. It was declared that self-governing dominions were to be "autonomous communities within the British Empire, equal in status, in no way subordinate one to another in any aspect of their domestic or external affairs, though united by a common allegiance to the Crown, and freely associated as members of the British Commonwealth of Nations."

The Free State government had always maintained that under the Treaty it had the power to legislate for itself in whatever manner it saw fit and rejected the British view that it remained a dominion and so had limited legislative competence.

The statute would repeal the Colonial Laws Validity Act 1865 which gave UK laws over dominions and colonies primary status. Whilst for many former colonies this was a positive result and allowed them to plot their futures from their own respective legislative apparatus, it further normalised the situation with Northern Ireland in that there was very little oversight by Parliament in London.
On 11th December, Patrick McGilligan the Minister for External Affairs released a statement welcoming the Statute;

"What is the significance of the Statute of Westminster in relation to the Irish Free State?

It is a solemn declaration by the British people through their representatives in Parliament that the powers inherent in the Treaty position are what we have proclaimed them to be for the last ten years.

It declares, in effect, that the Saorstát has powers to make whatsoever laws it desires, whether these laws purport to have internal or extra-territorial operation, whether they are repugnant or not to the law of England, whether they repeal old laws or enact new ones.

In a word, it declares that the powers of the Saorstát Parliament are equal in all respects to those of the English Parliament."[68]

1932

1932 brought a raft of activity in or affecting the Northern Ireland legislature. In February, a General Election was held in the South, sweeping Fianna Fáil, the party of Eamon De Valera to power. His republican policies mixed with his own and his colleagues' past caused dismay North of the border.

Indeed, one of the first acts of the new Government was to release over 20 republican prisoners in March.

One issue that would become hotly contested between the new Irish Government and the British Government was the issue of land annuities.

Even though the Boundary Commission agreement had relieved Ireland of its obligation to pay a proportion of UK public debt, the payment of annuities was still required and had been continued by the previous Government. De Valera had promised that he would not make the payments.

The annuities were loans made under the Land Acts by the Exchequer to house families in rural areas of Ireland.

On 22nd March 1932, the Free State Government informed their counterparts in Britain that they would legislate to remove the Oath of Allegiance from the Constitution. This was met with anger in Whitehall;

'In the opinion of his Majesty's Government in the United Kingdom it is manifest that the Oath is an integral part of the Treaty made 10 years ago between the two countries and hitherto honourably observed on both sides. They wish to make their standpoint on this question clear to his Majesty's Government in the Irish Free State beyond a possibility of doubt'[69]

The British Government also referred to the announcement that the land annuities would not be repaid in diplomatic cables, making clear the policy that land annuities were owed because of the Land Acts and should be paid.

The Constitution (Removal of Oath) Bill was introduced the next month, removing the requirement that elected representatives to the Dáil swear an oath of allegiance to the British monarch.

As retaliation for the withholding of the annuities due on 1st July, the British Government announced it would apply a 20% tariff to all Irish agricultural products.

In answering London's serve, Sean MacEntee, Irish Minister of Finance introduced the Finance (Customs Duties) Bill to impose over 40 tariffs on goods being imported to Ireland principally from Britain, thus beginning the Anglo-Irish Economic War.

In the North the month previous, Nationalist frustration with the Northern Ireland Parliament boiled over. Following a financial debate on the House on 11th May where Mr Devlin felt that the Speaker was constricting the ability of members to speak on key financial issues, he and his MPs withdrew from the House, not returning until early October 1933.

The day before the Free State Government informed the British of their intention to legislate for the removal of the oath, the Northern Parliament received details of a new Bill, the New Industries (Development) Bill which would effectively pay a sum of money annually to any new company who came and set up in Northern Ireland during what was a crippling period of economic stagnation in the two main industries.

Unemployment in shipbuilding by December 1932 would stand at 64.5%, whilst in linen it was steadily increasing to a high of 56% in July 1938.

The Bill also empowered the Ministry of Commerce to waive the rents of these new businesses by paying it to local authorities from Government coffers.

Only one business availed of the scheme, Shorts and Harland, which was formed in 1936. It received an annuity from the Government of £2,709.

Despite yet another initiative, unemployment continued to dog the Northern government throughout 1932. In April, the Home Affairs Minister revealed the huge increase in people seeking Outdoor Relief, which stood at 12,883 persons.

A resolution passed by the Ulster Unionist Labour Association summed up the demands of those seeking reform of the relief:

"While we appreciate the difficult position in which the Guardians are placed owing to the present regrettable and widespread distress, we feel it absolutely necessary that the amount given in the form of outdoor relief should be considerable increased."[70]

2,000 workers attended a protest meeting on September 30th in Belfast demanding, amongst other things, an increase in the rate of outdoor relief, schemes to be paid at union rates and an end to payment in kind. This was following meetings that had taken place in the South.

In the House, Jack Beattie was refused leave by the Speaker to bring forward a motion on unemployment during prorogation despite the Prime Minister being accepted to do so. In a fury, Beattie repeatedly removed the mace, representing the Monarch, from the Table, and was repeatedly asked to leave, refusing to do so until he received a ruling by the Speaker.

He eventually threw the mace on the floor of the House of Commons and left, the Sergeant-At-Arms having to replace the it.

The 1929 public works scheme initiated by the Government had largely failed to address the unemployment problem and exacerbated the problem of relief.

As expected, the protests and demands were ignored by the Guardians and largely by the Government, so the workers, both Protestant and Catholic, marched from Frederick Street Labour Exchange to Custom House on 3rd October where a meeting of the Guardians was held. Some 30,000 souls were in attendance.

The next day, workers blockaded the Lisburn Road and thousands rallied to the Workhouse to petition the Guardians who responded by passing the buck to the Government.

A riot began on the evening of 5th October and was met with a ferocious police response. An offer of increased rates put together by the Lord Mayor of Belfast was rejected and on 11th October, having armed the RUC with rifles and having the army on standby, the Government banned a planned rally by workers. Violence broke out in both the Falls and Shankill districts against police. One man, Sammy Baxter was killed by the RUC prompting no-go areas to be erected in areas across the City.

The following day a Catholic man was killed in the Falls by police. By the end of the riots, scores were injured from both sides of the community.

The Government had come up with the novel idea of increasing rates to workers by pillaging the Roads Fund, thus ending the relief disquiet.

"...the Ministry of Home Affairs promised large grants to Local Authorities in order to continue relief schemes, the grants being funded by the Road Fund."[71]

This was the only instance in the history of the Northern Ireland state that members of both denominations stood together against the Government and removed the ability of Unionist leaders to divide workers by using the religious card.

On 16th November, the new Parliament building at Stormont in East Belfast was officially opened by Edward, Prince of Wales. His visit was a spectacle not seen by the people of Northern Ireland since the visit of the King at the first meeting of the new Parliament.

The Prince was conveyed to Belfast onboard the MV Ulster Prince to Donegall Quay, where he was greeted by the Governor and Harbour Commissioners as well as Viscount Craigavon. Small planes flew overhead from nearby Aldergrove in formation.

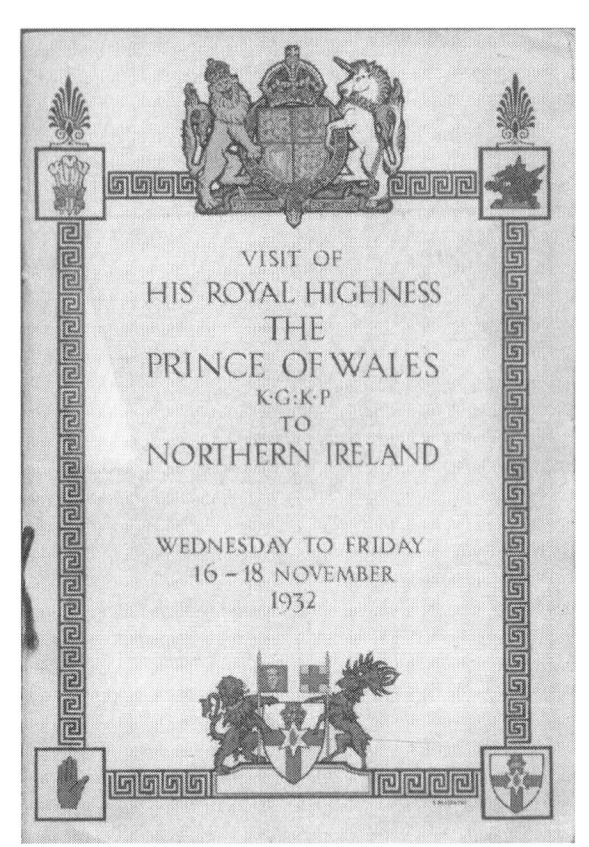

VISIT OF
HIS ROYAL HIGHNESS
THE
PRINCE OF WALES
K·G:K·P
TO
NORTHERN IRELAND

WEDNESDAY TO FRIDAY
16 – 18 NOVEMBER
1932

Nearby ships were decorated to welcome the Prince, and tiered seating had been provided at several points across the planned route of the Prince's procession.

On his first steps in Ulster, Navy ships in Belfast harbour sounded a 21-gun salute. The National Anthem was played by the Royal Marines Band which he then inspected.

From Donegall Quay to the Stormont site many thousands lined the route to see a glimpse of the royal bolstered by the presence of thousands of B Special officers.

At Parliament Buildings, loudspeakers had been provided to enable the many thousands of people to hear the Prince's speech. After taking the salute of the Royal Inniskilling Fusiliers on the promenade, he was met in the Great Hall by the Governor, the Prime Minister and the First Commissioner of Works, with the Imperial staircase looked on by a large Union flag donated by the Orangewomen of Toronto for the occasion.

Crowned with Britannia, the new building housed the House of Commons, Senate and administrative offices and offices for members. The Cabinet sat at the nearby Stormont Castle which doubled as the official residence of the Prime Minister, whilst Stormont House was used as the Speaker's grace and favour residence.
Nationalists boycotted the event. Elected representatives met in Belfast on Saturday 5th November and released a statement;

"We should betray the trust reposed in us by our constituents if we had hand, act, or part in the proceedings. We regard partition as a national evil, disastrous to the Six Counties, and injurious to the Twenty-Six."[72]

Speaking at the event, the Prince of Wales addressed the thousands of attendees;

"My Lord Duke
My Lords, Ladies and Gentlemen,
His Majesty the King, my dear father, being unable to be present in person, has charged me as his representative to perform today's ceremony of opening this building which is to be the home of your Parliament and administration.

More than ten years have passed since the first meeting of the Parliament of Northern Ireland, when my father expressed his confident hope that the important matters entrusted to the control and guidance of the Parliament would be managed with wisdom and with moderation, with fairness and due regard to every faith and interest, and with no abatement of that patriotic devotion to the Empire which you proved so gallantly in the Great War. Much has been achieved in that time, and hope has not been disappointed.

A promise was given by His Majesty's Government that a building should be provided worthy of the tasks which those were to labour in it would be called upon to perform, worthy of the people of Northern Ireland, their history and traditions. That promise has now been fulfilled. No-one can fail to be struck by the nobility and beauty of the fabric and the fairness of the site dominating a great part of your beautiful countryside near to the capital city of Belfast, of which you are justly proud, yet not so near as to be overshadowed by it.

It is a great pleasure to me to be among you today for the purpose of inaugurating this building and to convey the wishes of his Majesty for your welfare and prosperity. It is my father's earnest prayer that you will meet all those difficulties which confront the whole world, as well as your own special problems, with the courage, tenacity, loyalty and devotion which have always characterised the men of Northern Ireland and have made them famous in the annals of the Empire.

The responsibility of those who are entrusted with government and the making of laws can never be a light one. Heavy indeed is the burden that lies upon those who have to build upon new foundations. It is a matter for rejoicing that so many of those who have carried through this difficult task with such conspicuous success are still with you to give counsel and guidance in the difficulties which lie ahead.

In the name of and on behalf of his Majesty the King, I declare this building to be open. May the Blessing of Almighty God rest upon it and upon all those Ministers, Legislators and other public servants who labour therein.

It affords me much pleasure to convey this message from his Majesty the King; "I rejoice to think that the Parliament of Northern Ireland, at whose first meeting I was present, has now been provided with a worthy home. I ask you to assure the people of Northern Ireland of my heartfelt wishes for their continued happiness and progress.""

The opening itself cost £2,640 and commemorative medals were issued to mark the event.

The new home of Parliament was designed by Liverpool architect Arnold Thornley in Portland stone, measuring 365ft across, one foot for each day of the year in Greek classical theme. The building is adorned by laurel wreaths – which, depending on your outlook, represent either peace or victory.

The final cost of the building stood at £1.7 million. It had six floors measuring 100 feet high and is fronted by six pillars representing each county of Northern Ireland. The landscaping to the front and either side of what was to be called Parliament Buildings was were the cancelled Law Courts and Administrative building were to be housed.

The Central or Great Hall measured 26.85m x 14.31m and was adorned with a large golden chandelier which originally hung in Windsor Castle as a gift from the German Kaiser, but was removed after World War One, it is joined by two replicas which were produced by Harland and Wolff.

The interior walls of the new Hall were adorned with Travertine marble of cream, gold and walnut which also covered the main staircase and the carved features such as the clock. The balustrade of the staircase was made from bronze and designed with a six-pointed spoke throughout.

Its ceiling was protected by a secret waxing process utilized by Tabb & Co. of London and the colours remain as vibrant today as it did then.

Leading off the Central, or Great Hall were two rotunda outside the Commons and Senate Chambers 27ft in diameter. As part of the ingenious design by Thornely, four large light wells were created in the centre of the structure, finished with special light reflective tiles that would bring natural light to the offices at the centre of the building.

Four smaller light wells were created for the chambers, one at the north and south of the Commons and the Senate.

The House of Commons chamber was decorated with English walnut panels twelve feet high with the Table decked with gold Greek key inlays and blue benches in Moroccan leather.

In contrast, the Senate's walls were festooned with botticino marble and black columns topped with gilded gold craftwork with English walnut furnishings and rose coloured leather.

The Strangers Gallery of the Upper House had on its ceiling painted three figures representing the three major industries at the time - textiles, shipbuilding and agriculture which remain.

In all, the internal corridors were up to 300 feet long, and the building boasted over 500 doors and over 700 windows.

On the advent of the ceremony the building was formally handed over to the Northern Ireland Government by W. Ormsby-Gore, First Commissioner of Works.

PARLIAMENT BUILDINGS

Stormont Castle with the construction of Parliament Buildings in the background (PRONI, GOV/3/6)

PARLIAMENT BUILDINGS

Crowds on the Stormont Estate attending the laying of the Foundation Stone (PRONI, GOV/3/6)

PARLIAMENT BUILDINGS

21-gun salute from the sailors of HMS Caroline during the laying of the Foundation Stone (PRONI, GOV/3/6)

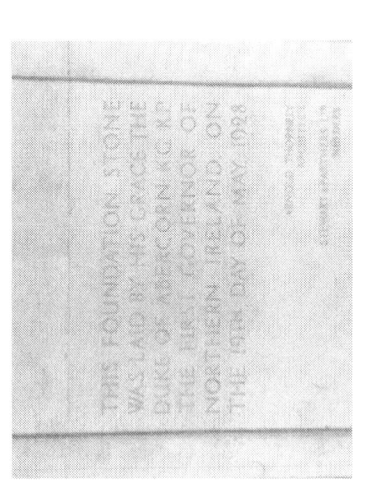

The Foundation Stone at the front façade of Parliament Buildings resting on the stone containing the casket, and below, the carved inscription adjacent to it at the entrance of Parliament Buildings celebrating the official opening.

Below: Members of the House of Commons attending the Senate, 1945 (PRONI, INF/7/A/5/44)

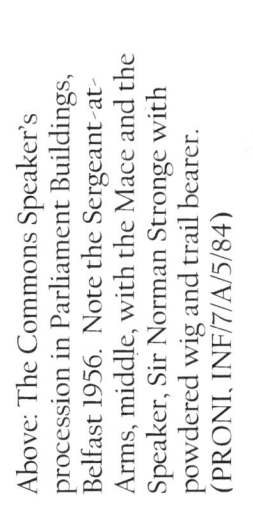

Above: The Commons Speaker's procession in Parliament Buildings, Belfast 1956. Note the Sergeant-at-Arms, middle, with the Mace and the Speaker, Sir Norman Strongue with powdered wig and trail bearer. (PRONI. INF/7/A/5/84)

Left: The Gift of Deed from the British Government of the Stormont Estate to Northern Ireland (July 1962) (PRONI, INF/7/A/5/98)

Right: Mr Arthur Henderson, Secretary of State for Air, Viscount Bangor (Speaker of the Senate) and Prime Minister Sir Basil Brooke at the unveiling of the inscription recording the thanks of the UK Government for the wartime use of the Senate Chamber by the R.A.F during World War Two (PRONI, INF/7/A/5/63)

Left: The Northern Ireland Senate sited in Union Theological College, 1921

Right, the Member's Rotunda of the Senate at Parliament Buildings

The Member's Rotunda leading to the Northern Ireland House of Commons/Assembly Chamber

IN MEMORY OF
CAPTAIN THE RIGHT HON SIR NORMAN STRONGE BT MC HML
MEMBER OF PARLIAMENT FOR MID ARMAGH 1938-69
SPEAKER HOUSE OF COMMONS 1945-69
SHOT WITH HIS SON JAMES BY TERRORISTS ON 21 JANUARY 1981

PLACED HERE BY PARLIAMENTARY COLLEAGUES AND FRIENDS

IN MEMORY OF
SENATOR JACK BARNHILL
MEMBER OF THE NORTHERN IRELAND SENATE 1962 - 71
DEPUTY SPEAKER OF THE SENATE 1967 - 68
KILLED BY TERRORISTS ON 12 DECEMBER 1971

"HONOUR, INTEGRITY, COMPASSION"

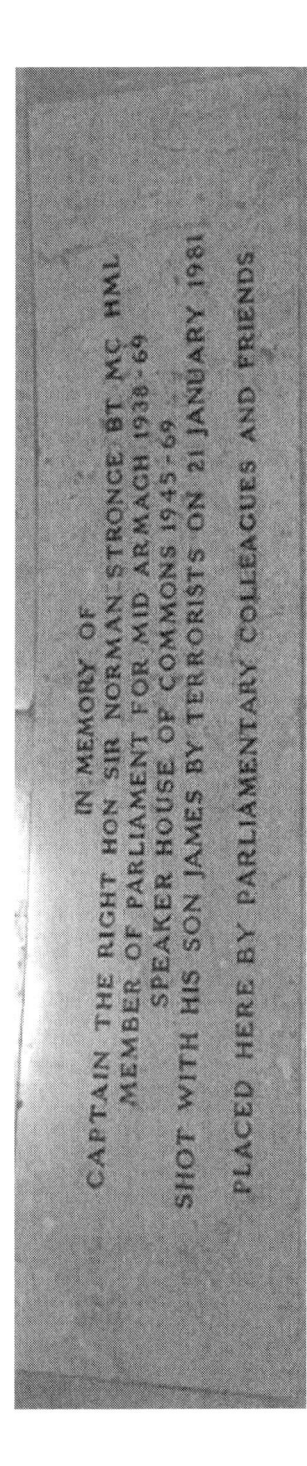

Engraving in the Member's Rotunda in remembrance of Sir Norman Stronge who was murdered by the IRA in 1981, below, plaque to remember Senator Jack Barnhill who was murdered in December 1971 in the Senate Rotunda.

IN MEMORY OF
SENATOR PADDY WILSON
MEMBER OF THE NORTHERN IRELAND SENATE 1969 – 72
KILLED BY TERRORISTS ON 25 JUNE 1973

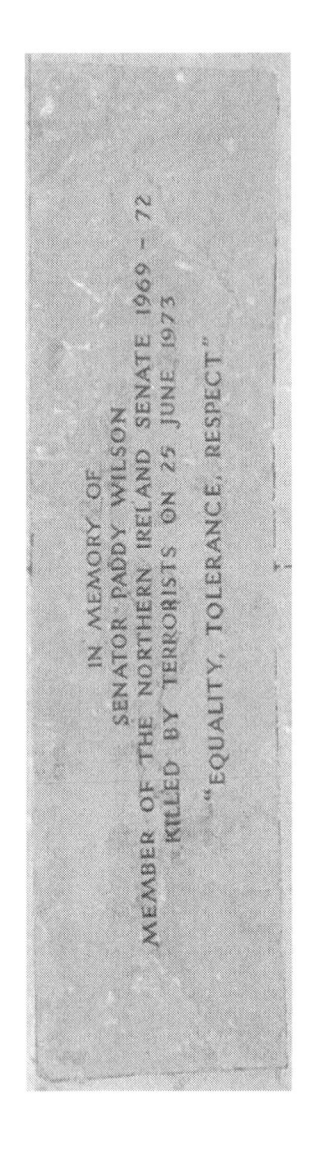

"EQUALITY, TOLERANCE, RESPECT"

Engraving in Parliament Buildings, Belfast to remember Senator Paddy Wilson who was murdered in June 1973, below, the tomb of Sir James and Lady Craig on the Stormont Estate. Pics courtesy of S Morrison.

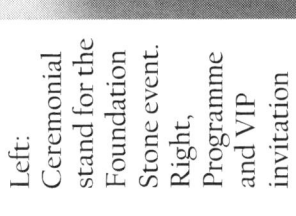

Left: Ceremonial stand for the Foundation Stone event. Right, Programme and VIP invitation

1933

The new building for the Royal Courts of Justice were opened on 31st May 1933 by the Governor. The building was designed by James Grey West with the eminent Sir Richard Allison as chief architect. Like Parliament Buildings, it was an opportunity to find work for the mass unemployed, and a Belfast firm in the form of Stewart and Partners were granted the contract to complete the project.

The original plans whereby the Court building would be situated alongside Parliament Buildings was due to be designed by Ulsterman, Ralph Knott.

When the plans changed, Mr Knott still completed the building of Stormont House, the Speaker's residence in 1926, the first of the Parliamentary Buildings to be completed on the Stormont Estate.

The foundation stone was laid in October 1929 by the Governor and in the presence of Rt Hon. George Lansbury, First Commissioner of Works for the Imperial Government. It stood on the location of an ad hoc potato market in Chichester Street and took over from the Crumlin Road courthouse as the Supreme Court of Ulster.

Finished in Portland stone with Irish granite pavings, the building primarily housed two Kings Bench Courts, a Chancery Court and a Court of Appeal with the small front building at Chichester Street used to house some small government agencies.

Much as with Parliament Buildings, the walls of the central hall are adorned with Travertine marble.

A snap election was called in the Irish Free State, strengthening the hand of Fianna Fáil.

A General Election was also held in Northern Ireland in November 1933, returning the Ulster Unionist Party to power, but marking a significant decline in the participation in elections across the province, with 33 of the 52 seats available being uncontested, the highest of any NI Parliamentary election.

In South Armagh, Paddy McLogan was elected as an Independent Republican, the first to sit as such, and Eamon De Valera returned to the House, taking a seat from Nationalists in South Down.

Independent Unionists returned three seats, but had a 7% increase in vote share, NI Labour stood three and returned two, and Nationalists returned nine, losing two seats.

One Independent ran for a seat in the University constituency but was not elected.

In the Senate, James Gyle was elected as the first Ind Unionist member, and Nationalists added two new members, Thomas McLaughlin and James McMahon to bring their total to five.

Fraught parliamentary relations continued in December in response to a question from Mr Hanna (UU, Larne) regarding the flying of the Irish tricolour, the Ministry of Home Affairs revealed that it had been banned effectively by the Special Powers Act where it might be used to breach the peace.

1934

Early in the new year Nationalism suffered a hammer blow when Joseph Devlin, the leader of Nationalism and leader of the opposition in all but name, died.

At the news of his death, the House paid a touching tribute to Mr Devlin across the benches, with the Prime Minister concluding his remarks saying;

"Those of us who knew him in public and in private life deplore the loss of a great Ulsterman, and we pay this small tribute to him here, and tender to his relatives our sympathy and our grief."

Only Viscount Craig, Mr Beattie (NIL, Belfast Pottinger) and Mr Healy (Nat, South Fermanagh) made speeches on this motion. Devlin was succeeded as Leader of the Nationalist Party by Thomas Campbell who won Devlin's seat in Belfast Central in a by election shortly after, resigning his seat in the Senate where he was the only Nationalist to have a Private Members Bill passed – the Wild Birds Protection Bill.

By May 1934, when the Loans Guarantee Act was allowed to lapse, the Northern Ireland government had guaranteed altogether £22,455,521 of which only £2,334,311 was outstanding by February 1942 and by the end of the decade all but £7,000 had been repaid.[73]

This demonstrated a huge success for the government and had helped to address the unemployment crisis of earlier years.

1935

An important if often overlooked piece of legislation was introduced in the House in May of 1935 – the Road and Rail Transportation Act. In essence, the railway and road transport industries had been operating on the basis of harsh competition and inefficient practices for several years, and the situation had now come to a point of government intervention.

The original oversight of the railways, given their cross-border nature, was envisaged by the Government of Ireland Act to be managed by the Council of Ireland. It was not until 1925 that the Ministry of Transport in London transferred responsibility for the railways to the Ministry of Commerce in Belfast when it became apparent the Southern Parliament would not be sitting.

It was not long after taking on responsibility for the railways that the first signs of distress came to visit on the Government. The Londonderry and Lough Swilly Railway was in dire financial straits and approached the Belfast Government for financial aid.

It was quickly followed by the Belfast and County Down Railway in June, which was on the brink of collapse. The Government was at pains not to intervene and instead commissioned an Interdepartmental Committee on transport in 1927 to make recommendations.

When it reported, the position was clear, companies should be allowed to collapse rather than relying on public subsidy. Due to the sharp rise in costs – especially in wages and the post-war slump, Stormont was not able to take on the sizeable debt of the companies involved.

"By 1934 the combined effect of the increasingly intense competition from the roads, deteriorating economic conditions a major railway strike in 1933 which lasted nearly three months, brought the railways almost to their knees."[74]

The government had called upon the talents of Sir Felix Pole, who had extensive experience in the transport industry, to compile a report on how to move forward. In briefing the House of the contents of the Bill in May, the Home Affairs Minister quoted from Sir Felix's report;

"The outstanding feature of the proposals submitted for consideration is that practically all parties recommend the government to take action in one form or another. Further regulation and co-ordination of the transport facilities are recognized as being necessary."

The Bill sought to create a Road Transport Board which would acquire road undertakings compulsorily. The railways would continue to operate but would do so alongside the roads in a Joint Committee that would have interests in each other's financial future and would co-ordinate rates.

The key tenet of this legislation was to continue the option for stable public transport at affordable prices lest the entire transport infrastructure in terms of public, goods and livestock transport collapse.

Whilst in theory the NIRTB seemed to be a resolution to the complex transport problems in Ulster, it was not long before the complaints from the public and from railway companies came rolling in. The idea of each venture having a financial stake in the others business was to act as an internal balance, what it was not envisaged it would do is to share out debt.

In the first year of operation the NIRTB reported losses of £100,000, and £160,000 in year two, all to be shared amongst the railway and road interests.

A committee was established under Sir William McLintock to investigate what could be done, such was the fury of the railway companies. However, it simply recommended what the Government was not prepared to implement – a single transport authority. The saga would continue in 1939.

The ugly scenes of sectarian destruction returned to Belfast in the summer of 1935 during the marching season. Workers and homes were attacked in the York Street area as early as 10 May, which prompted the government to instigate a curfew.

The next night, police officers were ambushed and attacked with stones from neighbouring streets and ran through houses to get to those attacking them. This was perceived by Protestants as a police riot by Catholic officers.

17th June saw shots being fired in York Street, which forced the Minister for Home Affairs to ban all processions apart from funerals in Northern Ireland.

It was widely seen in the loyalist community that this ban was aimed at the loyalist marching season. On 23 June the Lord Carson Flute Band paraded in breach of the order in York Street unobstructed. Four days later, the Home Affairs Minister rescinded his banning order.

On the 12th July, scuffles broke out in the Markets area after an Orange march, and a young Catholic man was arrested and charged with possessing a firearm. When North Belfast lodges returning home heard of the trouble, a riot broke out in Lancaster Street leaving two Catholics and two Protestants dead.

The next day 400 people attended Nelson street to deliver a wreath to the family of one of the dead Protestants. Led by the Billy Boys Band of Glasgow, the crowd entered the nearby Lower Dock area. 56 Catholic homes in six streets were destroyed.

On 14th July, realizing the severity of the trouble, the Army was despatched to the streets for the first time since the disturbances in 1922. Catholic evictions and looting were widespread.

The following three days saw large number of Catholics evicted from their homes in the Old Lodge area.

By the end of the concentrated violence by 22 July, seven Protestants and 3 Catholics lay dead, with 53 Catholics injured as well as 28 Protestants. On 24th the Army returned to their barracks.

Whilst the physical violence of the summer had ended, expulsions for workplaces of Catholics by Protestants continued. It is estimated that during the summer months 346 Catholic houses were abandoned, alongside 64 Protestant homes.

On 19th September, the ceilings of two rooms, 132 and 147 in Parliament Buildings, fell in. They revealed a major defect with the building and subsequent surveys revealed that by October, 118 ceilings were 'doubtful' – this number rose to 139 by November and was a major scandal for the contractors and the architect.

On 22nd October, Ulster lost one of its founding fathers when Sir Edward Carson died at home in England. He had last visited Belfast to see the unveiling of a statue in his honour outside the Stormont Parliament in July 1932.

HMS Broke conveyed Lord Carson's body to Belfast, and was drawn through the streets in a gun carriage, lined with thousands of mourners.

Craig and his colleagues alongside those in Britain were involved in arranging his State Funeral.

He was laid to rest in St Anne's Cathedral Belfast with soil from each of Northern Ireland's six counties.

The Chapter of the Cathedral wanted his body cremated, but Lady Carson and Sir James Craig refused.

1936

On January 20th, George V died in London and was succeed by Edward VIII. The Duke of Abercorn summoned the Parliament to meet on 24 January where a resolution on sending a message of condolence to the Queen and the new King were agreed.

As result of the coronation, local government elections were postponed until not later than 1st December.

A report by a Commission of Inquiry into the Civil Authorities (Special Powers) Act of 1922 and 1933 was completed by the National Council for Civil Liberties which caused widespread exasperation amongst government ranks in Belfast.

The conclusions of the report were as follows;

1. Firstly, that through the operation of the Special Powers Acts contempt has been begotten for the representative institutions of government.

2. Secondly, that through the use of Special Powers individual liberty is no longer protected by law but is at the arbitrary disposition of the Executive. This abrogation of the rule of law has been so practiced as to bring the freedom of the subject into contempt.
3. Thirdly, that the Northern Ireland Government has used Special Powers towards securing the domination of one particular political faction and, at the same time, towards curtailing the lawful activities of its opponents. The driving of legitimate movements underground into illegality, the intimidating or branding as law-breakers of their adherents, however innocent of crime, has tended to encourage violence and bigotry on the part of the Government's supporters as well as to beget in its opponents an intolerance of the 'law and order' thus maintained. The Government's policy is thus driving its opponents into the ways of extremists.
4. Fourthly, that the Northern Ireland Government, despite its assurances that Special Powers are for use only against law-breakers, has frequently employed them against innocent and law-abiding people, often in humble circumstances, whose injuries, inflicted without cause or justification, have gone unrecompensed and disregarded.

It concludes with a stinging condemnation.

"It is sad that in the guise of temporary and emergency legislation there should have been created under the shadow of the British Constitution a permanent machine of dictatorship – a standing temptation to whatever intolerant or bigoted section may attain power to abuse its authority at the expense of the people it rules."[75]

In response, Viscount Craig informed the House in a bad-tempered reply that "no importance should be attached to a document containing such misrepresentations. The Government believe that this grossly biased publication emanates from a similar source to other propagandists whole sole ambition is to see the establishment of an All-Ireland Republic"[76]

Whilst the Prime Minister may have been referring to the Liberal sympathies of some on the Commission, the Chairman, Edward Aylmer Digby was a decorated former senior official in the Admiralty.

This was the first time that an official publication for the readership of those in England openly and systematically criticized the Northern Ireland Government, and may have been able to go further on a wider remit.

Into April and May 1936, the barricades around the York Street areas erected during the trouble of the previous summer were still in place, a source of embarrassment for the RUC and the Minister of Home Affairs.

To the South, the Dáil moved to abolish the Senate of the Irish Free State in May.

In December, Britain faced a constitutional crisis following the abdication of Edward VIII to marry his divorcee lover, Wallace Simpson. He was succeeded by his brother, George VI.

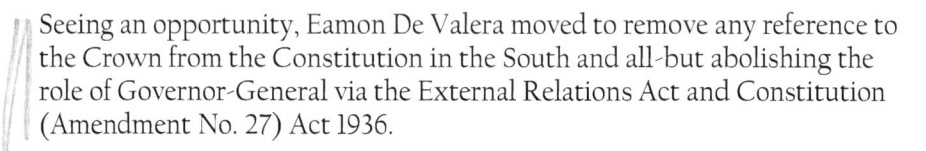

Seeing an opportunity, Eamon De Valera moved to remove any reference to the Crown from the Constitution in the South and all-but abolishing the role of Governor-General via the External Relations Act and Constitution (Amendment No. 27) Act 1936.

In a positive result for the Northern Ireland economy, the Air Ministry had created a new factory in Belfast which would be managed equally by Harland and Wolff and Shorts Brothers to manufacture new aircraft.

The Government secured the new site and costs of setting up the factory via use of the Loans Guarantee Act to secure £200,000 capital for the build as part of the wider UK re-armament effort.

1937

In July 1937 De Valera's Fianna Fáil retained power in the general election which also saw a referendum on the new Constitution. Eire was now the official name of the Southern state, but crucially, articles two and three of the new constitution caused outrage north of the border.

"Article 2
The national territory consists of the whole island of Ireland, its islands and the territorial seas.

"Article 3

Pending the re-integration of the national territory, and without prejudice to the right of the parliament and government established by this constitution to exercise jurisdiction over the whole territory, the laws enacted by the parliament shall have the like area and extent of application as the laws of Saorstát Éireann and the like extra-territorial effect."

These claims were tantamount to claiming the territory of Northern Ireland as being part of the jurisdiction ruled by the Republican terror Craig and his followers had fought for many years to distance themselves from.

The Speaker of the House was quickly disposed to rule out of order any discussion raised by Members of the topic – no doubt fearing ferocious opposition and a clash in the House with Nationalists. This issue crowned the list of grievances Unionists had with the southern state right through to the negotiations for the Good Friday Agreement in 1998 when it topped the list of unionist demands, which were eventually met by the incumbent Fianna Fáil government.

During the new King's visit on 28th July the IRA had attempted to assassinate the Monarch via land mine in Belfast whilst he visited Balmoral, further reminding unionists that the IRA hadn't gone away.

A statue of King George II was blown to pieces in May of that year in St Stephen's Green, Dublin as the External Relations Act 1937 was passed by the Dáil removing the post of Governor-General and in December the new Constitution of Ireland came into force, Eamon De Valera became Taoiseach and preparations for the election of the first Irish President were put in place.

The ramifications of the new Constitution were the basis for a snap election in the North.

3

1938-1965: Fragmentation

Following the unexpected election which was called solely to solidify the unionist base following the territorial claims of Eire, the UUP gained significantly at the expense of Labour and Ind Unionists, gaining three. Nationalists lost their seat in Mourne as the Unionist candidate ran unopposed.

In the Senate, Unionist domination continued. Nationalists returned four members, McAllister, McHugh, Maguire and McLaughlin – McMahon had died in 1936.

Actions in the new state to the south took precedence in 1938. Primarily, in April Douglas Hyde was selected as the first President of Ireland.

The economic war between Britain and Ireland lingered on until April 1938, with Ireland agreeing to make one payment of £10m in lieu of land annuities. In return, Britain would relinquish the so-called Treaty ports at Berehaven, Queenstown and Lough Swilly to Eire in order to end the economic hostilities and all tariffs would be lifted from all trade. Whilst the agreement was reached between the UK and Irish Governments, Craig and his Ministers lost no time in seeking concessions from Westminster given that the new agreement may have had effects on their state. He reported to the House on 26th April what Ulster had gleaned from the agreement.

Primarily, agricultural subsidies introduced in Britain which would be relevant to NI would now be paid for by the UK Exchequer.

The second, and most important concession was regarding the provision of the 1935 agreement on unemployment insurance in which the UK government would cover any cost of parity up to £1m pounds for services in NI. In 1938 the contribution was almost twice that, but the Exchequer waived the option to re-open the discussions on parity and wiped the almost £700,000 that the Belfast Government would owe.

Indeed, the UK Government agreed not to reconsider the unemployment agreement and would continue to pay up to £1m to Belfast in respect of unemployment insurance parity so long as the trade agreement remained in place.

Social services in NI would remain financed at parity levels paid for by London. Finally, re-armament contracts by the Admiralty would be directed to Ulster, and a factory possibly sited in Derry would be investigated.

Again, Northern Ireland benefitted from the pragmatism of the UK and Irish governments.

In June, Douglas Hyde was sworn in as the first President of Ireland. A week previous, a snap general election had given Ireland its first single party majority government under Fianna Fáil.

1939

George Leeke, Nationalist member for Mid Londonderry died in March, and the writ for a by-election to replace him was never moved, so the seat lay vacant until the next election.

In April, owing to conditions in Europe, the British Government re-introduced conscription with men aged 20 and 21 having to undergo six months military training. The month previous, the UK pledged to support Poland's independence and would act if its ally was attacked by Nazi Germany.

Despite boisterous optimism from Viscount Craigavon that Ulster would not be found wanting in its support of the UK's militarization effort, the UK Prime Minister excluded NI from conscription in the National Service (Armed Forces) Act.

Ulster had several military assets available at that time. The Royal Ulster Rifles, Royal Inniskilling and Royal Irish Fusiliers were stationed in Northern Ireland as well as the Royal Naval Volunteer Reserve Unit.

Financially, it was agreed with the Treasury that any outstanding expenditure in relation to hostilities would be paid for by the UK Government. On 25th August, the IRA detonated a bomb in the City of Coventry, killing 5 people and injuring 70 as part of sabotage operations in Britain aimed at securing a British withdrawal from Ireland.

Two men from Co Offaly were arrested and executed for the bombing.

Returning to the seemingly unsolvable issue of public transport, following criticism of the McLintock committee recommendation to create a single transport authority – opposed by the managers of the railways, Sir James Craig indulged in that age-old kicking of the issue into the grass by creating a Joint Select Committee.

It reported in August 1939 with simple recommendations – make the 1935 Act work and appoint a Minister to oversee it. The issue was then overshadowed considerably by events on the continent.

On 3rd September Germany invaded Poland and so began World War Two. Three days later the Governor, the Duke of Abercorn, stood down and was replaced by Lord Granville.

As a result of the war and to draw enemy attention away from the new Parliament Building, Viscount Craig made a statement to the House on 10th October with the acquiescence of the Speaker, limiting the sittings to two days a week for the foreseeable future, and also crucially announced that Mr Andrews his Finance Minister would now also act as Commerce Minister owing to the illness of Mr Barbour.

Despite pressure from Britain and the international community, Eamon De Valera set Ireland on a policy of neutrality. This was referred to as 'cowardly' by Craig.

In the South, the Emergency Powers Act was passed by the Oireachtas which established a state of emergency in the jurisdiction. This gave the Government the power to intern and censor the media as well as other controversial provisions. Protecting neutrality was De Valera's top priority and was especially worried that IRA action against Britain or in favour of Germany may end in Ireland being pulled into the war.

1940

In Britain, Neville Chamberlain resigned as Prime Minister on 10th May and was replaced by Winston Churchill.

Craig was keen to ensure that Ulster played its part in home defence and the general war effort. In May he met with officials in the War Office in London and on 28th he updated the House on the preparations.

The RUC and USC were to be given the duty of home defence, and a section of the USC would be established as the Ulster Defence Volunteers, like the Home Service in Britain.

There were 12,000 B Specials already available and armed, and County Commandants would be responsible for recruiting any others.

Agricultural output in Britain and NI was to be pooled, and whilst the shortage of flax from the continent continued, his Ministry would continue to try to address unemployment through munitions work.

The plan for the UDV was to have up to 30,000 men in total for across the whole province. Vehicles used by volunteers would have their access to petrol ensured.

Belfast already had anti-aircraft guns and anti-parachutist apparatus in place. The legislative apparatus in the form of the Special Powers Act allowed the Belfast administration to round up 'disloyal' members of the community and intern them in the prison ship Al Rawdah at Killylough – of course, this meant Nationalists and Republicans.

On 24th June 1940 a new Ministry of Public Security was established arising from the recommendation of an All-Party committee that had only first met just over a week previous. Mr J MacDermott (QUB) was appointed Minister and had responsibility to 'secure adequate protection to the public such as A.R.P civil defence, the constabulary forces, and the Ulster Defence Volunteers'.

Interestingly, it was proposed in the House that an all-Ireland Defence Council be established to deal with the defence of the entire island – not by a Nationalist, but by Mr Beattie of Labour. It was of course rubbished by the Prime Minister

It is generally accepted that precautions, with attention to air raid precautions, were inadequate up to this point. Underground shelters were not an option in many areas of Belfast due to the foundations of the City being of sleech.

"In the perilous days of 1940 a fearful people found little sense of leadership from the Northern Ireland Government."[77]

Following the cabinet meeting of 1st July, it was decided that the necessary steps should be taken to put the voluntary evacuation of the school children in Belfast into operation.[78]

A pre-registration scheme had been put in place by the Home Affairs department, and parents had registered upwards of 20,000 for evacuation should Northern Ireland come under sustained bombing. 10,000 children were eventually evacuated and by August 1940, just over 1100 had returned home.

On 7th September, the Luftwaffe began its ferocious bombing of London. The Blitz had begun.

On 25 September the Cabinet faced its first open revolt in the House. Mr Warnock (St Anne's, UUP) who had previously resigned office as the Parliamentary Secretary to the Ministry of Home Affairs due to the failure of the government to introduce conscription in Ulster laid the following motion before the House;

"That in the opinion of this House the Government of Northern Ireland, as at present constituted, is not the most effective instrument for the prosecution of the business of the State, either in relation to the war effort of the country or the ordinary business of good government, and that the welfare and prosperity of Northern Ireland, present and future, would be better secured by a reorganisation of the Cabinet."

Taking aim at the members of the Cabinet collectively, Warnock told the House that;

"I do not propose to say anything to-day except what the whole country is saying, but I can crystallise what I am going to say a little later on, by saying that in the entire country practically all over the Six Counties the same story has been told, that this Government has been too long in office and is in the main composed of tired and jaded men."

At this juncture, as Warnock outlined, five members of the Government and the Chief Whip had been in post for long periods, some over twenty years, unheard of in modern democracies across the Empire.

Dawson Bates had served since 1921 in Home Affairs, Craig as Prime Minister, Archdale in Agriculture, Barbour in Commerce since 1925 and Caulfield in Education for 12 years.

In his speech, Mr Warnock had said what many outside the Ulster Unionist Party had been saying since 1921 – that without an effective and representative legislature, the Executive would never be under threat of defeat and as such became complacent.

He used as an example of the feelings of some members, his own resignation and that of Alexander Gordon of East Down as Financial Secretary in June.

The Prime Minister angrily refuted the claims put to the House, using General Smuts as an example of elder statemen carrying on in their duties and personally attacking Mr Warnock for not raising concerns about war preparedness whilst having direct access to the Cabinet.

If only to demonstrate the strength of Mr Warnock's assertions, Craig died nearly two months to the day of the debate, on 24th November. He was 69 years old and had suffered ill-health for some time. He was replaced by 70-year-old John Miller Andrews.

Viscount Craigavon had died at home as a result of a heart attack following a short illness, succeeded in his title by his son.

At cabinet on 25th November, Ministers met to plan for the continuity of Government.

"Mr Andrews reported that by command of His Grace the Governor he had had an audience of His Grace that morning and that the Governor had asked him to assume the Office of Prime Minister. Mr Andrews said that although he fully realised the heavy responsibilities involved he felt it was his duty to accept His Grace's invitation.

In doing so, however, he appreciated that normally the leader of the Party which had a majority in the House, would be entrusted by the Governor with the duties of Prime Minister and accordingly his acceptance of office was contingent on the choice of leader by the Ulster Unionist Party."[79]

The cabinet agreed and accepted his offer to them to remain in their posts. The cabinet agreed that a subcommittee would be formed of the Minister of Home Affairs, Minister of Public Security, Lord Glentoran, the Secretary to the Cabinet, the Secretary to the Ministry of Public Security, Commander Henderson – Private Secretary to the Governor, Major May – Private Secretary to the Lord Mayor of Belfast, Sir W Hungerford, the Inspector General of the RUC and representatives of the Armed Forces to prepare a suitable - though not state, funeral after a service in Belmont Presbyterian Church.

Tributes poured in for the late Premier from the King, Governor, UK Prime Minister and from his colleagues in Ulster, the most heartfelt of those coming from the Minister for Labour John Gordon who said;

"Lord Craigavon was the greatest Ulsterman of his generation, and one of the outstanding statesmen of the British Empire. He lived for his beloved Ulster, and it may truly be said that he died in her service."

Two days after his death, the House passed the Craigavon (Burial) Act, giving the former Prime Minister the honour of being buried on the grounds of Parliament Buildings where his tomb and that of his wife remains to this day, enshrined in a Portland Stone tomb as per their wishes.

Andrews would continue to serve as Finance Minister as well as Prime Minister for the time being.

1941

Andrews appointed James Milne Barbour to the position of Minister of Finance on 16th January, promoting him from Commerce. Sir Basil Brooke (Lisnaskea, UUP) assumed Commerce, moved from Agriculture which was filled by Herbert Dixon (Bloomfield, UUP).

Brooke was from a wealthy dynasty in Fermanagh that had deep roots within the military and aristocracy in England. His sister went on to marry the Speaker, Sir Henry Mulholland.

Sir Basil had a well-known sectarian background, and had no qualms about making his positions on the minority clear.

"Sir Basil Brooke at a speech in Newtownbutler in 1933 told his audience, as reported by the Fermanagh Times; "There were a great number of Protestants and Orangemen who employed Roman Catholics. He felt he could speak freely on this subject as he had not a Roman Catholic about his place. He would point out that the Roman Catholics were endeavouring to get in everywhere and were out with all their force and might to destroy the power of the Constitution of Ulster. There was a definite plot to overpower the vote of Unionists in the North. He would appeal to loyalists, therefore, to employ Protestant lads and lassies."[80]

Also, in January a secret agreement was made between Britain and Ireland to allow RAF plans to use a corridor of airspace in Donegal to reduce travel time to the Atlantic.

A plan to evacuate Belfast of women and children known as the 'Hiram Plan' was proposed by the Public Security Minister in early 1940 but proved ineffective in mobilizing enough people out of the City – only around 4,000 by the time the Luftwaffe undertook its first air raid.

On 7th April, the first targeted air raid on Belfast took place, killing 13 people. The Luftwaffe dropped incendiary bombs on the dockland area and damaged the Shorts factory.

Eight days later, a major raid took place on Belfast by approximately 150 bombers. Residential areas as well as the docks and waterworks were badly damaged. 900 people lost their lives and up to half the city's domestic housing stock was damaged.

"Luftwaffe bombs had demolished 3,200 houses and damaged 56,600, nearly 4,000 of them left completely uninhabitable."[81]

The RAF had not attacked the bombers, and anti-aircraft weapons did not fire due to the belief that they may damage RAF aircraft. As part of a wider effort to dissuade the Luftwaffe from bombing key sites, a mixture of bitumen and cow manure was smeared across the exterior of Parliament Buildings.

Derry had also been bombed. A failed attempt to disrupt shipping in the Foyle had missed and two devices landed in the Messines Park area of Pennyburn killing 13 and injuring over thirty. It was the only enemy attack on the city during the war.

On 5th May, another raid took place in which 150 people were killed and extensive damage was inflicted on dwellings across the capital. In the South, the Government authorized its emergency services to cross the border and offer assistance following a telegram communicated by the Public Security Minister to de Valera.
"If the Northern Ireland Government was not strictly to blame for the lack of protection, its utter failure to respond purposefully to the suffering and to attempt to restore morale left it further exposed to condemnation from all parts of society."[82]

(The Senate Chamber being utilised as an RAF Operations Room, PRONI, CAB/3/G/181)

Even the British government had concerns about Ulster's readiness on defence evidenced by correspondence from the UK Home Secretary who wrote to Andrews on 13th May to underline concern about the use of resources.

The Government's woes were further compounded when an inquiry into functions of the Belfast Corporation uncovered serious malpractice and Dawson Bates was forced to appoint administrators to oversee executive functions. The Unionist grouping at City Hall were extremely powerful in the Party and they directed their fury at the Government.

The Repair of War Damage Bill was introduced in the House in September aimed at bypassing local government red tape for the repair of premises across the province affected by the war, with a particular focus on houses.

On 16th December Mr Beattie (Pottinger, NILP) brought another motion of No Confidence in the Government, citing the loss of Craig's seat to an Independent Unionist in North Down in the form of Thomas Bailie and the loss of Belfast Willowfield previously held by Arthur Black (UUP) to Harry Midgely, a Labour member, as a demonstration of the weak nature of the Executive.

The loss of Willowfield was a huge upset to Unionism who lost almost 40% of their vote in the constituency.

He lodged a stinging attack on the composition of the Government and its fitness to lead;

"Just think of the composition of this Government. It is largely made up of place hunters. There are cadging aristocrats, lawyers on the make, and juvenile soldiers who have thrown off their uniform to serve the King sleeping on the back benches. Add to these a few linen lords who have made a mess of their own businesses, a few grasping landlords, and you have the whole Stormont combination."[83]

With there being no seconder for the motion, it fell, as did Mr Beattie's motion from an earlier day that a Select Committee be established to 'devise ways and means to increase Ulster's war effort'.

1942

It is from April 1942 that we begin to see 'secret' sessions of the House sitting. This was particularly to protect information about war production and defences were motions would require detailed answers including sensitive information. Secret sessions were used four times during the 1942 sitting.

Thomas Stanislaus McAllister was again elected Deputy Speaker in the Upper House.

1943

The first hurdle of the year came following the death of the West Belfast MP Alexander Browne. In the subsequent by-election held on 9th February the Northern Ireland Labour Party stole the seat from under the noses of Unionism, overturning a majority of almost 14,000.

In early March, the House debated a motion by Mr Nixon (Woodvale, IndU) on the Government's attitude to the Beveridge Report. The UK Government had established a wide-ranging committee in the summer of 1941 to review and survey the provision of social services and insurance and to make recommendations.

Whilst the report proposed a wrap-around social service system, effectively the beginning of a purpose-built welfare state, the government did not accept the report in its entirety, arguing that the massive financial obligation it demanded could not be made until the war was over and an overview of public finances undertaken.

On 21 March, the Ulster Prime Minister announced that a new programme of social measures arising from the report would be put to the electorate at the next election, effectively kicking the proposals into the long grass, to the exasperation of Labour.

The Government adopted their 'London watch' stance and would not commit to implementing the recommendations of the Report until Westminster had considered them and moved on implementation.

Samuel Hall-Thompson (Clifton, UUP) put forward an amendment outlining the Governments view, defeating Mr Nixon's motion.

March also saw a breakthrough on the public transport front. Messrs Pope and Merrion, managers of two of the largest railways in Northern Ireland completed a report and submitted it to the government.

Its primary provision was to merge road and rail interests – which the government was opposed to. Again, the issue was moved off the radar.

The Ulster Unionist Parliamentary Party met on 19th March to discuss concern in the backbenches about the composition of the cabinet and the overall Government's performance, especially in the face of by-elections that had recently been lost to Labour and Independent Unionists.
At a meeting of the Parliamentary Party, it is alleged that a number of Minister were against Mr Andrews and public records uncover the sense of urgency and panic within the ranks of the Party.

On 31st March, Basil Brooke wrote to convey his fears that a cleverly worded motion of no confidence in the government would lead to a general election.

The Prime Minister had sought to arrange a meeting of the UUC on 16th April to support a Vote of Confidence in his government, but he was warned against this again by Brian Maginnis, MP for Iveagh;

"In my opinion, it is a constitutional axiom that unless a Prime Minister has the confidence and support of the majority party in the House of Commons, his position as Prime Minister is untenable. Unless he has such support, and it is apparent at the two party meetings held in recent months that such support is lacking for you, it is useless for him to appeal to any outside body and indeed such a course is constitutionally irregular".[84]

On first May, Sir Basil Brooke became the third Prime Minister of Northern Ireland, following Andrews' capitulation to the party backbenches. Ten days later, he placed a motion on a Vote of Confidence in his ministry. Mr Beattie put forward an amendment of the contrary and called for a General Election – it was easily defeated.

Brooke chose an entirely new Cabinet with all-new Ministers who had never served previously at the top tier of Government.

Maynard Sinclair (Cromac, UUP) was promoted from Financial Secretary to Finance Minister, as was William Lowry (Derry, UUP) who was promoted to Home Affairs Minister from Parliamentary Secretary.

Robert Corkey (QUB) was promoted to Minister of Education, again from a Parliamentary Secretary role (although Assistant). The Reverend Robert Moore (North Derry, UUP) was elevated to the Ministry of Agriculture. William Grant (Duncairn, UUP) who had also previously served as a Parliamentary Secretary and before his appointment as Minister for Labour, had served as Minister for Public Security.

Sir Roland Nugent was appointed Minister of Commerce from the Senate alongside Corkey.

Harry Midgley (Willowfield, CWLP) was appointed Minister for Public Security, the first time any Ministry had been held by someone who was a member of a rival political party.

The new premier was wary of the previous attacks that the Government was not decisive enough or indeed young enough in wartime and was convinced of the need to introduce 'new blood'.

1944

A rare event took place in the opening months of 1944, in that for the first time a Northern Ireland Prime Minister had effectively sacked a Minister in the form of Professor Robert Corkey in the Education brief.

The former Minister, a theologian, cited the opposition to his plans for religious education in schools for his departure, but the Prime Minister was quick to dispel this in an address to the House on 22nd February, effectively blaming the Minister for not adequately attending to his own Department.

It was a major scandal at the time, and especially during wartime when the Prime Minister continually faced accusations of leading an administration divided.

On 13th March the UK Government banned all travel between it and Ireland because of Dublin refusing to expel Axis power diplomats. This was a further effort by the Allies to compel Ireland into renouncing neutrality. On 10th, the US had gone as far as to say that Ireland's neutrality was aiding their enemies.

The same month saw Lt Col Samuel Hall-Thompson appointed as Minister of Education, soon to face an onslaught from members of the House on proposals to reform religious instruction in schools. Significantly, one of his handicaps in the view of his colleagues when seeking to address educational reform was that he was not an Orangeman.

In June Eamon De Valera led his party to a majority victory in the general election, amassing 76 seats. The same month (1st June) the new Ministry of Health and Local Government was formed in Belfast, headed by William Grant (Duncairn, UUP).

On 1st November the Housing (No. 2) Bill received its second reading in the House. It is widely recognized as a progressive piece of legislation. One of its key features was the creation of a Housing Trust, which, according to the Minister's speech that day:

"The Housing Trust which I propose to establish will be working in close contact with my Ministry. It will be able to experiment and engage in building by new methods, and thus be able to develop experience in meeting many of the difficult questions which are bound to arise."

In seeking to reassure Members that this would allow effective derogation of the responsibilities of local authorities to provide housing and that the Government would engage directly in financing and building homes, the Minister outlined in detail:

"The operations of the Housing Trust will be financed in full by the Government. The cost will be borne on the Estimates of my Department and will, therefore, come up for review every year. I have heard it said that since the houses to be built by the Housing Trust will not cost the ratepayers anything local authorities will be inclined to sit back and do nothing, leaving it to the Trust to come in and build the necessary houses in their area at Government expense. I want to make it clear at this stage that it is the statutory duty of every local authority in Northern Ireland to provide houses to meet the needs of its working people. The duty is clearly laid down in the case of urban authorities in the Housing Act of 1919, and in the case of rural authorities in an Act passed in 1906."

Around 40% of all local housing was built by the Trust in the coming decades, and areas such as Omagh, Dungannon and Armagh were of focus when local authorities failed to provide housing.

1945

Victory in Europe was proclaimed on 8 May 1945. On 25th May, the Prime Minister in proposing a message from Parliament to the King reiterated Northern Ireland's loyalty to the Union;

"I have used the expression "we in Ulster along with the people of Great Britain." We cherish our right to use that phrase. The truth behind it - our continued association with Great Britain as part of the United Kingdom - gave us the right to take part in this mighty struggle and gives us now the right to rejoice and to express our rejoicing."

Days later the U-boat fleet of Nazi Germany's Kriegsmarina surrendered at Lisahally port in Derry.

A general election was called for 14th June, and a UK election held weeks later. In Britain, Labour triumphed under Clement Attlee gaining 239 seats.

In Ulster, the perpetual majority of the Ulster Unionist Party remained, though it lost six seats. Nationalists returned ten members, unchanged whilst Labour gained a seat giving them two, being joined with the one seat gained by Commonwealth Labour, and one Independent Labour member in Jack Beattie (Pottinger) though Paddy Agnew lost his seat to a Nationalist in South Armagh.

Harry Diamond stood as a Socialist Republican in Belfast Falls and was elected, the first person to hold that moniker.

13 Unionists were elected unopposed alongside 6 Nationalists and 1 Independent Unionist. In South Down the Independent Unionist was defeated by a Nationalist.

A source of embarrassment for Sir Basil Brooke was the loss of Sir William Hungerford as Chief Whip, defeated in Belfast Oldpark by NI Labour Party candidate Robert Getgood.

The Senate saw the return of Labour with William Smyth gaining a seat. Nationalists were reduced to two and William McConnell-Wilton was elected as an Ind Unionist.

Sir Norman Stronge (Mid Armagh, UUP) was elected the new Speaker on 17th July. He was from a well-known aristocratic family who lived in Tynan Abbey, Armagh. He had allowed the RUC and military use of his home during the war.

Nationalists sought to regroup after the war. On 17th July, all Nationalist MPs and Senators met to discuss the policy of abstentionism, agreeing after some debate that it was time to end the practice. Their members took the Oath the following day and took their seats in the House of Commons and Senate in Belfast.

This was followed by a vote of the Fermanagh and Tyrone convention on Westminster in early August.

"By 113 votes to 23, [Anthony] Mulvey and [Patrick] Cunningham were instructed to take their seats at Westminster, and by 93 votes to 16 the Stormont MPs were also directed to abandon abstention."[85]

In August, it was reported to the House that Sir Robert Lynn, a former Deputy Speaker and widely respected member who had chaired the Lynn committee on education, had died.

Following complaints from across the Province during the war, the Government acted on the ability of workers from across the border – who at one time during the war were invaluable in construction and agriculture – to vote.

The Representation of the People Bill 1945 imposed a seven-year residency requirement prior to being granted the franchise. It is obvious that this was of the utmost importance particularly to border MPs, some of whom had relatively small majorities and did not want any upset to the local and national political picture.

"William Hungerford of the Ulster Unionist Labour Association denounced the invasion of rural districts by Catholic 'farm boys' from the South, who could become voters after only a few days working in the constituency. 'They have no stake whatsoever, not owning a blade of grass. Their power in the ballot box, however, is great'".[86]

Legislation was passed in Westminster for the compilation and upkeep of an imperial voters register and whilst the main aim of the NI legislation was to mimic this in using the Imperial register, the additional residency block was added.

Nationalists lost no time in giving the residency and electoral provisions against those in the South as 'Eire-phobia'.

In October, an issue which would later become of serious contention, housing in Derry – was raised in Oral Questions with the Minister making clear that even when 250 houses had been allocated to the Derry area, the Corporation had not progressed the plans and the Minister could not inform the House where or when the houses would be built. A month later in updating the House, the Minister again reiterated that no plans had been received by his Department from the Corporation.

On 16th October, Robert Getgood (Oldpark, NILP) raised a motion in the House decrying the state of housing and attempting to force the Government to begin building new homes immediately, and crucially, to force local authorities to seize empty properties and house families in them.

He outlined that most of housing in Northern Ireland required repair, and up to 42,000 were 'not worth repairing'. In his speech he outlined the dire state of housing across Northern Ireland as outlined in the government's own report, but interestingly, referred on record to the political interference in housing building for electoral reasons;

"It is, therefore, no cause for surprise that, with a Government so reactionary in outlook and so lackadaisical in their methods, the rural councils in Northern Ireland should follow their evil example in the matter of housing. For instance, only 43,000 cottages were built in the 20 years before the war, while in County Fermanagh, where housing is the worst in Northern Ireland, not a single cottage has been erected since 1922, and County Tyrone is little better. Indeed, a leading Tory some years ago advised the, councils not to build cottages, as many of them were likely to be occupied by their political opponents. The fewer the houses the fewer the votes, and therefore the fewer their opponents in the rural councils. What a mentality!"

In defending the Government, Unionist members cited a motion passed by the Ulster Unionist Labour Association which declared support for the Housing (No. 2) Bill's approach to addressing the housing problem.

Mr Nixon (Woodvale, Ind U) revealed that in 1939 the current Prime Minister when Minister of Commerce had signed an order under Defence Regulations to stop the manufacturing of bricks in Northern Ireland which was now contributing to the housing crisis – it caused significant embarrassment for the Premier.

In responding, the Minister outlined that by June 1946, 4,000 new houses would be built under the Government's plans, despite acknowledging a report by the Housing Committee of the Planning Advisory Board that 100,000 new houses were needed.

The fears of Nationalists in relation to the residence and work permits was confirmed in an answer to an Oral Question by Campbell to the Minister of Home Affairs on 18th October. Asking why the Minister revoked the residence permits of up to 20,000 natives of the south, Mr Warnock referred to the Residence in Northern Ireland (Restriction) Order 1942 which effectively required, much like the employment permits, anyone not native to the North prior to 1st January 1940 to have a permit issued by his Ministry to reside in the state.

It was yet another reactionary attempt to remove any electoral threat by an influx of potential anti-partitionist voters particularly to border counties despite the Ministry of Labour openly granting work to tradesmen from the South due to a labour shortage of bricklayers and other craftsmen in Ulster.

Indeed, during an adjournment debate in November 1941 Mr Henderson blasted the Minister of Labour about 'Eire workers';

"The Minister of Labour will have to account for his action in this matter when the Willowfield election takes place. I will make it a point to be there to find out if he is speaking and taking part in elections. I am glad the Prime Minister has come in. I want to know why the people of the Free State are allowed to come up here to take the work of the Ulster people who have stood faithfully by this Government. What is the cause of this change of policy? You have linked up electricity and now you are linking up the people, North and South. Why do not you give employment to your own people first? Why are unskilled workers allowed to come here from the Free State and take the work of unskilled labourers of Northern Ireland. I am prepared to take the Minister of Labour to where he will find unskilled workers doing labourers' work here."

This issue was further raised in the Imperial House in 1947 by Mr Mulvey of Fermanagh and Tyrone when he queried why 'some' NI residents who returned to the province were granted their full citizenship and franchise rights, whilst others in the same situation were granted only ongoing citizenship. He did not refer to Nationalists but the application of this practice to Nationalists who left for work and then returned is not out of the question.

Up to 200,000 Irish citizens emigrated to Britain and Northern Ireland during the war to work and to serve in the armed forces. Throughout the period 1945-47 the Dáil was filled with angry members demanding the Taoiseach act on the residency permits, with he himself exclaiming;

"It is a matter of great regret to me that the proposal has been brought forward. It is based on no better principle than that on which so many European peoples are being violently displaced. Our people keenly resent the implications of the proposal; it is an example of the expedients by which the policy of the unjust partition of the country has to be maintained."[87]

In one of the only instances of violence in the House itself, Harry Midgley assaulted Jack Beattie in the House on 30th October after an acrimonious debate with the Speaker. Midgley had fallen out with the NILP sometime before and was referred to as a 'galoot' by Mr Beattie.

In November following election victories, Eddie McAteer (Mid Derry, Nat) whose brother Hugh was to become Commander-in-Chief of the IRA and Malachy Conlon (S Armagh, Nat) held a public meeting in Dungannon with a view to uniting Irish Nationalism into one platform.

"Finally, at a meeting of all Nationalist MPs and Senators it was agreed to summon a province wide convention in Dungannon for 14th November with the:

"primary purpose to promote a united effort to consolidate all Anti-Partitionist forces in the Six Counties and to launch an organisation of the people as a democratic body, having for its objects, the independence of Ireland, the well-being of all the people, the fostering of an Irish outlook...and the promotion of co-operation among all creeds and classes.""[88]

400 delegates attended the meeting and a fund was established to fund the new body, with £1000 raised immediately.

Many Nationalists began to question the merit of abstentionism after the war. James McGlade who would become a senior member of the APL commented "we have had enough of abstentionism". Both had taken the Oath to be able to take their seats in Westminster.

The Anti-Partition League was to be led by Conlon and James McSparran (Mourne, Nat) as its inaugural chairman. It was joined in Britain by the Friends of Ireland group of Labour MPs led by Hugh Delargy. The two groups collaborated on the issue of ending partition in Ireland.

Conlon, it must be said, had some made some statements in public that followed him throughout his public career. He had made numerous anti-Semitic comments linking it with communism and Russia.

On 13th November the Chairman of Ways and Means Mr Stevenson (QUB, UUP) resigned due to ill health and was replaced by Thomas Bailie (North Down, UUP).

The newly formed Anti-Partition League faced its first great hurdle of confidence when Thomas Campbell, the Nationalist MP for Belfast Central, resigned his seat in order to become a County Court Judge.

1946

The first legislative item brought before the House in 1946 was a new Housing Bill. The main provision of this was effectively an admission by the government that it needed to assist other avenues of house building. For the first time, it legislated for financial assistance to be given to housing associations and their building schemes.

This was timely given the fact that families had begun to squat in the Nissen huts at Springtown Camp in Derry vacated by US Forces, such was their cramped conditions at their family homes.

In recognition of the role of the Parliament Building during the war when the Senate chamber was used by the RAF as an Operations Room, the UK Government determined that the contribution would be remembered in perpetuity and the balustrade of the Senate was inscribed as the image below demonstrates.

THIS INSCRIPTION RECORDS THE GRATITUDE OF HIS MAJESTYS GOVERNMENT IN THE UNITED KINGDOM FOR THE USE OF THIS CHAMBER AS AN OPERATIONS ROOM BY THE ROYAL AIR FORCE DURING THE SECOND WORLD WAR

It joined the 6ft 7" statue of Viscount Craigavon which was erected in the year previous on a Mourne granite plinth at the top of the stairs in the Great Hall.

In June, following the death of Westminster MP and Independent Unionist James Little (Down), the Ulster Unionists took the seat with a majority of almost 22,000 and now held both Co Down seats.

On 21st the by-election took place in Belfast Central to replace Campbell and given the state of the Nationalist party in the City, the seat was simply abandoned. It was won by Labour, leaving the Nationalists no seats in the capital and largely confined now to the west.

The Government launched a White Paper on Transport, finally conceding the need to merge rail and road interests into a unitary authority. Work would begin in earnest to create legislation for the new authority.

Yet another Bill deemed by Nationalists to solidify the Unionist state was presented to the House, the Elections and Franchise Bill. Cahir Healy described it as an 'an outrage to democracy'.

The Bill sought to determine the manner of the allocation of the franchise in local government elections to those who were effectively householders. Given the state of housing throughout the province and the propensity of local authorities to ignore Catholic housing needs, it was to disenfranchise many as in basic terms a local government house could potentially mean a vote.

"During a debate in June 1948 on a motion proposed by Diamond calling for 'one man, one vote' in all elections, Healy raised the speech made by E. C Ferguson, MP for Enniskillen on 9 April at a meeting of the Unionist Association of Fermanagh. With the Prime Minister present, Ferguson had declared that 'the Nationalist majority of the county stood at 3,684 and that they must ultimately reduce and liquidate that majority."[89]

Springtown and the provision of housing there reached cabinet level in August;

"The Minister of Health and Local Government circulated a memorandum on the position at Springtown about which a deputation from the Londonderry Unionist Association had interviewed him on the previous day.

The Association proposed to press the Derry Corporation to rescind the undertaking they had given to manage the camp and to re-house the occupants when necessary. If the Corporation reversed its previous decision, there would be no other authority to manage the huts and it had hitherto been a principle of Government policy not to undertake direct housing responsibilities, the alternative of ejecting the occupants who could not be allowed to remain on the premises in their present insanitary condition was most unpalatable".[90]

On September 2nd the Irish Government allowed the Emergency Powers Act 1939 to expire and the Defence Forces Regulations 1940 was revoked. The Northern counterpart in the Special Powers Act lingered on.

A further legislative resolution in education was introduced to the Commons on 15th October the Minister of Education proposed that the new Education Bill be read a second time. As outlined in his speech to the House, all previous Education Acts would be repealed.

The terms 'primary, secondary and further' education was first introduced to statute replacing elementary and technical. Secondary school would begin at eleven, and selection would take place particularly for grammar schools.

The issue of religious education is touched upon – school assemblies will include prayers and all schools will offer religious teaching.

Nursery school provision is included in the Bill, following from the success of war nurseries and establishes provision for special education. School meals are made a compulsory service and free books and other items are made available in primary and intermediate schools.

Crucially, the grant to voluntary schools, mainly of whom are catholic-led, is raised from 50% to 65% and access to universities is given for the first time via a grants system.

"Victory for Lt Col. Hall-Thompson's policy meant his personal defeat. On 14th December 1949 the Grand Orange Lodge of Ireland discussed education and it became known that the Minister was to resign. Announcing this the following day, the Prime Minister promised to review the whole system."[91]

4th December 1946 saw an important motion put to the House by Mr Healy (S Fermanagh, Nat).

"That in the opinion of this House the gerrymandering of local government electoral areas, whereby minorities of electors are enabled to elect a majority of the public representatives is undemocratic and unfair, and a public inquiry should be held into the whole matter."

A motion of gerrymandering, the fixing of electoral boundaries to ensure a Unionist majority had long been a bone of contention for Nationalists across Northern Ireland, especially in areas like Derry where a city with a Nationalist majority elected a majority Unionist local authority.

Speaking of his constituency, he outlined a bizarre outline of the beginning of gerrymandering in Fermanagh to demonstrate his point;

"We [Nationalists] held it [Fermanagh] again from the introduction of Proportional Representation until 1922, when this Government issued a sealed order abolishing the county councils and appointing as a paid commissioner a legal gentleman who was afterwards a Member of this House.

We are not like the Government and other bodies-guilty of misappropriation, jobbery or fraud. The Government did not like our opinion and watched for an opportunity of getting rid of us. The county secretary was interned. When he was interned one Department of the Home Office wrote him a letter telling him that unless he turned up at the office of the county council on a certain day he would be dismissed.

While one Department of the Home Office was writing him to that effect another Department notified him that they could not release him under any circumstances. What a comedy for the world outside, but what a tragedy for the people in the toils of such a gang of political manipulators."

During the speech, Healy and other Nationalists members outlined the statistical basis of their claims of gerrymandering and its historical basis.

In Derry in 1920 for example, there were 8,868 anti-partitionists which would have elected 21 councillors to the 6,340 of all other electors which should have elected 19 councillors. Following the abolition of proportional representation for local government elections, and a reinstatement of the wards of 1898, Catholics with a majority over all other electors of 1,219, were in the minority by 8 councillors.

In the same City in 1928 the North Ward has a Nationalist majority, but when the Local Company Franchise Act was enacted, Unionists were given an artificial majority of 2014 votes.

In another change, in 1936 the Londonderry Corporation had submitted a revised local government scheme which would further rejig the number of wards and councillors. It was put to a public inquiry and rejected, however, statistical information from the inquiry was then used by the Ministry to devise a new scheme.

It was felt that 40 councillors were too many, and the Ministry reduced the number by half. The basis for this was the poor law valuation and population. The North ward had a lower population but a higher valuation, and as a result would have two aldermen and six councillors elected, as would South. The Waterside ward would have one alderman and three councillors.

1937 saw Derry's five wards reduced to three. The East ward was added to North, and a large section of North added to South and West wards. As a result, 9,527 anti-partitionists elected 8 councillors, whilst 7,506 others elected 12 councillors.

Cahir Healy in speaking on the motion also referred to other Nationalist-majority areas where gerrymandering was prevalent.

Lisnaskea had a clear majority of Nationalists of 4,223 over all others, and yet elected 15 councillors to 16 of others. The situation in Enniskillen was worse still. Nationalists had a majority over Unionists of 78 voters, yet they elected 9 members to the Unionists 17.

In the Enniskillen Urban ward, 2,100 unionists elected 14 councillors against a Nationalist electorate of over four times that, who elected eight members.

Restrictions on how many people could occupy part of a tenement house were introduced which meant that every separate part of a house had to be separately rated to be given a vote. It was not uncommon to have a large building with 14 families living there, with one or two votes for the whole population.

His motion was defeated by 26-14 on 10th December.

Following meetings across the country, the Anti-Partition League had appointed Sean O'Gallagher as its first full-time organizer.

1947

On 28th January, the issue of housing reared its head again, this time in the shape of Mr Eddie McAteer (Mid Derry, Nat) asking the Minister of Health and Local Government why the Derry Corporation was refusing to allow the Ministry to take over the Belmont camp in Derry and convert it into housing for those squatting there.

The Minister refuted the claim, and instead informed the House that the Corporation were offered assistance from the Ministry to convert the huts into temporary housing, providing the Corporation took over the management of them, which they declined.

Derry Corporation had 1,680 applications for housing at this time and had only provided 63 houses in the two-year period preceding the question, and 61 of these were described as 'temporary prefabricated bungalows.'

In April following the first annual convention of the Anti-Partition League, Eddie McAteer was elected Vice-chairman. On 21st Jack Beattie raised for the first time the possible dis-arming of the RUC. His raising of the issue incensed Unionist members, culminating in the comments of Hugh Minford (Antrim Borough, UUP) on 20th May;

"so soon as hon. Members opposite can give a guarantee for the peace of Ulster then so soon shall we require fewer police".

The Safeguarding of Employment Bill was the brother of the 1945 Representation of the People Act. Irish workers from over the border had the right to vote effectively removed by the latter, and now the Safeguarding Bill sought to remove their right to work in Ulster.

It would now be against the law for anyone to work, or for a business to employ someone without a permit issued by the Ministry of Labour. The premise behind the Bill from the Government's view was to provide protection for residents from competition for jobs.

However, it was clear to some members the effect of the bill. Mr Beattie referred to it as embodying 'discontent and narrow bigotry'.

On 13th June the Northern Ireland Bill received its second reading in Westminster. The Bill was aimed at extending the legislative power of the Parliament of Northern Ireland. It is important on its own merits, but also because of the debates that took place on its passage which demonstrated the new partnership between the Irish Anti-Partition League and the Friends of Ireland Labour group of MPs.

The Unionists, however, put as much effort into debunking the claims of the anti-partitionists. The cabinet meeting on 20th March had agreed that the Ministers of Home Affairs and Health and Local Government would be in the House of Commons on the night of the second reading for discussion with their MPs and that their departmental officials would be in attendance to brief Home Office ministers and staff.

The Minister of Home Affairs was himself personally completing a paper on the Special Powers Act, the franchise laws and the gerrymandering allegations which he was to send to their MPs in London. It was also agreed that the Ulster Unionist Party would set up an internal committee to counter propaganda from anti-partitionists.

During the debate, Hugh Delargy MP (Manchester Platting, Labour) referred to a leaflet that was issued to Westminster MPs by the Northern Ireland Ministry of Home Affairs which he described as a 'monument of ruin' that contained the 'gravest distortions of truth'. It referred to the IRA re-organising after the war.

He also referred to a rebuttal pamphlet sent to Members by the Anti-Partition League, taking the opportunity to inform and lobby members on the situation in Northern Ireland.

During his speech he took the opportunity to take aim at the use of the Special Powers Act. He was followed by Mr Mulvey the Member for Fermanagh and Tyrone who protested about gerrymandering and the myth of an oncoming insurrection.

"The Government in Northern Ireland, in connection with the gerrymandering of the franchise, have made the position there the most undemocratic in the British Commonwealth today."

He also referred to discrimination in public recruitment.

The legislation itself had some key provisions. Oddly, Clause 1 enabled the Government of Northern Ireland to 'make provisions for hydro-electric, drainage, water and other schemes to be operated on both sides of the border in conjunction with the Eirean (sic) authorities'. From a Government who continually exercised its wish never to be part of that polity and whose members frequently attacked it in the legislature, this arrangement would seem out of place.

Clause 6 gave the Northern Ireland Parliament the power to enable a new proposed authority to take over Great Northern Railway property and to join in the operation of through service in Eire. This would follow on from the Road and Rail Transportation Act of 1935.

Clause ten gave the Northern Ireland Parliament the power to alter subordinate legislation passed by the Imperial Parliament after 1920 which the Government of Ireland Act had prohibited hitherto.

The efforts of Nationalists and Labour supporters in Westminster had served to highlight for the first time since partition, the state of Northern Ireland to an English audience via Westminster.

On 24th September, the Health Services Bill received its Second Reading in the House. The Minister lauded it as the outcome of;

"a common consensus of opinion that the time is ripe for a complete overhaul of our health services and the adoption of an ambitious and bold new design."

The Bill followed Britain in creating the National Health Service in Northern Ireland providing for all manner of health services under a General Services Board for general practice, and the Hospital Authority for acute services.

Nationalists reacted angrily to the provisions in the Health Services Bill which would effectively place the Mater Hospital under the responsibility of the new Hospitals Authority. It was feared that this would erode the Catholic ethos of the hospital.

Some Unionist MPs at Westminster voted against Labour legislation on welfare whilst members of the Northern Ireland Parliament were left in no doubt that they must, however much embarrassment it caused the party, vote for the measures before them.

The new services would cost £1.75m per year from the passing of the Bill. Specialist and acute services would be budgeted at £3m per annum with a total per annum cost of around £5m and the local authority charges set at £250,000. National Insurance would contribute £1m per year towards the total cost, the rest having to be found by the Exchequer.

The General Services Board would set about creating locally based health centres and county health committees. Local authorities would have certain services such as nursing homes and health visiting placed under their control as envisaged in the 1946 Act.

In seeking to address an elephant in the room for Nationalists whilst also taking advantage of the relative peace in Northern Ireland during this period, Eddie McAteer moved a motion in the House at the end of September that 'the time was now ripe for a general amnesty for all prisoners in Northern Ireland sentences for political offences'. It was bound to heighten tensions in the House.

Internees following the war had been released by the Northern Government and McAteer sought to use this goodwill as a means of leverage for the prisoners in the Crumlin Road Jail.

"I repeat the statement which I made here many months ago, that if we unlocked every door in the Crumlin Road Prison, if we allowed out every prisoner there, whether political or otherwise, there would not be a ripple on the calm pool of public peace in the Six Counties."

The Minister Mr Warnock, whilst accepting the change in general tone of the motion, refused to contemplate an amnesty, informing the House that those behind bars were members of the Irish Republican Army and have such have not refuted their stated aims.

Whilst Ireland was at the time of the motion a peaceful place, the Unionist Government was not willing to contemplate releasing prisoners from a time of turmoil, some from the time of the 1922 unrest.

Indeed, the primary tool of the government in quelling the unrest, the Special Powers Act, had already transformed from a peace keeping measure into a political weapon aimed at all things Nationalist and Republican, whether that be processions, papers, emblems or commemorations.

On 3rd December, the Prime Minister outlined his Government's post-war economic plans to the House. A key tenet of Ulster's contribution to alleviating the economic crisis was in agriculture which did not affect any dollar deficit.

Sir Basil Brooke outlined that the Government in Belfast would seek to increase agricultural output in the form of 13.5 million gallons more milk, 8,000 tonnes more beef, 36,000 tonnes of more pig meat and 35 million dozen more eggs by 1951-52.

Since 1935 the proportion of exported goods to the total of all goods manufactured in Northern Ireland rose by a quarter. The direction of labour that was taking place in the UK to exporting industries did not transfer to Northern Ireland.

The Government's plan rested on three strands. Primarily, reducing unemployment, which would prove difficult given industry had a shortage of steel for new factories. Secondly, attracting females back into work who had ceased working in munitions establishments after the end of the war. The Prime Minister urged employers to investigate nursery provision to allow this to become a reality.

The third objective was to maximise Ulster's share of raw materials. This would prove immensely difficult given the shortage of these even for the Imperial Government.

It is clear from the tone and way the Prime Minister delivered his speech that this crisis was of a proportion not seen since after the 1929 crash, and in my opinion was one of the most detailed – and honest – economic briefings given to the House since its inception.

1948

4th February saw Fianna Fáil lose power in the south, with the formation of the first inter-party coalition consisting of Fine Gael, the Labour Party, Clann na Poblachta, Clann na Talmhan and the National Labour Party.

2nd March against fuelled tensions in the House with a motion for the House to have to annually approve the Special Powers Act, Franchise Act, Trade Disputes and Trade Unions Act as well as the Method of Voting and Redistribution of Seats Act. It was proposed by Harry Diamond (Falls, SRP) and soon felt the wrath of the Ulster Unionist opposition.

At one time, the Minister of Home Affairs seem to accuse the proposer of being 'a pal' of Adolf Hitler until 'he was beaten' – the Minister also refers to himself as 'Caesar'.

The business of the House descended into anarchy, with the Minister referring to the banning of a St Patrick's Day march in Derry because of the use of a Republican flag. At the cabinet meeting the month previous the decision had been taken to ban the procession by the Ancient Order of Hibernians through the city following discussions with the Unionist Mayor of the City. 30,000 people and 100 bands were expected to attend.

"So long as this Government lasts, and so long as I am Minister of Home Affairs, I shall not permit the Republican flag to be carried through Derry city."

It was met with cries of 'No surrender' by one Mr Downey of Labour. Rev McManaway (City of Derry, UUP) went further, by stating that if the march being referred to had gone ahead, 'we' would have stopped it.

Despite the acrimony however, the Home Affairs Minister had informed his colleagues at Cabinet that he proposed to surrender his powers under the Special Powers Act which infringed upon the liberty of the individual.

Continuing his crusade on housing allocation, on 15th June during Oral Questions to the Minister of Local Government, Eddie McAteer asked the Minister about unaffordable rents for the tenants in the Creggan Estate, Derry and was informed that the Housing Trust was due to build 250 houses soon in the area, and that rates in the area were due to come down. In response, Mr McAteer referred to this as the continued 'economic blockade of Derry'.

The Transport Act was put to the House on June. It created the Ulster Transport Authority which would undertake both rail and road interests. The Belfast and County Down, NIRTB and NCC railways were all acquired by the Authority.

Despite concerns from the transport sector, the Commerce Minister was optimistic in his view that the new authority would 'pay for itself'.

A source of significant embarrassment to the government took place in September. In issuing an order to ban all parades in Belfast to stop a commemoration of the 1798 rebellion, the Minister of Home Affairs was not aware that the Cumberland Orange Lodge had its annual church service in Bloomfield.

Technically, their procession was banned, but they ignored the order and rather than being subject to the full force of the law, the Minister publicly apologized that they had been put to such inconvenience.

On 21 December 1948 the Republic of Ireland Act was signed into law in Ireland. It was described as 'An Act to repeal the Executive Authority (External Relations) Act, 1936, to declare that the description of the State shall be the Republic of Ireland, and to enable the President to exercise the executive power or any executive function of the state in or in connection with its external relations.'

Effectively, the legislation removed any remaining semblance of link to the United Kingdom including the powers of the monarch and vested any powers as head of state with the President.

The UK Government reacted to the passage of the Bill with legislation of its own in the form of the Ireland Act 1949 which will be outlined in the following section.

The Northern Ireland Government wasted no time in seeking to extract concessions from London on the constitutional position of the state arising from the new Republic's moves.

1949

February saw a general election held in the North. Prime Minister Sir Basil Brooke made clear the reason for the snap poll;

"We are going to the country on one question only: whether this country is determined...to remain an integral part of the United Kingdom"[92]

The Anti-Partition League had ushered support from across the political spectrum in Dublin, and all parties sought to assist in the cost of fighting the Northern election by utilizing church gate collections.

Whilst helpful to the Nationalists, it was used as a rod by the Unionists as a demonstration of interference by both the Southern establishment and the Catholic Church.

The Labour vote collapsed, with its two members both losing their seats. Frank Hanna in Belfast Central of Independent Labour held his seat, however.

Harry Diamond retained his Falls seat as a Socialist Republican and was joined by two Independent Unionists and two Independents. A Communist Party member ran against Baron Glentoran in Bloomfield but was decidedly routed.

In Pottinger, Jack Beattie of Ind Labour lost to the UUP candidate Sammy Rodgers. In all, the UUP gained four seats to give them 37, the Nationalists held all their nine although they gained a massive 17.6% increase in their vote.

14 UUP candidates and two Nationalists were returned unopposed.

In the Upper House, Unionists dropped to 17, their lowest number since the foundation of the state. McConnell-Wilton retained his seat as the sole Ind Unionist and Smyth as the sole Labour member. They were joined by five Nationalists – John McNally, Charles Bradley, Louis Lynch, Paddy O' Hare and Gerry Lennon.

Major George Thomson took the reigns as Clerk of the Parliaments.

9th March saw the Social Services (Agreement) Bill receive its Second Reading in the House. It formalizes an agreement between the NI Finance Minister and the Chancellor of the Exchequer in enlarging previous re-insurance agreements to cover all social security entitlements in Northern Ireland.

The new Joint Authority for social services and general insurance purposes would ensure that parity is maintained between both jurisdictions. The Northern Ireland Government will contribute to the UK cost of insurance and will then be refunded up to 80% of the excess cost of parity. It was yet another agreement that ensured Northern Ireland remained able to maintain parity of entitlement and services to the UK at a reduced cost overall.

The Irish Government continued its policy of neutrality, refusing to join the new NATO in April.

Days later, the British Government introduced the Ireland Act. It has two provisions – firstly recognizing the Republic of Ireland, and secondly and more crucially, outlining that the constitutional status of Northern Ireland within the United Kingdom would not change unless the Parliament of Northern Ireland agreed otherwise.

However, it also removed the one unifying issue for Unionists in the North – the spectre of the border.

Given the electoral nature of Northern Ireland at the time, the latter provision was referred to as the 'unionist veto'.

It caused widespread anger amongst the Nationalist community in the North – whose name was almost changed to Ulster – and amongst the Government in the Republic who felt it was in some form retaliation for the passage of their 1948 Act.

On 10th May in an unusually frustrated manner, the Taoiseach brought forward a motion to the Dáil in protest at the British Bill.

"Dail Eireann, Solemnly re-asserting the indefeasible right of the Irish nation to the unity and integrity of the national territory. Re-affirming the sovereign right of the people of Ireland to choose its own form of Government and, through its democratic institutions, to decide all questions of national policy, free from outside interference. Repudiating the claim of the British Parliament to enact legislation affecting Ireland's territorial integrity in violation of those rights, and Pledging the determination of the Irish people to continue the struggle against the unjust and unnatural partition of our country until it is brought to a successful conclusion; Places on record its indignant protest against the introduction in the British Parliament of legislation purporting to endorse and continue the existing partition of Ireland, and Calls upon the British Government and people to end the present occupation of our Six North-Eastern Counties, and thereby enable the unity of Ireland to be restored and the age-long differences between the two nations brought to an end".

Days later, Anti-Partitionists from across Ireland held a rally in Dublin. 100,000 people attended to hear the Taoiseach exclaim to Nationalists in the North that;

"the Irish nation was working for them and with them."

The following day, Mr Nixon of Belfast Woodvale who had long been a thorn in the side of the Government since his election, died.

In contrast to the heretofore financial predicaments of the administration in Belfast, the 1949 is a suitable candidate to demonstrate the reawakening of Ulster's economy from the doldrums of the 1920's and 1930's. In its first budget, the Northern Ireland Government had effectively no means of implementing policy that were not mirroring that of Britain.

As has been documented, since then major agreements such as that on re-insurance lifted huge sections of expenditure from the shoulders of Belfast's coffers.

From staring into the abyss of bankruptcy just after partition, the Minister of Finance got to his feet on 17 May 1949 to announce a standalone capital budget of £27 million – close to £1 billion in today's climate.

The vast majority of this would be to finance a massive school building programme – some £15m. £4.5m was to be injected into industrial building programmes, £2m on improvements in agriculture, with just under £2m spent on health and infrastructure with the balance on education and transport.

The Minister, Maynard Sinclair was a canny financial operator and recognised the basic requirements for the Northern Ireland economy were not just growth based on the relationship with the mainland, but structural changes in the domestic economy.

"Our chief problem is to attract industries employing male labour. Many of these industries must not only bring their raw material from Great Britain, but must send a large proportion of the finished goods to that market or to Great Britain ports for trans-shipment abroad, and this adds to the cost of production. If we are to succeed in our efforts to bring new industries to this country to absorb our unemployed male labour there are three essentials, apart from any financial inducements we may be able to offer. First, the retention of the established high reputation of the skill of our workpeople; second, the continuance of our comparative freedom from strikes; and third, a conviction that under no circumstances will Northern Ireland cease to be a part of the United Kingdom."

Despite this pragmatism, however, the Unionist government still insisted on paying an imperial contribution – this year alone it would amount to £20 million. £235 million had been paid into the contribution since partition, and despite the cheerful outlook for Northern Ireland arising from the Minister's capital programme, taxes on some foodstuffs were raised.

This issue had given succour in recent years to those proponents of Dominion status for Northern Ireland, effectively self-rule within the Commonwealth, but in securing the post-war agreements on welfare, those arguments had been dealt a critical blow.

In the House, members – all Unionist, raised concerns about Northern Ireland receiving its 'fair share' of raw materials for example, one member commenting that if Ulster was home to one-forteith of the UK population, then that same proportion of resources should be allocated to the province, especially with the effort being made by Parliament to ensure that Ulster paid its way.

On 15 August the Minister of Local Government and Health, William Grant, died. He was replaced by the first woman to hold Ministerial office, Dame Dehra Parker (S Derry, UUP).

1950

The thorny issue of addressing the state of the railways in Northern Ireland occupied the cabinet in May. A memo by the Minister of Commerce outlined the dire state the Great Northern Railway found itself in.

It was losing £250,000 per year and it was estimated that even if the Transport Authority had stepped in and taken over, this loss would rise by £50,000 due to higher wages for UTA staff.

The cabinet refused to allow the UTA to purchase GNR holdings for the time being.

5th December saw the second reading of the Re-equipment of Industry Bill which aimed 'to provide for the payment of grants towards expenditure incurred in reequipment or modernisation schemes. The extent of the grant will be an amount not exceeding one-third of the expenditure on such machinery and equipment included in a scheme which has been approved by my Ministry.'

The Government had long been lobbied on such a provision especially owing to the post-war slump but was extremely slow to action.

1951

The Republic's coalition government fell at the end of May resulting in a hollow victory at the polls for Eamon De Valera who would lead a minority FF government.

On 19th June the Public Order Bill was introduced. Controversially and considering a growing number of marches and processions by Nationalists, it would require anyone who wanted to organize a procession to inform a senior RUC officer with 48 hours' notice. It sought to replace Regulation four of the Special Powers Act.

If that officer believed the march may constitute or contribute to a breach of the peace, he could re-route it, and the final intercession being from the Minister who could further ban the march to prevent disorder.

Interestingly, the Bill itself did not apply to funerals or processions 'customarily held along a particular route' – i.e. Orange Order marches.

Two court judgements had recently tied the hands of the Ministry regarding public order – one decreed that the handling of the tricolour in public did not constitute a breach of the peace and the other ordered that highways were to be for the use of any section of the community after a nationalist band parading in Tyrone was attacked.

The legislation was passed but the debate lasted almost three days with scathing criticism coming from both sides of the House particularly over the issue of processions in Derry.

Whilst the debate on the Bill raged on, Eddie McAteer brought forward a motion that the Londonderry Corporation was in breach of Section 5 of the Government of Ireland Act 1920 – effectively that it was discriminating against people based on their religion. Whilst he did not then move the motion, the Prime Minister did welcome Mr McAteer's offer to put in writing to him the specific issues of dissatisfaction.

1952

On 18th March during speeches on the Consolidated Funds Bill, Mr McAteer (Mid Derry, Nat) raised the issue of disorder in Derry on St Patrick's Day. He informed the House that the RUC in the City had surged towards a crowd in the City who were in good spirits, but dispersing.
In the House, Eddie McAteer outlined his criticism of the RUC;

"At the junction of Shipquay Street and Castle Street, Derry, at the conclusion of a happily peaceful meeting which the majority of the citizens enjoyed yesterday, the crowd were dispersing. A section of them not in processional order by any manner of means-in fact, most of them were on the sidewalk going down Shipquay Street-came to the intersection with a street called Castle Street.

There we saw a Crossley load of police officers who immediately jumped out on to the street and began surging their way through the crowd. I was right on the spot. I appealed to officers whom I am prepared to name, if necessary, to keep back out of Shipquay Street and I said I would guarantee that there would be no trouble. But it was clear to me that the police were determined to take advantage of the opportunity for a full dress rehearsal of the anti-riot precautions and exercises which they have been carrying out in Victoria Barracks in these past few weeks. In other words, the helpless people of Derry are simply to be used as guinea-pigs for the new tactics, or the perfection of the old tactics, of the R.U.C. Despite my warning to officers who seemed to be in charge, the police surged out amongst the crowd of people and started pushing them here and there, and, as the old story says, "Your Honour, that is how the row began."

Naturally, the Minister of Home Affairs rebutted, accusing of Mr McAteer of seeking to stir trouble in the City centre whereby a meeting he was addressing then marched past Strand Road police station with a tricolour and then attack police officers with stones and pieces of coal, such was the discourse when any specific incidents were raised in the House.

At the beginning of December Lord Granville retired from the Governorship and was replaced by Lord Wakehurst.

On 10th December Harry Diamond attempted to amend the Repeal of Necessary Laws Bill by seeking to include the repeal of the Special Powers Act.

In his speech he outlined the even current members of the House were previously held for breaking the draconian legislation – Eddie McAteer, Cahir Healy and the proposer himself.

Like many other attempts to address the Special Powers Act, the move failed.

It was however, a year of personal satisfaction for Brooke who was created Viscount Brookeborough.

1953

It is widely accepted that 1953 marked the beginning of the overt use of state apparatus for purely political outcomes. Nationalists contend that this had always occurred which research shows, but this year is seemingly when tempers boiled over in the House and when constitutional issues constantly came to the fore between parties, even more so since 1922.

At the end of January Major Sinclair, Minister of Finance, was tragically killed in sinking of the ship MV Princess Victoria. He was to be later honoured by the naming of the Pavilion at Stormont after him.

During this month at a special meeting, Sinn Fein decided to contest the next Westminster elections of 1955 but would not take any seats won.

On the 6th February, King George VI died in London. He was succeeded by Queen Elizabeth II.

Despite being resolute in their determination over some years not to purchase railway holdings, in 1953 both governments north and south agreed to purchase the Great Northern Railways interests in their jurisdictions, and the GNR Board remained, but five years later the nationalisation was complete, when the Board was dissolved and the Transport Authority assumed full management control of the GNR, bringing an end to a decades long complex thorn in the side of the Governments side – or so it was hoped.

Losses of around £1,000,000 had been incurred just on the northern section of the company and the Belfast administration.

A Tribunal had been established in 1951 to investigate the heavy losses of the Ulster Transport Authority and on 28th April the Minister provided the report to the House.

"The plain truth is that the transition from the era of the railway monopoly is still proceeding, and an economic scheme of partnership between rail locomotion and the road motor vehicle is still proving elusive."

Railway lines across Down were closed in 1950 with more being closed in Derry and Antrim to follow. Rail services had been for many years incurring massive losses and the UTA was now registering losses which would compel action by the Ministry of Commerce.

Many members were not happy at the plan to acquire GNR, but the freight aspect of the business was essential for commerce and could not be allowed to falter.

October saw the general election held whereby the UUP consolidated its strength in the east of the Bann, gaining one seat leaving them with 38.

For the first time, two Anti-Partition candidates won seats. Charlie McGleenan in South Armagh and Liam Kelly in Mid Tyrone – both taken from Nationalists.

NI Labour returned no members, whilst Murtagh Morgan of Irish Labour shocked the UUP by taking the Docks seat with less than a 200-vote majority. In Belfast Clifton the former Education Minister Samuel Hall-Thompson lost his seat to an Independent Unionist.

In the Falls, Harry Diamond regained his seat, sitting as a Socialist Republican. 21 Unionist candidates ran unopposed, the highest number since 1933, as did 3 Nationalists.

The Senate saw a straight split between Unionists and Nationalists for the first time. Although John Donaghy was elected as an Independent, he was a Catholic and largely voted with Nationalists.

In December, the Speaker received correspondence from a judge in Omagh to inform the House that Liam Kelly, the Anti-Partition member for Mid Tyrone was being returned for trial on charges of sedition.

1954

On 10 February the new Flags and Emblems (Display) Bill received its second reading. The aim of the legislation was simple: to protect the Union Flag as the flag of Northern Ireland and to ensure that 'provocative emblems' would not be shown in public.

During the election campaign, the Prime Minister made a pledge to his followers that he would protect the Union Flag. Naturally, the Irish Tricolour was deemed to be a provocative emblem as it had effectively been banned in 1933 under the Special Powers Act;

"Any person who has in his possession, or displays, or causes to be displayed, or assists in displaying or in causing to be displayed in any public place ... any emblem, flag or other symbol consisting of three vertical or horizontal stripes coloured respectively green, white and yellow purporting to be an emblem, flag or symbol representing the Irish Republican Army ... an Irish Republic ... or... any ... unlawful association shall be guilty of an offence."[93]

Cahir Healy used the debate to take aim at the power of the Orange Order over the Government, by stating that Ministers were acting in accordance with instructions from lodges and able to brief them that Nationalists for example would not be able to walk the Derry Walls on St Patrick's Day even before the House had even seen the Bill.

Whilst the legislation did not expressly refer to the Irish tricolour, it was clear to Nationalists that this was the target of the Bill, as well as the individual freedoms of citizens who were not of a Unionist persuasion. Several members referred to the 'Dungiven incident' as being the precursor that prompted action by the authorities.

The Bill was strategically introduced to fill the gap left by the under-fire regulations of the Special Powers Act. When one sees the nature of processions and material banned under that Act, it is clear as to the nature of the Flags and Emblems legislation.

Mr Hanna (Central, NILP) was forthright in his view of the Bill, describing it as;

"the most bare-faced piece of discrimination yet attempted by the Government. The cant, humbug and hypocrisy with which it has been supported in this House will deceive no one who really understands the situation and background of events. It has been recognised for a long time by political observers that all has been far from well in the Unionist Party camp, and the basic reason is probably not very hard to find."

The debate on the Bill was one of the most acrimonious in the history of the legislature.

On 12 June, the renewed IRA carried out an arms raid at Gough Barracks, signalling the resurgence of the organization following a relatively peaceful period in Northern Ireland.

During the raid a group of soldiers were held hostage whilst over 300 rifles were seized. It was the first IRA raid on an Army establishment since during the War of Independence.

On 18 May following the fall of the minority FF government in Dublin, a general election was called which returned a Fine Gael/Labour coalition.

1955

On 26 May the UK held a general election, the first in which Sinn Fein contested seats, though on a policy of abstentionism. Much to the dismay of the Unionist government in Ulster, Republicans took two seats in Westminster, Mid Ulster and Fermanagh and South Tyrone.

Thus, began an electoral saga. The two Sinn Fein MPs, Philip Clarke and Thomas Mitchell were both deemed ineligible to sit in the House due to them being currently serving sentences for 'treason felony' arising from an IRA operation to steal arms in Omagh in October 1954 where they were captured.

Col. Robert Grosvenor, the second highest polling candidate in Fermanagh and South Tyrone was deemed elected, however in Mid Ulster, a by election was called which Mitchell again won. He was again declared ineligible and Charles Beattie of the UUP, the runner-up was declared elected.

However, Beattie held an office of profit under the Crown which disqualified him from election to the House of Commons, and a further by-election was held in May, this time returning George Forrest, an Independent Unionist was elected.

Despite all of this, Sinn Fein had amassed almost a quarter of the vote polled.

Unionism re-gained West Belfast when Florence McLaughlin, the sole female candidate in Northern Ireland, took the seat from Irish Labour with a massive majority.

Unionists in Stormont made no attempt to disguise their anger at the Sinn Fein candidacy. Hugh Minford (Antrim Borough, UUP) referred to anyone who voted for the two SF candidates as a 'disgrace to civilisation'.

The basis for the future onslaught of economic reinvigoration attempts made by the government began at the appointment of Lord Chandos as chair of the new Northern Ireland Development Council whose role it was 'to promote new industries and to reduce unemployment.

This coincided with two important developments at Westminster. Firstly, the concession by the Treasury to the principle of 'leeway' proposed by the Joint Exchequer Board which allowed the government in Belfast to reconfigure its relationship with subvention and access funds beyond its means. The second significant shift came after the publication of the Hall Report.

"Between 1945 and 1951 a total of £75.17m was spent by the Northern Ireland Government on industrial subsidisation. Between 1952 and 1957 this went up to £139.29m and it shot up to £292.25m between 1958 and 1963."[94]

On 14th December the Republic of Ireland was admitted to the United Nations.

1956

In mid-December, the IRA officially mounted Operation Harvest, often referred to as the Border campaign. Since the issuing of General Order No. 8 by the IRA Army Council in 1948 – that no offensive action was to take place in the Republic of Ireland, the focus of the organization and its leaders shifted north.

Several strategic locations were targeted on 12th, including the bombing of a BBC transmitter in Derry, the Magherafelt courthouse which was burned to the ground as well as a 'B' Special's post in Newry.

Launching the campaign that day, the IRA accompanied armed actions with a public statement;

"Spearheaded by Ireland's freedom fighters, our people have carried the fight to the enemy...Out of this national liberation struggle a new Ireland will emerge, upright and free. In that new Ireland, we shall build a country fit for all our people to live in. That then is our aim: an independent, united, democratic Irish Republic. For this we shall fight until the invader is driven from our soil and victory is ours."

Two days later, the RUC station at Lisnaskea was attacked with bombs and gunfire, luckily there were no casualties.

On 18th, Hugh Minford brought an adjournment motion before the House following the raids – the Opposition were not present. He praised the Prime Minister who the night before had made a televised address on the atrocities, and the new Minister of Home Affairs Walter Topping (Larne, UUP).

He accused the British Government of not doing enough to ensure that people coming from the Republic to carry out attacks in the North were prevented from doing so.

He called on the Government to exclude SF members from being elected to the House and from disallowing those republicans who have gone over the border from coming back.

"We as Protestants must establish peace in this country."

The Minister informed the House that two police officers had been injured in the raids but were recovering, and that six arrests had taken place.

"It is astonishing that those who are responsible for these acts of violence have not yet learned that bullets cannot shoot beliefs. We believe in Britain and in the British way of life. We are British and British we will remain."

The Irish Government did issue a statement outlining that it would do all within its power to take necessary steps in addressing the issues.

One week later and in the reactionary style of the Belfast Government, the Special Powers Act was used to intern hundreds of republican sympathisers.

Interestingly, the Prime Minister in his speech made clear that no-one should take the law into their own hands and that there should be no advocacy towards others to carry out retaliation.

He informed the House that he received information that the UK Ambassador in Dublin had been obliged to convey the anger of Her Majesties Government about the armed raids.

Regulations were introduced to intern suspects, and further consideration was being given to introducing further powers under the Special Powers Act to close roads and to impose a curfew in border areas.

On 30th, a further attack took place on the RUC barracks in Derrylin, killing Constable John Scally.

The 1956 Housing (Misc. Provisions) and Rent Restriction Act laid bare the ever weakening hold the Government had over its backbenchers. The legislation effectively allowed private landlords to raise their rents. Warnock resigned in protest and future Finance Minister Ivan Neill abstained but was later forced to publicly recant.

1957

In January, the Irish Government arrested senior members of the IRA leadership to avoid a diplomatic incident with Britain. On the first of the month, an IRA unit arranged to attack an RUC/B Special barracks in Brookeborough, Co Fermanagh. Several members were killed and a large number of RUC and B Specials backed up by the Army pursued the unit until they reached the border.. It was a significant target given the name of the town.

One of those killed, Sean South from County Limerick was given a huge funeral in his home town attended by thousands of sympathisers.

On 27th February, Mr Porter (Clifton, IndU) suggested during an economic debate that;

"there are groups of people in the areas concerned who, if given the proper powers and protection, would be willing to form themselves into a volunteer force to protect their own areas."

The Republic went to the polls on 5th March, and Sinn Fein won four seats – the first time in the Republic and they amassed almost 66,000 votes. Eamon De Valera took up the role of Taoiseach for what would be the last time when FF gained an overall majority.

Some cross-border roads had spikes installed such as the Belleek to Pettigo road and the road from Newry to Omeath in order to hamper the actions of IRA columns moving vehicles across the frontier using smaller roads.

On 4th July, another RUC officer was killed, this time in an ambush on a barracks in Forkhill, Co Armagh and another injured. The officer who was killed was a Catholic.

As a result of this, the Republic joined the Northern Government in interning republican activists which had a devastating impact on the ability of the IRA to carry out cross-border operations.

By October, the House was informed that over 200 incidents had taken place because of the armed campaign, causing damage more than £600,000. The Minister of Home Affairs informed the House that 41 people had been convicted 'and have received sentences of imprisonment amounting in all to 217 years'.

November saw the largest loss of life for the IRA during the campaign as four members were killed when preparing a bomb for transport to Northern Ireland in Edentubber, Co Louth.

This resurgence of the IRA, long the fear of the ruling Unionists – or at least used as an excuse to retain security apparatus in the form of the Special Powers Act – was certainly used to justify regressive policies such as internment and the destruction of cross border roads, many of which were not repaired until decades later.

When a new source of employment came to the West in the form of a new Du Pont factory in Maydown outside Derry, it looked like the economic prospects for Northern Ireland might be turning. However, ever concerned about their base, Unionists put a plan in place that would protect them.

"When the American owned chemicals plan, Du Pont, was sited in Derry in 1957, it was arranged that the Unionist Party would nominate the personnel manager in charge of recruitment for the first two years of operation. The intention was to ensure a 'proportionate' employment of protestants."[95]

1958

In February, the Government found itself embroiled in the platers strike at Harland and Wolff. With unemployment a recurring problem, the Minister of Labour and National Insurance was keen that his Department become an arbiter in the dispute over pay.

A general election was held in March, returning the perpetual Ulster Unionist majority. However, the election saw the return of NI Labour who had won four seats – all in Belfast.

Nationalists returned seven, whilst the Independent Unionist in Belfast Clifton lost to the UUP.

In Iveagh, the vigilante group Ulster Protestant Action that was formed in 1956 in response to IRA activity ran A.H. Duff as an Independent Protestant Unionist. Although failing to get elected, their candidate received over 40% of the vote.

Frank Hanna of Independent Labour held his seat in Belfast Central and Charlie McGleenan did not stand in South Armagh, with an Independent Nationalist taking his seat.

The normal contesters were joined by the new Ulster Liberal Party whose leader, Albert McElroy ran for a seat in Queen's but narrowly lost out. The senate election of the previous year kept the profile of the House the same as in 1953.

By April, 136,000 working days had been lost in the Harland and Wolff strike.

The economic problems kept on coming for the Stormont government. In a reply to the Queen's Speech on 3 April, Robert Simpson (Mid Antrim, UUP) stated;

"Altogether the post-war years have been very unhappy ones for the linen industry. The Korean War and the Suez crisis gave spurts of short lived prosperity, but currency difficulties, import restrictions and taxation have resulted in long periods of gloom."

That year, the workforce involved in the linen industry was around 45,000, two thirds less than in 1907. Production after the war had reached 230 million square yards but had now slumped to only 38 million square yards.

The difficulties of the global textiles industry to procure chemicals needed to manufacture Rayon, a synthetic fibre that was cheaper and hard wearing had kept the linen industry afloat during the conflict in Korea but then collapsed. It 1951 it employed about 76,000 workers in Northern Ireland, seven years later it had dropped to 51,000.

The economy further revealed the inability of the Unionist Party to look outside its own ranks and identify policy implications for people outside the Stormont bubble.

"Against a background of economic gloom in the Provinces industrial heavy industries, the Unionist Party appeared too distant from working class concerns and even more damagingly, insufficiently equipped to deal with the problems."[96]

With hundreds of IRA members now interned without trial in both the North and in the Republic, the campaign of violence steadily wound down. However, some incidents did cause serious damage such as the crashing of a freight train into Derry train station and the destruction of Ulster Transport Authority vehicles in Dungiven.

By May, 187 people had been interned in the North with a further 66 people having been convicted. Three police officers had been killed and a further 15 injured. The Home Affairs Minister in updating the House on the disturbances, also revealed that the Army had played an 'invaluable part' in addressing the violence.

On 1 July, an IRA member was shot dead at Clontivrin on the border when their unit was stopped when approaching the Great Northern Railways line. He was shot dead by police who were returning fire. According to the Minister of Home Affairs, another man was subsequently found in searches who had been injured in the shooting and was believed to be an IRA member from Monaghan going by the name of Trainor.

1959

Internment in the Republic had been so successful in addressing the Border Campaign that in March, the Irish Government ended the practice.

On 11th March the last internees were released from the Curragh Camp, following its operation for 20 months where several escape attempts – some successful, took place.

On 23th June, Sean Lemass took over as Taoiseach from De Valera who had stood down and ran for President of Ireland, for which he was elected. He took office from June 25th.

The IRA campaign in Northern Ireland had effectively run out of steam, with little activity in 1959 compared to previous years despite the murder of an RUC officer in South Armagh and the attempted murder of four more by landmine. It had only served to strengthen the view in Unionism that Catholics were a threat.

"In May 1959 MP for Antrim, Nat Minford, demanded security screening of civil servants and wanted the percentage of Catholics employed to be made known."[97]

1960

March saw the ambush of an RUC contingent by IRA members, this time operating in Irish territory and firing across the border to Rosslea. No casualties were reported, and it was one of the last overt actions of the Campaign.

Throughout the rump of the IRA campaign, there was just 26 minor incidents compared to the 200 per year in previous years.

1961

On 22nd March the Government, jittery about the rising unemployment rate and faltering of the shipyards, set about proposing a motion of confidence in itself for the work it was doing to get Ulster back to work.

The debate lasted several days, with genuine concern shown by all sides on the precarious situation the Ulster worker found himself in.

On 4th May the Government appointed Sir Herbert Brittain to head the Joint Study Group whose job it would be' to examine and report on the economic situation in Northern Ireland, the factors causing the persistent high unemployment and what measures can be taken to bring about a lasting improvement'.

The group was to be made up of senior economic officials from both the Northern Ireland and UK Governments – the last real dip in the Northern Ireland pool for London whose patience with seemingly shielding Belfast from the economic realities of the day had long since run out.

By 1st June however, the committee had not yet met. Sir Robert Hall took over as Chair of the Group following Brittain's death.

On the same day as the announcement of the JSG, the Minister of Health and Local Government informed the House that his Department had been sent documents alleging impropriety by some members of Belfast Corporation, namely taking part in debates regarding transactions between the Corporation and companies those members had interests in.

The papers were sent to the Attorney General who advised that a public inquiry should be instigated to investigate the claims, which the Minister announced that day and would be chaired by Robert Lowry, QC.

October saw another Irish general election. Based on a crisis around the refusal of Ireland's application to the European Economic Community. Sean Lemass lead a FF minority government and significantly, Sinn Fein lost all of four seats it had previously gained.

By the time November came, the IRA campaign was unofficially over. The combined efforts of the Governments of Northern Ireland and the Republic had stamped out active units by increased border patrols, internment and in the Republic, the use of special military courts.

1962

On 26 February, the IRA officially called off its Border Campaign. In Stormont, the Minister of Home Affairs Brian Faulkner (E Down, UUP) stated;

"May I remind the House that at the beginning of the campaign the I.R.A. and other "splinter" groups announced their intention of overthrowing the Government of Northern Ireland and having its territory incorporated by force of arms in the Republic of Ireland. In meeting this threat, we have at all times had the utmost support from the Government at Westminster, and the full co-operation of the Services in this area, for which we are grateful.

We are, in fact, more firmly established than ever as an integral and indivisible part of the United Kingdom."

In seeking to consolidate the space that had been created by the ending of the IRA campaign which they opposed, Catholic bishops met with the Unionist Lord Mayor of Belfast for the first time since partition.

John Sholto Fitzpatrick Cooke, a war veteran with the Royal Navy Volunteer Reserve, took over as Clerk of the Parliaments, having served in Stormont since 1947 when he worked with the Speakers team, and subsequently as Clerk Assistant from 1953.

In March 1962 during a discussion on an inquiry into the Belfast Corporation, Phelim O'Neill raised the issue of Ministers disclosing their external interests to give confidence to the House and the public that no questionable dealings were being undertaken. Work would commence under O'Neill.

On 31 May a general election was held. The UUP lost two seats but held their majority at 34 seats – 20 of these were elected unopposed. Labour held their four seats and gained almost 10% on their last electoral performance. Ulster Liberals took a seat in Queens at the expense of the Unionists and Harry Diamond held his seat in Falls.

Irish Labour gained a seat in Belfast Dock with Gerry Fitt who would go on to play a significant political role.

The Senate saw the return of Labour again, with one seat and four Nationalists. The Independent, Donaghy, also retained his seat.

This was mathematically a frightening election for Unionism. The Labour Party had come within 8,000 votes of them in Belfast. 67,450 votes to 60,170.

On 28th June the Local Government Minister announced the findings of the inquiry into Belfast Corporation.

The report uncovered widespread practice of members of the Corporation not disclosing interests when dealing with matters of public finance, and caused a public outcry, as well as a feeling of anger within the powerful UU group at City Hall towards Stormont.

The outcome of the inquiry was for the first time a code of conduct for council members in law which sought to protect the interests of the Corporation against allegations of impropriety.

At the cabinet meeting held on 3rd October, Ministers were kept up to date about Northern Ireland's role as part of the UK within NATO when Central Control in Armagh was utilised in an exercise in September.

Locked in the grip of the Cold War, the cabinet discussed putting civil defence plans in place in the form of the UK government plans. Interestingly, however, the cabinet approved that Derry, previously a dispersal area in the event of a thermonuclear attack, was effectively downgraded, and it was determined that it would not be under threat like Belfast. Of course, we now know since the fall of the Soviet Union that due to intelligence signal equipment in the surrounding hills and the military base at Ballykelly, Derry was indeed a target should the war turn hot.

This file at the Public Records Office had been marked closed prior to the enquiries of the author, it is now opened to the public.

In a major hit to the plans of the cabinet for the economy, a paper delivered to the cabinet outlined the dire straits the Shorts factory found itself in, despite being granted aid previously. The UK government through the Ministry of Aviation had apparently 'regarded Shorts as relatively inefficient and expensive and it now seemed unlikely that a contract for the modified 'Belfast' aircraft would be placed'.[98]

The plant had been built with grant-aid from the government free of charge and was now facing closure, which not only would have been a major embarrassment, but would increase unemployment in and around East Belfast, a unionist heartland.

The Treasury had suggested that of the £10-12 million required to keep the business afloat, the Northern Ireland Government should contribute £5m which would cause difficulty with the opposition.

Officials were to travel to London to try and secure the full £12 million needed and the position of the Belfast authority was to be made clear – that it would strongly resist any suggestion that it should take over the firm.

On the overall Hall report, the Education Minister acknowledged that the UK Government were now pursuing a strong economic policy, pursuant to the aim of joining the Common Market and that Northern Ireland's economic priorities would not necessarily float to the top of the governments priorities.

In fact, the feeling of Ministers was that given their counterparts in London would not countenance special treatment for the province, it should seek to persuade London to take responsibility directly for the unemployment problem in Ulster – which was rejected.

1963

In February, Sir Robert Matthews published his plan to create a new city in North Armagh and to radically change the development of Northern Ireland. In his report, a new city we now know as Craigavon would be created and Belfast's growth would be addressed to protect rural hinterlands.

"An outline plan and report were published in December 1965. It was expected, by 1981, to cover 6,000 acres and have a population of 100,000. Targets included 26,000 new jobs, half in manufacturing, 18,750 new homes, 16 primary and 8 secondary schools, 25 new churches and a 1,000-bed regional hospital."[99]

A boundary known as the Matthews Line was drawn up to stop the creation of new homes in the suburbs of Belfast and the focus would now be on creating the new city between Lurgan and Portadown which would have the potential to attract significant foreign investment.

"On 6 July it was announced that the new city would be named 'Craigavon' after the Unionist hero and first Prime Minister of Northern Ireland. The Opposition was incredulous. Joseph Connellan interrupted Craig's announcement with 'A Protestant city for a Protestant people.'"[100]

The Belfast Regional Survey and Plan exposed the inequity of the planning process and raised the concerns of members that economic development was now in the ownership of the East of the province under the Government.

Naturally, Nationalists and Socialists MPs poured scorn on the report as a fantasy. Geoffrey Cupcott, the head of the design team for the new City, under immense pressure from both an economic and political standpoint, resigned from the project, apparently stating that the new City should be abandoned in favour of developing Derry, serving only to heighten Nationalist suspicion of the plan.

Speaking on a motion of censure again the Minister of Development brought by T. W. Boyd after the Minister openly criticised the National Plan at the Labour conference in Blackpool, Patrick Gormley (Mid Derry, Nat) told the House on 7th October 1965 that Copcutt had resigned because the Registrar-General had told him he had to ensure that the new City was free of non-Unionists, which he rightly rejected.

"Recently I heard the details of the Copcutt resignation and I am seriously perturbed by this matter. This is a thing that any sane person in Northern Ireland must be perturbed about. An emissary came on behalf of the Cabinet to Mr. Copcutt and said: 'You had better see to it in the planning of this city that you will not have an influx of people who will be anti-Unionist and of the Catholic persuasion. If you fall down on that you will have to pack your bags' Mr. Copcutt's answer was 'I shall pack my bags now'.

The person who gave that ultimatum to Mr. Copcutt was the Registrar General. This is the double talk which we have in Northern Ireland, that is the outcome of secret meetings."[101]

On 26 March, the Prime Minister resigned citing increasingly poor health.

"Within the narrow confines of his own criteria for success, Brookeborough's achievements over 20 years were substantial; the Unionist Party maintained essential unity; the anti-partitionist project was thwarted, and a potentially difficult post-war relationship with Britain under Labour was managed."[102]

Brookeborough had been ill for some time with an ulcer and had spent time in hospital prior to resigning, however this was not the only reason for his stepping down.

A serious threat to his leadership had come to the fore when it had been discovered that Lord Glentoran had been a director of a bank that had benefitted from government contracts. There had been fury in the Parliamentary Party with ten prominent MPs including future Prime Minister Chichester-Clark publicly demanding he divest from his interests. The old gentleman's club establishment was experiencing, not for the first time, that its time at the top of the Party had ended.

It took several bad-tempered Cabinet meetings and an internal UUC committee to force Glentoran to rectify the embarrassing situation, and it seriously weakened Brookeborough, poster boy of the aristocratic leadership.

He was to be replaced by Captain Terence O'Neill (Bannside, UUP) who immediately set about reshuffling his Cabinet and ensured he did not suffer the same PR disaster over outside interests by creating a cabinet code of conduct.

Jack Andrews, son of the late James Miller Andrews was promoted to Finance Minister. William Craig took over in Home Affairs, and Brian Faulkner moved to Commerce.

Speaking of his predecessor who would remain an MP, Captain O'Neill stated;

"He has done much for Ulster not only during his Premiership, but indeed before when he was Minister of Agriculture and Minister of Commerce. But in my opinion his greatest achievement was in the constitutional field with the passing of the Ireland Bill at Westminster soon after the war. Under this Act the Constitution of Northern Ireland received additional and valuable safeguards because it transferred the power of decision from Westminster to Stormont."

A rapprochement between Belfast and Dublin, but also significantly, between the worker and the Government, took place under O'Neill's premiership. The arrival of O'Neill constituted a major shakeup in Ulster's administration. Not only did it have a new Prime Minister, but a new Cabinet Secretary as Brookeborough's had left with him.

O'Neill, who was born and raised in England, had held a commission in World War Two and as such retained his military rank as Captain. His time as Prime Minister of Northern Ireland is widely regarded as the beginning of the business-like and competent management of the state and its lingering problems, particularly in the economic arena.

During his tenure, a raft of reports would be commissioned on structural issues within the economy, and some that had been ordered by his predecessor would report giving a clearer picture of the challenges facing the new government.

A report on the general economic outlook of the state was undertaken by K.S. Isles and Norman Cuthbert and reported in 1957, the first of the key reports to inform the administration. It had been commissioned by the then Minister of Commerce Sir Roland Nugent and was presented to Lord Glentoran in June 1955.

The "practical objective of the report is to assess across Northern Ireland's economic condition, and to examine the factors limiting its economic development, in order to throw light on the broad problems of economic and industrial policy."

The report itself ran into almost 650 pages and was a work of statistical marvel which produced information on everything from employment hotspots to the prices of linen in the United States compared to Ulster.

A key report was published by Sir Robert Hall in 1962 following the work of a committee he was tasked with chairing. Controversially, one of its key findings was that emigration from Northern Ireland would continue to rise – a key economic factor but also one which caused fear amongst the ruling Unionists particularly in the border areas where increased emigration of Protestants might upset their local – and even the overall regional political makeup.

"The Hall report, despite the contemporary vogue for regional planning, was unadventurous and suggested little more than lower wages and higher emigration. This was not simply a report in the mould of Isles and Cuthbert. It was significant because its preparation was the arena for a struggle between the Northern Ireland government and the British Exchequer."[103]

It was little wonder the economy would become O'Neill's focus. Between 1961-4, 11,500 jobs disappeared in the shipyards alone. As previously referred to, the second of the significant events that took place in this period was as a result of the publication of the Hall Report.

Westminster had long tired of the never-ending demands on time and resources from Northern Ireland regarding the economy. In the old politics of the pre and immediate post-war period, the personality of a Minister, the circle he had assembled and indeed his social status were to some extent the tools of the trade. Brookeborough was of this generation.

However, Hall represented a sudden end to that relationship. His style had resulted in the door being closed by London. It effectively ended the begging bowl nature of the UK-Ulster relationship he personified.

No longer were treasury officials and political figureheads in London afraid of their actions, or lack of action, leading to unrest in Ulster.

In a historic albeit understated manner, the 30th April saw Billy Boyd of the Northern Ireland Labour Party take up the role of Deputy Speaker of the House and Chairman of Ways and Means, the first non-Unionist to do so.

May saw the second reading of the new Housing Bill which sought to build on relative success in conversions since the mid 1950's by creating a standard scheme of improvement grants which could be used to provide hot water, baths or showers and other modern amenities.

Ministers interests in external firms benefitting from government contracts again came to the fore in the summer. It was discussed at Cabinet level and on 20th June the Cabinet Secretary circulated a draft code of conduct for members. During the cabinet discussion, concern was raised by some members about firms they had interests in being able to apply openly for industrial development grants.

This and other issues such as the status of doctors as part of a practice becoming office holders was brought before the cabinet on 25th, and it was agreed that arising from previous concerns, firms in which ministers had interests could apply for grants as long as this was done "openly and with the full disclosure of the facts to Parliament".[104]

O'Neill was perfectly aware of the need to remove this thorny issue from his inbox.

"The Prime Minister said that Unionist backbenchers as well as the Opposition and the press expected rules to be formulated with out further delay".[105]

In October following a review of the capacity of Queen's University from 1963-68 to provide University places, the Government announced the Lockwood Committee would be established under Sir John Lockwood to investigate the provision of higher education in Northern Ireland. Its report was to become one of the most controversial in the history of the state.

On 22nd, the Prime Minister announced a major economic inquiry on 'the useful scope of economic planning and co-ordination' with the purpose of 'producing a plan bringing together foreseen developments in different sectors, examining our performance and indicating directions in which progress might be made'. It would be known as the Wilson Report.

O'Neill oversaw the creation of the first Economic Council, and so began the establishment of O'Neillism – a byword for a new, practical, confident Ulster.

1964

On 17th January a precursor to the Northern Ireland Civil Rights Movement was formed known as the Campaign for Social Justice. It aimed to highlight the discrimination against the minority in housing, public employment and other areas of public life. It published its first pamphlet on 5th February entitled 'Northern Ireland: The Plain Truth' which sought to demonstrate the discrimination faced by Catholics in areas all over the North, for an audience outside of the state.

The CSJ was to be chaired by Patricia McCluskey who was to go meet with the Tánaiste and Attorney General in Dublin soon after the launch to explore the possibility of taking a test case to the Commission on Human Rights in Strasbourg or the Northern Ireland courts. Whilst legal aid for the case was refused, Dublin felt the campaign may contest the decision in the High Court and seek to highlight further in legal terms the discrimination suffered by Catholics.

In February after lobbying in London, the Treasury released a further £52m to the Province to build new roads and complement his focus on the economy. It constituted the first of O'Neill's accomplishments as Prime Minister.

Early in 1964 the housing situation in Derry in particular, boiled over. The remaining 100 or so families at the Springtown Camp had marched through Derry demanding housing on 28 January. When this was raised with the Minister for Local Government by Eddie McAteer, he revealed that the Londonderry Corporation had sought to force the Londonderry Rural District Council to take responsibility for the accommodation given it was outside the city boundaries, which the Ministry rejected.

The Minister responded to concerns on 27 February by outlining that 3,346 new houses had been built in Derry since 1944 (roughly 167 per year), 303 under construction. In March, however, he rejected the suggestion of appointing the Housing Trust to address the housing issues in Derry.

It was continually contested by residents that the Londonderry Corporation would not house them within the City boundary as it would upset the electoral math of the district. This is in line with the Minister's refusal to allow the Housing Trust to address the systemic issues in the City.

In London, Labour backbenchers established the Campaign for Democracy in Ulster, which would campaign for reform in the province and prove pivotal in later years.

Early deliberations by the cabinet on the Lockwood report in July focussed on the response of the Government on the location the committee might choose to place a new university in. Work on the flagship policy of a new city was forefront in the minds of Ministers.

"While the Committee should not be asked to override educational considerations, it should be told clearly to give due regard to the political, social and economic issues involved in the New City plan".[106]

On 6th September during the general election campaign, a tricolour was erected in premises supporting Billy McMillen in West Belfast. Technically whilst illegal under the 1954 legislation, the RUC did not act as it did not believe this would cause a breach of the peace in a Nationalist area.

However, the Reverend Ian Paisley, a firebrand Protestant preacher and his followers demanded that unless the flag was removed they would remove it themselves. This prompted the RUC to intervene and remove the flag, starting several days of rioting in the City.

During the disturbances, over 80 premises, both domestic and commercial were damaged and up to 40 police officers injured.

Harry Diamond, member for Falls was quick to attribute blame on the Government and the RUC;

"Let me say this, and I am going to place the responsibility where it belongs for these actions in Divis Street. This community can afford many things and it has afforded in the last 18 months the brashness of the hand and the rule of this Prime Minister. But I say to the party on the opposite side of this House, and it is its responsibility, that we cannot afford any longer that brashness.

It is its responsibility because its authority and its majority and its support in this community are going to depend upon that. As I say, for that brashness, that ham-handedness, that inexperience which resulted in this action the other day, which could set the entire community at each other's throats and which has already discredited us throughout the world, this Prime Minister is responsible."

The incident in Divis Street and the entrance of Rev Paisley into the public discourse was the first time in many years that Belfast had seen such widespread violence and the long-premeditated fear of violence had been realized by the Government.

Unionist candidates won all 12 seats in the UK general election held on 15th October.

In another significant move away from the rigid policy platforms of Brookeborough, the Belfast Government recognized the Northern Ireland Committee of the ITCU which represented many workers in the North after securing enhanced freedom for the committee within the trade union movement.

The Economic Council established by O'Neill had six seats for representatives of the trade unions but could not accept the nominations of the chair of the Northern Ireland committee due to its membership of a union run from Dublin. This key issue of autonomy was laboured between the government and the ITCU for over a year when the Council was boycotted by them.

Finally, in June, both sides were able to agree to move forward when the constitution of the ITCU delivered appropriate autonomy to the NI committee.

It was one of few pragmatic moves by the administration and helped with the ongoing problems with labour that would continue to dog Ulster during the period.

On 1st December the Governor, Lord Wakehurst, stood down and was replaced by Lord Erskine.

Lockwood continued to focus the minds of the cabinet in December and its meeting on 21st examined the recommendations arising from the committee's recommendations. It had chosen to site the new university in Coleraine as opposed to the North West and the ramifications would be considerable.

"As to location, the Committee had sought an area of reasonable tranquility, with a sufficient surrounding population, with local authority willing to help (e.g. by making a gift of a site) and with existing accommodation available for students and others. Using these criteria, they had selected Coleraine.

This raised the peculiarly difficult problem of Magee University College. In considering the future of the institution, certain facts should be borne in mind. At present those students seeking degrees had ultimately to attend Trinity College, Dublin for a period. There were 322 full-time students, but only 188 came from Northern Ireland and the balance from Great Britain, the Irish Republic and further afield.

As more university places were provided in Great Britain, it was to be expected that the demand from that source for places at Magee would decline substantially."[107]

It is also notable that Ministers referred to Magee as a 'derelict institution'.

4

1965-1972: Endgame

1965 can be said to be the year the Terence O'Neill's practical politics began to swing into action. On the first day of the year he created the Ministry of Development and appointed William Craig (Larne, UUP) as Minister and renamed the Department of Health and Local Government as the Department of Health and Social Services in line with his modernisation of the public service.

In January, O'Neill invited Sean Lemass to Stormont. He joined the Taoiseach in Belfast on 14 January and made a statement to the House on 19th referring to Mr Lemass as a 'realist' at the meeting which 'could not have been more pleasant'.

O'Neill's attitude drew congratulations from Nationalist and Labour members of the House, but Unionist members were silent. Indeed, Ian Paisley and his supporters had attended Stormont and threw snowballs at the car of the Taoiseach.

"Paisley and O'Neill represented two directions for Northern Protestants; the one forward to new arrangements and new relationships; the other backward to the old longstanding traditions and Shibboleths."[108]

In February, however, Hugh Minford put forward a motion in the House expressing the hope that the meeting would promote a spirit of co-operation and friendliness between the two Governments.

Of course, the Prime Minister did not receive widespread support from those in his own party. Mr Warnock and Mr Boal did little to hide their disapproval of his meeting with the Taoiseach.

On 9th February, the Prime Minister returned the courtesy of the Taoiseach and visited him in Dublin. Eddie McAteer suggested to the Prime Minister in a debate on the visit that a joint session of the House of Commons and the Dáil should be held, in replying O'Neill stated that the House and the Senate had not even had a joint session and it was best not to stretch themselves too far.

Between these two dates on 2nd February, the Nationalist Party accepted the role of Official Opposition in the House for the first time. Eddie McAteer's correspondence with the Speaker announcing the move was read to the House and R. H. Connor was appointed Opposition Whip.

In updating the House, the next day, the Prime Minister made clear that no political or constitutional matters were discussed with the Dublin Government, only that of practicality.

On 19th January the Minister of Commerce Brian Faulkner revealed the Members of the new Economic Council of which he was chair. It had links with the Irish Congress of Trade Unions for the first time since its inception.

On 17th February, the Wilson Report was published. It had been announced in October 1963 and had a wide-ranging economic scope. The Economic Development Programme as it became known, was adopted by the government in full in a White Paper and its recommendations sought to map out the way forward for the Northern Ireland economy in the round.

The programme aimed for 40,000 jobs in manufacturing between 1970-75, house building and industrial training for school leavers.

General infrastructure improvement such as a massive house building programme, a multi-million-pound road building scheme were all aspirations in the report that the government shared.

Growth centres outside of Belfast were to be developed and a focus was to be put on industrial training centres to ensure skills were available in the province for the future workforce.

It was to be financed by £445m of public investment, backed by a further £455m of supposed private investment. It was never going to be easy however, especially given the extremely limited scope for the Stormont administration to plan economically.

Following the publication of the Lockwood Report on 10th February, shades of all political opinion in Derry were incredulous. The University for Derry committee organised a protest in the City on 18th February led by the Unionist Mayor of the City, Albert Anderson. Both he and Eddie McAteer led a convoy to Stormont of some 1,900 vehicles to impress upon the Government the range of feeling about the decision to locate the new University in Coleraine.

On 3 March the report of the Lockwood Committee came before the House. The Report recommended that the new University be established in the Protestant-majority town of Coleraine, rather than Derry which had already the Magee College, or either of the other two widely-referenced destinations – Craigavon or Armagh.

In his speech to the House, the Prime Minister said of the Report;

"The Lockwood Committee therefore followed the task through to its logical conclusion. In deciding what the nature of a second university should be, it examined the related question of where a university of that particular character might best be located. It did so with no preconceived notions for or against any area. Submissions were received from the areas which wished to be considered as possible locations, and at the end of the day the Committee decided to recommend Coleraine. It would be difficult indeed to justify setting aside such a recommendation, linked as it was with the general scheme of the Committee's Report."

Both Nationalists and Labour members expressed outrage at the decision not to site the new University in Derry. Mr Bleakley (Victoria, NILP) attempted to amend a motion in the House calling endorsing Derry, but it fell.

It seems almost obvious that members of the government knew the decision to award the University to Coleraine rather than Derry would cause consternation as they had an abundance of information to attempt to rebuff allegations that Derry was being overlooked for government projects.

It is at this point that we can add University to the issues of the franchise, housing, employment and policing as grievances for the Nationalist community right across the North. What had transpired however, was that rather than seeking to support their native city's claim to the bounty from Lockwood, Londonderry Unionists sought to block it.

"In May 1965 Dr Robert Nixon, Unionist MP for Down stated that 'the Prime Minister himself told us that leading Unionist citizens in Derry were against new industries and the new university coming to Derry, and indeed that the siting of Coolkeeragh power station there was against their advice and wishes."[109]

At the cabinet meeting on 31st March, it was revealed that the Trustees of Magee had refused to come to Belfast to meet the Minister, and instead demanded he meet them in Derry.

March also saw an Irish general election where Sean Lemass's Fianna Fáil won an outright majority.

On 9th May, O'Neill met with Prime Minister Harold Wilson in London where it was believed the Prime Minister urged him to address discrimination in the region.
It could be no coincidence then that at the July cabinet meeting the Minister of Home Affairs informed members he would for the first time in many years, relinquish powers allocated to him under the Special Powers Act.

At that time 39 regulations were in place, and he was to dispose of twenty-one of these immediately, with the option to reinstate them at some point in the future.

The powers to stop and search persons, vehicles or premises was to be abandoned alongside the power to intern, impose a curfew and control vehicles.[110]

Another major report was laid at the feet of the government in July, when the Benson report was concluded. It had been commissioned following the continuing losses incurred by the Ulster Transport Authority primarily in railway holdings.

It was to truly mark the end of the extensive accessibility to rail in Northern Ireland. All lines but three, the Belfast-Larne Harbour, Belfast through Portadown to the border and Belfast-Bangor were to be mothballed and closed within three years.

It was a major culture shock to the people of the province who had been able to utilise a railway infrastructure since partition. From 1965 onwards, 108 rail halts or stations were closed throughout Ireland, 26 in the North alone. The Authority itself was to be privatised and broken up by 1965 and the rail infrastructure was to be replaced by investment in roads.

Motorways that even predated their counterparts in Britain were to be laid by a multi-million-pound programme. The recommendations in the report particularly affected the west of the province, where Derry would lose access to the Republic via rail, and large parts of the rural access to other areas would be critically curtailed.

In August, the British Home Office appointed Oliver Wright to represent the views of the Government to the leadership in Belfast, as well as reporting to London the administration's actions in restoring order. This was the first time since partition that the UK Government had placed an operative in Belfast to report directly back to Westminster on Northern Ireland.

In the November general election, the UUP won 59.1% of the total vote, and gained two seats, bringing them to 36. Nationalists returned nine, and Harry Diamond was joined by Gerry Fitt who was previously on a Labour ticket. The National Democratic Party formed in 1965 following a failed experiment in Nationalist unity. It took a seat in Belfast Dock with John Joseph Brennan.

Sheelaugh Murnaghan took a seat in Queen's unopposed for the Liberal Party.

The Upper House saw two Labour members returned, with four Nationalists and Donaghy as the Independent, the UUP retaining its large majority.

On 15th December 1965 Britain and Ireland signed the Anglo-Irish Trade Agreement that would create a free trade area between the two nations. For the Irish, the agreement constituted a step forward in its quest to become a member of the EEC after being rejected earlier.

1966

In February when discussing the Estimates, it was revealed to the horror of Members that the recent renovation of Stormont Castle would cost the taxpayer £59,014 – with the internal painting costing £8,000 alone, tarnishing O'Neill's image as a reformer.

On 7th March the Minister of Home Affairs issued two orders under the Special Powers Act – the first banning any march commemorating the 1867 Fenian Rebellion, and the other banning the Republican Clubs which he described as being the same organization as Sinn Fein. Three days prior, the British Home Secretary met with the UK Prime Minister following reports of possible violence at 1916 commemoration events.

On 31st March the UK general election was held and Gerry Fitt, Stormont MP for the Docks area of Belfast was elected to represent West Belfast.

The modern-day Ulster Volunteer Force emerged on 21st May. It issued a statement outlining that known IRA men would be 'executed'. Six days later, the Ulster Volunteer Force was banned by the Government.

Its first victim was an elderly Protestant woman after a petrol bomb attack on a Catholic-owned bar in the Upper Shankill went awry and set her home alight.
It shot and killed a Catholic man named as John Scullion on 27th May and murdered Peter Ward and injured a further two in June.

On 6th June, the Rev Ian Paisley led a procession through Belfast City Centre to protest about the Presbyterian Assembly with banners stating such things as 'No Money for Rome' and 'The Pope is No Christ'. It caused uproar in Nationalist areas and when it deviated from an agreed route, the RUC did not intervene.

This was one of several incidents which the Reverend led, and the House seemed united in their abhorrence of such events, summed up by the Member for South Armagh, Mr Richardson;

"The Prime Minister is not here but the Minister of Home Affairs is in his place. The Government should step in and put an end to this man's career and his followers."

Two days later in Parliament Buildings, Gerry Fitt was accosted by two members purporting to be from Paisley's Ulster Protestant Action. They had been signed into the Distinguished Strangers Gallery by Mr McQuade (Woodvale, UUP).

Paisley had used his influence throughout the year to create the Ulster Constitution Defence Committee which targeted O'Neill specifically and his détente policies towards the Republic in particular. It would go on to play a role in the opposition on the streets to the Civil Rights Movement in the form of the Ulster Protestant Volunteers.

In the South, Lemass had been replaced by Jack Lynch as Taoiseach.

The Government were forced to act owing to the riots led by Paisley's supporters in attacking Catholic businesses in Belfast city centre, and it was agreed at cabinet on 25th July that the Minister of Home Affairs would make an order banning all processions within 15 miles of Belfast City Hall for three months to end the turmoil.

Discussions between the Belfast and London Governments took place in early August as the flare up of violence sat increasingly uneasy with the Labour Party.

Harold Wilson praised the Stormont Ministers for their role in addressing the 'difficult and delicate' situation at Easter but informed them that his backbenches and that of the Liberals, with some Conservative support, were concerned with some areas of affairs in Northern Ireland.

The British Prime Minister was sanguine in his approach, yet clear – "a real effort should be made to meet some of the grievances which had been expressed, otherwise Westminster would be forced to act".[iii]

Ministers were under no illusion. At their own cabinet meeting four days later, the Minister of Agriculture commented that a threat seemed to be hanging over Northern Ireland from London, a comment which the Prime Minister concurred with.

1967

On 7th February Miss Murnaghan (QUB) sought to introduce a Human Rights Bill, her second attempt of four in total. It sought to create a human rights commission and had previously sought to make unlawful discrimination a criminal offence, however Unionists argued that the 1920 had provided this and the Bills never passed the second stage.

The Northern Ireland Civil Rights Movement was formed in Belfast on 9 April. It was the successor to the Campaign for Social Justice and demanded an end to discrimination in Northern Ireland against Catholics in housing, employment and the vote. It was around this time that the Official Opposition began appointing Spokespersons in the House.

Days later, a group of Labour MPs, members of the Campaign for Democracy in Ulster, visited the province to see first-hand the conditions of the minority and to meet with stakeholders – including the Ulster Unionist Party, who refused to meet with them.

The summer of 1966 could be seen to be the beginning of the 'awakening' in Britain about the governance of Northern Ireland. Several MP's, newspapers and television programmes focused on the claims of the minority and on 27th April the Prime Minister seemed to agree with them, expressing concern about the governance of the province in the House of Commons.

November saw the creation of the Derry Housing Action Committee (DHAC). It was formed with the simple aim of addressing the lack of adequate houses for mainly Nationalists in the Derry area and regularly disrupted Londonderry Corporation meetings to protest at the lack of action on sustainable housing.

Meetings between UK ministers and Terence O'Neill following these high-profile concerns did not deliver immediate change and fuelled the realization amongst the Catholic minority that this may be the time to seize on any opportunity to have their grievances addressed by the British Government and not Stormont.

On 20th December, the government established a Boundary Commission that would draw the boundaries of the newly formed constituencies arising from the dissolution of the Queen's University seats. Three members of the Westminster Commission were to oversee the work.

1968

8th January saw a further meeting between O'Neill and the Taoiseach, but their agenda did not include the political disturbances in the North, rather there were a number of Ministerial discussions regarding North-South co-operation on issues such as foot and mouth disease and electrification across the border.

The House lost a crucial voice when Viscount Brookeborough resigned his Parliamentary seat on 13th February.

On March 25th the DHAC stormed the monthly meeting of Londonderry Corporation and sat-in on the meeting to protest the lack of housing in the City.

20th May would be the day that many hard-line Unionists took their public revenge on Captain O'Neill. He was attacked with flours and eggs whilst leaving a meeting of the Woodvale Unionist Association. Days before, Unionists won the by election in Londonderry City.

One of the first and most public protests held by the Civil Rights Movement began on the morning of 20th June when Austin Currie (W Tyrone, Nat) joined the Gildernew family and others in squatting into 9 Kinnaird Park, Caledon in protest at the house having been allocated to a Miss Emily Beattie, a 19-year old Protestant girl with no dependents. He was encouraged to make headlines to attract interest in the situation in Ulster by Labour MP for Manchester Blackley, Paul Rose who was also the chair of the Campaign for Democracy in Ulster.

Internal documents show that the Crown Solicitor wanted charges brought against the MP and two others for the protest. They were forcibly evicted by the RUC and the Nationalist Party voted the next day to support Currie's actions at their Annual Conference.

The case against Currie and the others was thrown out based on the fact they had only occupied the premises for less than four hours though documentation shows that an appeal would be lodged against this decision.

24th August was to be the day of the first Civil Rights March, from Coalisland to Dungannon, although the march was banned under the Public Order Act from entering Dungannon by an order signed by Mr Skerritt, the District Inspector of the RUC.

Around 1,500 people were present at Coalisland and in reaching the police cordon speeches were made by prominent MPs such as Gerry Fitt, who, according to a police report, stoked tensions in the crowd by saying that 'but for the presence of women and children I'd lead the march into the Square'.[112]

Loyalists held a counter demonstration on the day, and the RUC kept the two factions apart, with the march passing off relatively peacefully. It prompted a strange response from the Minister of Home Affairs, he released a statement the next day clarifying the situation regarding the RUC actions at the march and clarified that these 'were not sectarian'.

A week later after a planned DHAC protest in Derry's Guildhall, one of the organisers, Eamon Melaugh, contacted the Civil Rights Association and invited them to march in Derry.

On 8th September as per the Public Order Act the RUC were informed that the Civil Rights Association were to hold a march on Saturday 5th October.

On 1st October the Apprentice Boys of Derry announced plans to hold a march during the same date and time as the Civil Rights march. This gave the government the excuse that the original march could lead to a breach of peace, and two days later the Minister issued an Order banning all processions and marches from the City centre or waterside areas of the city.

A document from the Home Affairs Ministry briefing the Home Office in London on the banning of the march alleges that a fifty-strong contingent of the Liverpool Branch of the Apprentice Boys were to come to the City to attend an initiation at the Apprentice Boys Memorial Hall on Society Street which is yards from the City Walls – however, the document then notes that alternative arrangements for the Liverpudlians had been made and that there would be no threat of violence – subsequently it stated that the RUC had received complaints from residents which upheld the Order.

On 5th October the planned march began with marchers assembling at Duke Street in the Waterside area of Derry. Around 300 people had gathered to take part. The congregation included an RTE television crew who captured the now well-known scenes of the RUC baton charging the marches before the march had even started. This is described by many as the start of the conflict in Northern Ireland as widespread rioting took place in Derry following this event. Several Westminster and Stormont MPs were in attendance and were injured in the violence.

Police insisted they were attacked by missiles from marchers prior to batons being drawn.

The organisers of the march were arrested under the Public Order Act the next day and a special court session held were they were remanded on bail. Due to continued rioting and a large congregation in and around the Diamond, the special court was held in the Strand Road police station.

Documentation from the local hospital shows that because of the disturbances on 5th and 6th October, a total of 85 people were treated in the Emergency Department.

On 8th October the Taoiseach gave a speech in Clonmel outlining his view that partition was the root cause of the disturbances in the North.

"Partition is the first and foremost root cause. And Partition arose out of British policy. The methods necessary to maintain Partition against the wishes of the vast majority of the Irish people and local majorities in areas like Derry City, that is: gerrymandering discrimination in jobs and housing, suppression of free speech and the right of peaceful protest, could not be continued without the political and the huge financial support received from Britain."[113]

With the violence ongoing in Derry, in Belfast a demonstration led by Queen's students aimed at protesting police brutality in the North West was undertaken on 9th October. It was met by a counter demonstration led by the Rev Ian Paisley. Following the demonstration, the People's Democracy organization was formed.

The Derry Citizens Action Committee was formed on the same day, led by Ivan Cooper with a local teacher named John Hume as vice-chair. It aimed to bring together organisations in the City to address social problems.

15th October saw the Nationalist Party withdraw from their position as the Official Opposition at Stormont. The next day, the Minister of Home Affairs, William Craig brought a motion before the House condemning the 5th Oct march.

He praised the actions of the RUC and despite the images of marches being attacked being broadcast all over the world, he made the following statement;

"None of the news media, either in written reports or visually, presented a strictly chronological, accurate report of what happened and why. The result of this was that the people of Northern Ireland and further afield were given the impression that the RUC in carrying out the terms of the order which I had made acted precipitately and with scant regard to that high standard of behaviour which they had set out over the years."

He then went on to summarise the series of events and in a bizarre episode, referred to a letter from Mr O'Connor of West Tyrone which outlined the injuries suffered by Eddie McAteer at the march following a report from his doctor that outlined personal details such as an injury to his groin as a result of the baton charge.

The Minister then went on to sum up his views;

"My order has been represented as a ban on free speech and on free assembly. As a member of a democratic Government I deny this."

On 30th Jack Lynch met the British Prime Minister in Downing Street and suggested an end to partition in order to end the upheaval in the North, which was naturally rebuffed. Interestingly, however, the Prime Minister said he 'recognised' the problems faced by Catholics in Ulster.

A meeting took place in Downing Street on 4th November between the Prime Minister and his NI counterpart flanked by Cabinet ministers.[114]

Minutes from the meeting show Harold Wilson would not directly become involved in the affairs of the Ulster Government but was not shy in threatening to review financial arrangements the Treasury had with Belfast if the situation in Northern Ireland was not satisfactorily addressed.

He stated that the Government found the situation in Derry and the issue of the local franchise 'irksome' and significantly, pointed out that the use of the Special Powers Act gave rise to international criticism.

He urged that a Parliamentary Commissioner be appointed (which had previously been rejected) to allow grievances to be raised by MPs especially in a system where one party would always be in Government.

For his part, O'Neill sought to demonstrate his willingness to address community relations by pointing out his Government had attracted DuPont to Derry which would have a majority Catholic workforce. He also referred to the Electoral Law Bill which was progressing through the House, abolishing the Queen's University seats and the business vote.

It was the first time in decades that the UK Government had sought to involve itself in the governance of Northern Ireland and demonstrated to the senior Unionist Ministers the need for urgent reform.

A Northern Ireland Cabinet meeting held on 7th November at Stormont Castle demonstrated the panic that had gripped Government following the meeting with the Prime Minister and the speedy reforms that would be needed in order to avoid a confrontation with Westminster.

Unlikely by chance, the following day the Londonderry Corporation agreed to Nationalist demands for a transparent point-based system of housing allocation in the district.

13th November saw a ban on all marches apart from 'customary' processions until the 14 December. This was defied by the DCAC two days later when a massive procession and sit-down protest took place in the Diamond area of the city.

Support for the basis of Derry's revolt came from an unlikely quarter in the form of Edmund Warnock when he wrote to Terence O'Neill on 13th November;

"If ever a community had a right to demonstrate against a denial of civil rights, Derry is the finest example. A Roman Catholic and Nationalist city has for three or four decades been administered (and none too fairly administered) by a Protestant and Unionist majority secured by a manipulation of the ward boundaries for the sole purpose of retaining Unionist control.

I was consulted by Sir James Craig, Dawson Bates and R.D. Megaw at the time it was done. Craig thought that the fate of our constitution was on a knife-edge at the time and that, in the circumstances, it was defensible on the basis that the safety of the State was the supreme law. It was most clearly understood that the arrangement was to be a temporary measure – five years was mentioned."[115]

A further meeting of the Cabinet on 20th November with senior police in attendance to brief Ministers on the disturbances in Derry gives rise to an exceptional quote;

"In response to a question from the Prime Minister, the police view was given that unless the heat could be taken out of events by political means, the law and order situation could get completely out of control".[116]

At the same meeting a letter was discussed from the UK Prime Minister outlining that if the Ulster Government did not introduce universal suffrage, it would be imposed on them by Westminster.

The Ministers of Commerce, Agriculture, Home Affairs and Education were opposed to being forced to act on the franchise, especially if the Government in Belfast offered a package of other reforms, indeed the Ministers of Commerce and Agriculture commented that;
"that a "package" of other reforms should be agreed, and that at a further visit to Downing Street Mr. Wilson should be clearly told that a move to universal adult suffrage was not politically feasible at present. This would at the very worst have the merit of demonstrating to the Party some willingness to avoid complete surrender on all issues."

On 22nd November O'Neill announced five major reforms which the Government would implement – a development commission to replace the Londonderry Corporation; a Government Ombudsman; that housing allocation would be based on need; the Special Powers Act would be abolished as soon as was practicable and reform of the local government franchise.

Days earlier, the Nationalist Party adopted a policy of civil disobedience at its conference.

"In just forty-eight days since 5 October 1968 the Catholic minority had won more political concessions than it had over the previous forty-seven years."[117]

The Governor, Lord Erskine, stood down on 27th November and was replaced by Lord Grey of Naunton.

The Special Powers Act at this stage had created almost 100 regulations which the state used to occupy any space in public life that may, in their view, pose a threat to the Constitution.

A cursory glance at the work by LK Donohue demonstrates the extent to which regulations under the Act had been used primarily to suppress freedom of speech and assembly of Nationalists and Republicans, even those seeking to demonstrate their identity in the most peaceful of ways at graveside commemorations.

Almost 100 processions and marches had been banned over the lifetime of the Act, nearly all Easter Commemorations and certainly anything politically Nationalist.

Six days later the Electoral Law (NI) Act 1968 became law, abolishing the University seats and the company vote, establishing for the first time 'one man, one vote' in local government elections. Crucially, a Boundary Commission was also established.

A civil rights march in Armagh was stopped by the RUC on 30th November due to a counter demonstration by Ian Paisley and Major Bunting, for which both were arrested.

On 4th December, the Minister for Development when briefing the House on the Second Reading of the New Towns Bill, informed members that the Development Commission taking over from the Londonderry Commission would take over the powers of the Corporation as well as the Rural District Council for the purposed of implementing a development plan. Members of the Corporation were effectively sacked, and the Mayor's ex-officio seat in the Senate was temporarily returned as empty.

Five days later, the juggernaut of demands, meetings and protests prompted O'Neill to deliver a televised speech stating famously 'Ulster is at the crossroads'. The DCAC resolved to end all marches and demonstrations for a period of one month following the address to give the government breathing space and as an act of good will.

Two days later, following extensive interventions by William Craig the Home Affairs Minister on the legal interpretation of Westminster's powers under section 75 of the Government of Ireland Act – despite having this clarified by the Attorney General, the Prime Minister relieved Craig of his ministerial duties, creating him as some form of loyalist martyr to his followers.

1969

People's Democracy had started a march from Belfast to Derry on 1st January mirroring the famous Selma to Montgomery march of the Civil Rights Movement in the United States. It began with a small group of people but grew to many hundreds in the next three days.

Several English MPs contacted the Prime Minister in Belfast to ensure that marchers were not hampered, and that the RUC gave them adequate protection.

There was sporadic violence throughout the march when attacked by loyalist demonstrators, prompting the new Minister of Home Affairs Captain Long to issue a press statement urging restraint.

However, on 4th January the march reached the Burntollet bridge a few miles outside Derry. A loyalist mob of several hundred awaited them, joined by – according to sources – off-duty B Special officers. Loyalists hurled rocks and missiles at the marchers, and pictures revealed that RUC officers who attended the scene, mingled with the loyalists and did not arrest any. When the march reached low ground, they were stormed by the mob, and deserted by the RUC.

Dozens of people were injured by metal bars and glass and required hospital treatment. Marchers accused the RUC officers attached to the march of not protecting them, especially when they entered Derry and were again attacked at Irish Street, a Protestant estate in the Waterside.

The new Minister after being questioned in the House confirmed that only four people would be charged.

When the march arrived at its destination, the RUC broke up the planned rally, and so began several days of serious rioting in the city.

The Prime Minister issued a statement the next day seemingly blaming the marchers for undertaking a 'foolhardy' enterprise aimed at bringing further shame to Northern Ireland. For once, Eddie McAteer agreed with him that the march should not have taken place and indeed elements within the Civil Rights Association had warned against it.

In the Cabinet meeting on 6th, the RUC gave a worrying assessment of the situation in Derry, informing Ministers that "considerable strength, possibly even involving the use of firearms, would be required to re-enter the area in the current atmosphere".[118]

At the meeting, Captain Long sought permission of the Cabinet to meet John Hume to attempt to calm the situation.

Significantly, the Cabinet agreed that the regular RUC officers should now be bolstered by a mobilization of the B Specials, much to the dismay of the Irish Government.

On 8th Frank Aiken, the Minister of Foreign Affairs in Dublin met with the British Ambassador regarding the Northern Ireland situation. In the note of the meeting, the Minister was asked his views on whether the British should grant any Belfast request to use troops, this was flatly rejected.

The 15th saw Captain O'Neill announce an inquiry into the disturbances across the province to chaired by Lord Cameron which the Irish Council of Churches had called on him to instigate. The day before the announcement of an enquiry, the Prime Minister submitted a memo to the Cabinet about the general political situation, recognising how his Government were being viewed from afar;

"What have we to lose by such an inquiry? As things stand it is all too widely accepted throughout the United Kingdom that a sectarian Government, directing a partisan police force, is confronting a movement of idealists."[119]

In it, he acknowledged that the use of the RUC to address what was a political problem would have limited effect. He also informed colleagues that if the government sought troops the Home Office would refuse this.

He proposed an inquiry that would investigate all aspects of the problems facing Northern Ireland and "could hardly fail to bring out in an objective way the real difficulties of the situation and the real aims of some of those involved".[120]

His proposal of a Royal Commission established by the Governor would concede a critical demand to the Civil Rights Movement but would also seal his political fate.

The House attempted to continue debating issues such as fisheries, housing and social services but it was now clear that 'disturbances' would from here on, take precedence over all other matters in Parliament.

The next day, Deputy Prime Minister Brian Faulkner resigned from O'Neill's government, landing a crushing blow. He was followed two days later by the Health Minister which piled pressure on the Prime Minister, who was forced to call an election to regain any political authority he had left. It was announced for 24 February 1969.

The election was an anomaly. Unionists were split into opposing Pro and Anti-O'Neill camps, and indeed some even stood against one another. Whilst the Unionist majority held firm, O'Neill's opponents gained over 20% of the vote and 13 seats. He was re-elected Prime Minister days later.

Independent Pro-O'Neillers won three seats but significantly, Eddie McAteer lost his seat in Foyle to John Hume. It was a watershed moment for the direction of Nationalist politics.
People's Democracy also fielded candidates and although none were elected, they captured almost 25,000 votes.

The Upper House did not see a spill-over of change, the only change from the previous election was Donaghy switching to Nationalist membership.

March saw the establishment of the Cameron Inquiry and the legislation passing through Westminster that would allow a Commission.

For two weeks from the end of March, loyalists piled the pressure on O'Neill by seeking to destabilise public amenities across Ulster, on one occasion causing a blackout across Belfast as part of a bombing campaign.

On 17th April following the death of long-standing Unionist Mid Ulster MP George Forrest, Bernadette Devlin, a 21-year-old member of People's Democracy stood as a Unity candidate against the widow of Mr Forrest and took the seat. It sent shockwaves across Unionism. Devlin was the youngest woman ever to have been elected to Westminster.

Over the following weekend, rioting in Derry intensified and an innocent man named Sammy Devenney was severely beaten by police officers in his home, resulting in a heart attack and later death. He was one of the first fatality in this phase of the political upheaval.

The UVF bombed the main water supply to Belfast the next day, seeking blame apportioned to the IRA. Troops were despatched from their barracks across the province to secure key civic amenities.

Wednesday 23rd April saw the end of the O'Neill premiership. His party had voted narrowly to introduce universal suffrage in elections, but it proved hollow when James Chichester-Clark, the Agriculture Minister, resigned following the result. It was the same day that the promised Parliamentary Bill came to fruition, with the hope expressed in the House that Sir Edmund Compton would take up the post of Commissioner.

The Taoiseach paid tribute to O'Neill and commented that he believed him to be sincere in his wish to promote a spirit of toleration and understanding in Northern Ireland.

On 3rd March the Cameron Commission was established under the Chairmanship of Lord Cameron assisted by Sr J.H. Biggart and Mr J.J. Campbell. It would investigate and establish the reasons for the violence in Derry on 5th October and following days. 152 complaints were made about the police following the 4th and 5th January the previous year, there was 630 officers on duty and 25 of those were injured.

20th March saw a significant event in the House. Following a ruling by the Speaker on the Public Order Bill – which was in fact out of Order, Captain Brooke was allowed to put the Question to the house in the middle of the debate, effectively guillotining the debate to evade Nationalist input. What followed was a demonstration of unity that until now many Nationalists had been unable to harness.

It is reported in Hansard that;

'Mr Carron, Mr Cooper, Mr Devlin, Mr Hume, Mr Kennedy, Mr Keogh, Mr O'Hanlon and Mr O'Reilly staged a sit-down protest and sang 'We Shall Overcome'.

John Hume brought forward a motion on 22nd April regarding the violence in Derry regarding the attack on Sammy Devenney and the surrounding events;

"The Government are not governing. As we have said repeatedly, they are intent on the struggle within the ranks of their own party".

Chichester-Clark succeeded O'Neill as leader of the Ulster Unionists and Prime Minister, yet despite his opposition to the reforms O'Neill had pursued, he committed to implementing them, and started with a general amnesty for all those being held on offences relating to demonstrations since 5th October 1968.

He appointed Jack Andrews, son of former Prime Minister John Miller Andrews as Deputy Prime Minister. William Long was appointed to Education, Phelim O'Neill moved into Agriculture and Brian Faulkner became Minister of Development.

On 7th May a secret communique was issued from Belfast to Westminster seeking the Government's view on requesting military intervention in Ulster should the government grant universal suffrage. It was not satisfied with the result of its communications, that the GOC in Ulster would be required to seek permission from London on the use of military resources and then communication would take place on a governmental level.[121]

On the same day, the first meeting of the newly formed Cabinet Security Committee took place. As part of the membership which included the Prime Minister, Development Minister, Education Minister, the Inspector General and John Taylor MP representing the Minister of Home Affairs.

Minutes from the meeting show that a proposal had been put forward by the Civil Rights Association to hold local elections under universal suffrage in some specific areas of the province, but the Prime Minister was more concerned that rivalry between NICRA and militant Protestants was giving an advantage to the IRA.

The Minister of Development is quoted in the papers as saying that 'immediate legislation granting one man one vote was vital'.[122]

A Development Commission set up to replace the Londonderry Corporation was to be headed by Mr Brian Morton it was announced. Unionists were furious, and Gerry Fitt wasted no time in expressing his view;

"This commission means in fact "you have made it impossible for us to control this city, but we are going to make sure you do not control it, so we will abolish the Corporation and put in a commission.""

Throughout June, the security situation stabilized and the Act which allowed complaints to be made against government departments was passed by the House. However, the beginning of the traditional marching season raised tensions despite plans by the Army to withdraw on 16th June.

The Rev Ian Paisley as leader of what were identified as 'militant Protestants' by the Cabinet, sought to meet the Prime Minister to put forward plans for a march in Newry on 26th July. The Inspector General was very worried that a counter demonstration would take place but it was agreed that the Prime Minister and Minister of Home Affairs would meet the Reverend.

Militarily, the 1st Batt the Light Infantry would be replaced temporarily by the Royal Regiment of Wales and the 1st Batt the Prince of Wales Regiment were leaving for their base in July.

On 14 July, Francis McCloskey of Dungiven was the first civilian to be killed when he was assaulted by a police officer. Significantly, Sammy Devenney died three days later after the new Prime Minister mobilized the B Specials across the province.

Events leading to the 14th in both Derry and Dungiven on 12th and 13th July "had stretched the resources of the RUC to the limit" according to the Inspector General who had decided to alert sections of the Special Constabulary who would be armed only with batons to be on stand by for duty alongside the RUC.[123]

Following a meeting with the Home Secretary in London, the Prime Minister agreed to allow the Apprentice Boys march in Derry on 12th August to proceed, prompting what we now refer to as the beginning of the 'Battle of the Bogside'.

Barricades were erected around the route of the march and the Civil Rights Association provided stewards to minimise disruption. Prior to the march, the Derry Citizen's Defence Association was established to defend the Bogside area against attack from militant protestants on the route and to ensure no incursion into the Bogside.

Resources such as stones and petrol bombs had been stockpiled by DCDA should trouble break out and when RUC officers sought to enter the Bogside as a result of confrontation with marches, these were despatched and a two day running battle between residents and the RUC, then B Specials took place.

Huge re-enforcements of police were sent to Derry to the tune of 3 District Inspectors, 10 Head Constables, 40 Sergeants and 246 Constables as outlined by the Inspector General to the Cabinet Security Committee on 14th July.

On the day following, there were some minor disturbances in Derry around the Bishop Street area. Strangely, local unionists had sent a telegram to the Prime Minister stating that troublemakers had been coming from over the border which was denied by the Inspector General.

13th August saw the Taoiseach making a public intervention in a televised address. He made clear that the Stormont administration was no longer in control of the security situation and uttered the famous words – the Irish Government can no longer stand by and see innocent people injured and perhaps worse'.

This statement gave hope to Nationalists that assistance would come from the Dublin Government, perhaps even in the form of military intervention.

On 14th August, the Inspector General of the RUC issued correspondence to the General Officer Commanding in Northern Ireland asking for his troops to despatched to Derry as after several days of sustained rioting, his officers were exhausted.

Parliament had been in recess until October but was recalled to discuss the disturbances in Derry in particular. The Prime Minister posed a motion condemning the violence, praising the police and calling on those with influence in the City to work to end the violence.

In his speech, the Prime Minister stated;

"This debate will test to the full our ability to rise to the level of events. Are we in this House prepared to lead the community back to peace?"

He directed the blame for the onslaught of violence squarely on the shoulders of the residents of the Bogside for attacking the march.

"the people in Britain and elsewhere who are watching these events should waken up to the reality of what is happening here. This is not the agitation of a minority seeking by lawful means the assertion of political rights. It is the conspiracy of forces seeking to overthrow a Government democratically elected by a large majority"

In his remarks he also took aim at the Taoiseach's intervention;

"History will record in how responsible and neighbourly a way we have tried to conduct our relationships with the Irish Republic. All that has been brought to an end by this intervention. We must and we will treat the Government which seeks to wound us in our darkest hour as an unfriendly and implacable Government, dedicated to overthrow by any means the status which enjoys the support of a majority of our electorate. I am sure many hon. Members who heard Mr. Lynch's remarks will have shared my intense anger and resentment at their tone and content"

In response, Gerry Fitt made a crystallising speech that summed up the feelings of the people of the Bogside and beyond. He ended his speech with the following statement;

"The party, the Government and this Parliament no longer have any relevance in the affairs of the Irish people and I intend to make that clear in my actions from now."

Field hospitals were to be established and protected by Irish troops along the border to treat the wounded and at the Cabinet meeting on 15th August, the Dublin government hinted at a British-Irish peacekeeping force in the North.

The Irish Government also set about utilizing the United Nations and bringing the issue of the Six Counties before the Security Council to discuss a peacekeeping force.

Security oversight was effectively handed over to a new Joint Security Committee from 16th August. The new committee was recommended by the General Officer Commanding and Minister of Home Affairs, pulling together members of the Cabinet committee, Chief of Staff, Inspector General, Secretary to the Cabinet, the Security Liaison Officer at NI Command Headquarters and the County Inspector of the Crime Special Branch who would meet daily.

This committee focussed the attention of the inner workings of the government and the work even of Parliament was largely from this point bogged down in debates and adjournment motions relating to disturbances.

It was at this first meeting that the Minister of Home Affairs proposed that the access to the Falls area from the Shankill be 'sealed off' and that certain smaller and unapproved border roads should be spiked or closed by the military.
On the 19th following a meeting with the UK Prime Minister, the General Officer Commanding in Ulster took control of the security situation including command of the RUC for security operations.

Full command and control of the B Specials was also granted to the GOC. The Irish government were not impressed, especially by the declaration by the two governments following the London meeting which was vague and did not provide urgent proposals to address the underlying issues.

The arrival of troops was welcomed by the residents of Derry who saw them as an intermediary that was not under the control of the Stormont regime. From 19th August the 4th company of the Queen's Regiment were moved to the city alongside the B Squadron of the Life Guards with the 1st Batt of the Hampshire Regiment being held in reserve in Ballykinlar.

Indeed, on 27th August the security situation had calmed so much that the British Home Secretary visited the City to survey the situation.

Two days later, the Stormont government released a further communique outlining this time the plans for addressing the grievances of the Catholic population in housing and other areas. It was seen by many to be too late, and it had effectively lost control of the wider province at least in security terms.

An IRA statement reminded the British troops that if it was used to suppress 'the legitimate attempts of the people to defend themselves against the B Specials and the sectarian orange murder gang then you will have to face the consequences'.

Two weeks later saw the erection by the Army of the first 'peace line' in Belfast separating Catholic and Protestant neighbourhoods. These remain today despite comments at the JSC that 'there would be no question of the peace line becoming permanent'.

Perhaps just a coincidence, but the same day as the Home Secretary's visit, the Government in Belfast announced the establishment of the Scarman Tribunal which was set up to investigate the violence around several incidents;

(1) during the month of March 1969, at the electricity sub-station, Castlereagh;

(2) during the month of April 1969, at Kilmore, Co. Armagh; Silent Valley and Annalong, Co. Down, and Clady, Co. Antrim;

(3) during the month of April 1969, at or near ten post offices in the city of Belfast;

(4) during the months of July and August 1969, in the cities of Londonderry and Belfast;

(5) during the months of July and August 1969, in the town of Dungiven;

(6) during the month of August 1969, in the city of Armagh and in the towns of Coalisland, Dungannon and Newry;

and (7) during the 17th, 18th August 1969, at Crossmaglen, Co. Armagh; and resulted in loss of life, personal injury or damage to property.

Sir Leslie Scarman would chair the tribunal, with one Protestant, William Marshall, and one Catholic, Mr George Lavery presiding.

On 12th September the Cameron Report was published, followed by the Hunt Report on policing. To the horror of the Stormont government, it recommended disarming the RUC, disbanding the Specials and creating a local regiment under the control of the Army in Ulster.

It's sixteen points outlining the causes of disorder clearly pointed to the maladministration by Unionists locally and province wide of housing, the franchise and employment.

"The Government's announcements on the reform of local government franchise - the 'one man one vote' issue - reform and readjustment of local government administration, including electoral areas and boundaries, introduction of a comprehensive and fair 'points' system in the allocation of Council built houses and the introduction of special machinery to deal with complaints arising out of matters of local administration, go a very considerable way. not only to acknowledge the justice of the complaints on these points but also the expediency and necessity of providing remedies for them."[124]

The JSC had decided on 22nd September that the ban on processions would be extended for a further three months, and were faced with the prospect of closing the Stormont Estate due to press statements by Ian Paisley calling on his supporters to possibly hold a meeting outside Parliament Buildings – something the Speaker refused to accept.

A week later, the Chief of Staff informed Ministers that a new assertive policy would be rolled out by the Army in that soldiers would no longer seek to keep warring factions apart, but would now prioritise dispersal and arrest of troublemakers.

Northern Ireland Ministers met with the UK Home Secretary over the 9th and 10th October and as reflected in their communique issued on 10th, the Northern Ireland Government had in fact conceded to implement many public policies that it had hitherto resisted, the most important of these was a central housing authority that would undertake the allocation of all housing throughout the province and remove the ability of local government to engage in questionable practices.

Harold Wilson insisted on a change of the leadership of the RUC and Arthur Young was appointed Chief Constable in the place of Mr Peacocke who had resigned.

The communique also included economic provisions that would prove, in the short term at least, very important. The Industrial Development Acts would now provide grants to repair premises arising from riots and civil commotion and the grants payable under the Act would be raised by 5% for a period of three years.

An anti-discrimination clause would be included in all government tenders, and it would become an offence to incite religious hatred – despite the fact a Bill had been previously brought to the House on the issue and defeated.

Robert Simpson was appointed as the first Minister of Community Relations in October. On his appointment he sought to gain credibility across the Nationalist community by resigning as a member of the Orange Order.

Following the acceptance of the Hunt report by the government in Belfast, the determination of Ministers was to ensure that the RUC and Army re-entered the Falls and Bogside areas. Some felt so strongly about the necessity for this that the Ministers of Home Affairs, Development and Education said they would consider their positions if the move was delayed.

11th November saw Royal Assent granted to the Community Relations Act which established the NI Community Relations Commission which would work to foster better relations across communities.

By 25th November, most of the demands of the Civil Rights movement had been met when the electoral franchise became universal and the legislation creating a commissioner for complaints became law with John Benn taking up the role.

On 17th December Brian Faulkner initiated the Macrory Review of Local Government in Northern Ireland. It had a wide remit, including looking at housing, reshaping of local government generally and the range of services it provided.

Two weeks later, the Ulster Defence Regiment which would be part-time and under the control of the military commanders in Ulster, was formed and became operational on 1st January 1970.

During the significant rioting and disturbances across Ulster in the preceding months, the republican movement had remained patient and had not engaged in any formal way against the forces of the state.

However, on 11 January, the Sinn Fein organization and the IRA split on the issue of abstentionism. A significant number of delegates to the Sinn Fein Ard Fheis in Dublin voted to end abstentionism, paving the way for the split of a hitherto united republican front.

The split created two organisations and mirrored the split in the IRA – those who left the main SF party were now referred to as Provisional Sinn Fein, whilst the other was called Official Sinn Fein.

Days later on the 26th, O'Neill resigned his parliamentary seat. Two days later, the first major upset of the reform programme was made public.

Despite the findings of the Cameron Commission that allegations of misconduct of RUC officers in Derry in January 1969 were substantiated, 16 members of the RUC had the charges against them dropped.

March saw the further degradation of control of the Stormont administration. Five members of the Ulster Unionists including the former Minister of Home Affairs, William Craig, were expelled from the party. On the 8th, a bomb was left at the home of Stormont MP, Austin Currie.

The Police Act was passed, which disarmed the RUC and created an RUC Reserve as well as a civilian oversight authority in the Police Authority, which Nationalists never engaged with. Overall security strategy would be managed by the Joint Security Committee – comprising the Army, RUC and the Authority.

Serious rioting continued in Belfast and Derry in April.

Chichester-Clark, like O'Neill, had serious opposition from the Protestant community for introducing these reforms and this came in the form of Ian Paisley who had won a by election following the elevation of O'Neill to the peerage. He won the Bannside seat in Stormont.

On 21 April the Alliance Party of Northern Ireland was formed and sought to attract liberal cross-community support. It would encompass many of the members of the former Ulster Liberal Party.

On 30th April, another part of the reform puzzle was moved into place with the second reading of the Social Needs Bill. It was described by the Minister as 'community first aid' and sought to address the remedial problems around poverty and low living standards. It is seemingly the first practical piece of legislation from the Government that recognizes that 'the problems which this Province must solve in the community relations field cannot be regarded as separate and distinct from the economic problems which we also face'.

May saw the Republic seemingly sucked into the turmoil in the North when Neill Blaney and Charles Haughey, two former senior Government ministers were sacked by Jack Lynch for their involvement in an arms importing scheme for the IRA in Northern Ireland. Their trial continued until October and both were acquitted but it gave credence to the thoughts of Ulster Protestants that the Irish state was assisting a rebellion in Ulster.

The Macrory Report on local government was published on 29 May, seeking to totally reform the state of local government in Northern Ireland. 26 new regional councils would be created, but many powers such as housing would be vested in Parliament.

June saw a general election in the UK. Ian Paisley was elected to Antrim North, Bernadette Devlin held Mid Ulster, Gerry Fitt in West Belfast and Frank McManus in Fermanagh South Tyrone. All remaining eight seats were taken by Ulster Unionists. With Paisley elected to Westminster, he suffered his first suspension from Stormont on 2nd July for challenging the Speaker.

27th June saw the IRA engage in the civil strife for the first time. Loyalists and Nationalists fought pitch battles in Belfast and when Loyalists entered the Short Strand area, with no troops to protect them or their property, the IRA took up position in St Matthews Church. Five loyalists were killed by their actions.

The following day, exactly as it had been in the 1920's, 500 Catholics were forced from their jobs at Harland and Wolff by loyalists.

3 July saw an end to any goodwill the Catholic inhabitants of Ulster had towards the military. A 24-hour curfew was imposed on the Falls area of Belfast and extensive house searches were carried out, many in a manner that only served to increase anger.

20 days later the Stormont Government – waiting until after the traditional Orange marching season, imposed a ban on all marches and processions in Northern Ireland.

20 August 1970 saw the created of the Social Democratic and Labour Party led by Gerry Fitt with John Hume as his deputy. Many sitting and former Nationalist MPs at Stormont joined the party.

Five days later, the Minister of Home Affairs resigned and was replaced by John Taylor who was especially critical of the government reform programme.

On 12 November, the Northern Ireland Housing Executive was created. It would act as the central housing allocation body in Ulster and would allocate homes based on a transparent points system.

1971

In February, Chichester-Clark met with Cardinal Conway, the first time this kind of meeting had even taken place between a Unionist Prime Minister and a senior Catholic cleric.

A few days later on 4th March, six rounds of .303 ammunition were found in Stormont, prompting a security review.

Following a meeting with the British Government on 16 March regarding the security situation and the Northern Ireland Government's request for more troops, Chichester-Clark resigned on 20th, citing the lack of engagement and support from the British Government after they offered a further 1,300 troops for Ulster.

He was succeeded three days later by the former Deputy Prime Minister under O'Neill, Brian Faulkner. On 22 June he initiated a reform of Ministerial positions in Stormont, which was a precursor to allowing Nationalists to serve in Government, despite his own public commentary on Catholics;

"It is apparent that anti-Roman Catholicism shaded over into with anti-Irish nationalism. Faulkner told a 1960 Orange demonstration in Comber: 'When we in the Unionist Party defend ourselves against the political attacks of the Nationalist Party we are perforce defending ourselves against the Catholic hierarchy.'"[125]

On 30th March the Prime Minister proposed a vote of confidence in his government. Amendments were proposed by Gerry Fitt and also by the Rev. Ian Paisley who took aim at the government's security policy;

"deplores the failure of the Prime Minister to give to the country the facts about the resignation of his predecessor, to rearm the police in danger areas with weapons of sufficient power to defeat the I.R.A assassins, to use effectively all forces available to put down subversion, to acknowledge the valid criticism about the law and order situation, especially with regard to the no-go' areas, to reverse the suicidal policies of the previous Government in the security field and condemns him for accepting the advice of Lord O'Neill of the Maine on the appointment of Mr. David Bleakly as Minister of Community Relations".

The SDLP withdrew from Parliament on 16 July after two men had been shot by the Army in the Bogside area of Derry and no inquiry was established following eyewitness statements that contradicted the statement of the Army that the men were armed.

On 22nd June, in an attempt to reform Parliament, parts of a development paper were brought forward that would create standing committees for Social Services, Environmental Services and Industrial Services were the chair of two would be an Opposition member. It did not have the desired effect of bringing Opposition members enthusiastically on side.

On Monday 9 August, internment was re-introduced in Northern Ireland and almost 350 people were arrested as part of Operation Demetrius – mainly Nationalists – on the first day. The government felt that this would address the security problems and specifically the activities of the IRA, but it fed into further anger in the Catholic community as it saw the move as directed solely at them.

Brian Faulkner's television address was perceived as lacking in feeling about the gravity of the policy he had just introduced.

The lists of suspects provided by the RUC were out of date, and those leaders of violent Republicanism who were so keenly sought were able to escape and evade internment. 450 names had been on the lists drawn up, including people like Ivan Barr who headed the Civil Rights Association's Executive. It was to be an exceptionally flawed operation and forced many peaceful Nationalists to become further estranged from both the UK and Northern Ireland Governments.

Over the 9th and 10th August serious rioting took place in Belfast and many families were forced to flee their homes. It was an escalation even from the burning of Bombay Street two years previous which had left a deep scar on the consciousness of Nationalists in the City.

As part of Operation Demetrius, the Parachute Regiment were sent to the Ballymurphy estate in Belfast to undertake an arrest operation. 1 Para had been despatched to the area and over the next two days, 11 civilians including a priest brandishing a wide cloth whilst attempting to administer the last rites to a man who had been shot, had been shot dead by the soldiers.

22nd August saw over 200 Unionist councillors withdraw from their respective councils over the imposition of internment.

In September, several loyalist groupings came together to form the Ulster Defence Association. On 26th, David Bleakley resigned as the Minister for Community Relations citing lack of progress on any new cross-community initiatives by the government. The Prime Minister assumed the role of Minister of Home Affairs whilst the House was in summer recess.

Four days later, Ian Paisley and Desmond Boal formed the Ulster Democratic Unionist Party which would become the DUP.

On 5th October a new sitting of Parliament began, boycotted by the SDLP after the refusal of the authorities to hold an inquiry as to why two men had been shot in Derry by the Army.

Ironically, the 11th November saw Faulkner tell the House that the UK Government were not contemplating direct rule for Ulster.

On 4th December, McGurk's Bar was bombed by the UVF. The building collapsed, killing fifteen Catholics, including two children and injuring a further 17. It was followed that night by intense intercommunal violence at the nearby New Lodge interface.

On 12th December an Official IRA team crossed the border from the Republic into Strabane. Their target was Senator Jack Barnhill, an Ulster Unionist member of the Northern Ireland Senate and respected businessman.

The armed gang rang the doorbell of the house, answered by the Senator, who after scuffling with one of the men, was shot dead.

They placed an explosive device in the house and left. When it exploded it destroyed entirely the building. He became only the second serving member of the Northern Ireland Parliament to be killed during this period. In the House, the Prime Minister lamented;

"It is almost fifty years, Mr. Speaker, since a Prime Minister of Northern Ireland has had the sad duty of moving such a Motion in this our Parliament. In recent months many innocent people -men, women and even babes in arms have lost their lives in the brutal terrorist campaign.

Now this wickedness has struck at a respected colleague, at a man whose sincere political views were always expressed with courtesy and gentleness. The I.R.A have claimed that Senator Barnhill was shot when he struggled with men who came to destroy his home. We may never know the precise circumstances, because truth is as unknown to such men as mercy. What we do know is that a man was shot down at his own door by those who came with evil intent."

It was the second time that a member of the Parliament had been killed, the first being W Twaddell.

Days later, another Senator was targeted. Edith Taggart was a UUP senator and when gunmen attempted to enter her home in South Belfast, her husband confronted them and was slightly injured, shots were fired but did not hit anyone.

Attacks on members of the judiciary also took place.

1972

A march was organised for Magilligan Strand on 22 January. The destination for the march was the internment camp at Magilligan where hundreds of men were being held without trial.

As marchers approached the wire fencing that had been erected by the Army on the beach, they were fired upon by soldiers using rubber bullets without provocation. This served only to further alienate the Nationalist community and the liberal NICRA against the armed forces.

On 30 January the Civil Rights Association continued with plans for a march against internment in Derry which had been banned under the Public Order Act. Organisers made it known that troublemakers were to stay away, and stewards were put in place to try and separate the younger marchers from the Army at specific flashpoints.

Unbeknownst to the organisers or the marchers, the decision had been taken at the highest levels to bring the Parachute Regiment into the City to undertake an arrest operation, the same battalion as had been used in Ballymurphy. Free Derry had been established behind 29 barricades erected around the Bogside area to keep the RUC and armed forces out of the area, an embarrassment to the political leadership in both in London and Belfast.

Between 10 and 15,000 people took part in the march which set off from Creggan to the Guildhall along the planned route. When the lead vehicle reached William Street in the city centre, a decision was made to reroute to Rossville Street as the army had blockaded the route to the Guildhall.

At the William Street barrier, some marchers threw stones and debris at the patrolling soldiers, who returned fire with CS gas and rubber bullets. 1 Para lay in wait in a building overlooking William Street, and stones were thrown in their direction. They opened fire with live round, hitting two men on waste ground near their position.

Minutes later the arrest operation began when armoured vehicles sped into the area from behind the barriers. Colonel Derek Wilford in command disobeyed a direct order that only one company undertake the operation on foot and not chase the marchers to identify and arrest known rioters.

Taking a position across from the rubble barricade at Rossville Street, the paratroopers targeted and shot dead six people, wounding a seventh who were throwing stones at their position.

A group of people were chased into an open courtyard where the troops again first, wounding six and killing one who was shot in the back whilst running from the area.

At the carpark in Glenfada Park, soldiers fired killing two men and injuring four. Beyond the carpark, four more civilians were shot dead.

In less than 12 minutes over 100 rounds had been fired by 1 Para. 26 people had been shot, with 13 killed on the day, and another who would die months later from their injuries.

In the British House of Commons, the Home Secretary did not mince his words;
"The G.O.C. has further reported that when the Army advanced to make arrests among the trouble-makers they came under fire from a block of flats and other quarters. At this stage the members of the orderly, although illegal, march were no longer in the near vicinity. The Army returned the fire directed at them with aimed shots and inflicted a number of casualties on those who were attacking them with firearms and with bombs."

The view of the British Government was clear, the Parachute Regiment had only fired when fired upon. Bernadette Devlin was in the House and had been in Derry the previous day. The Speaker refused to allow her to speak as was convention for Members who had witnessed an event first hand, and she walked across the floor of the House and slapped Mr Maulding.

Anger on both sides of the border boiled over, and on 2nd February the British Embassy in Dublin was burned to the ground following the funerals in Derry of those killed. It is thought over 100,000 people took to the streets of the Irish capital that day, many carrying black flags.

Workers in the Republic undertook a general strike, and the Irish Government moved on its demand from August 1969, going to the United Nations to demand a neutral peacekeeping force in Northern Ireland.

The day before, the Prime Minister appointed Lord Widgery, the Lord Chief Justice to head an inquiry into the events of Bloody Sunday. His report in April would lay the blame of the deaths in Derry at the door of the marchers and vindicated the paratroopers, to widespread fury branding it a 'whitewash'.

Two weeks later, John Taylor a junior Minister in Belfast, was shot six times in his car in Armagh, although he survived.

On 4th March the IRA bombed the Abercorn Restaurant in central Belfast, killing two and injuring almost 130 people. The attack caused widespread revulsion given the two victims were women and some children had been injured.

On 21st March, Brian Faulkner went to London to be informed of the imposition of Direct Rule. Three days later, the Prime Minister publicly announced that Stormont would be prorogued and that the Northern Ireland Government had threatened to resign if security powers were transferred to Westminster.

The Northern Ireland (Temporary Provisions) Act was introduced in the House of Commons on 27th March and created the Northern Ireland Office which would oversee London's direct rule of the province. He stated in his speech to the House of Commons on 24th;

"Parliament will, therefore, be invited to pass before Easter a Measure transferring all legislative and executive powers now vested in the Northern Ireland Parliament and Government to the United Kingdom Parliament and a United Kingdom Minister. This provision will expire after one year unless this Parliament resolves otherwise. The Parliament of Northern Ireland would stand prorogued but would not be dissolved.

The present Prime Minister of Northern Ireland has agreed to continue in office until this legislation is passed.

The increased burden which this transfer of responsibilities will entail means that it will no longer be possible for my right hon. Friend the Home Secretary to discharge these duties in addition to his many other responsibilities. A new Office of Secretary of State for Northern Ireland is, therefore, being created. My right hon. Friend the Lord President is to be appointed to this office, together with the necessary junior Ministers. He will be empowered by the new legislation to appoint a commission of persons resident in Northern Ireland to advise and assist him in the discharge of his duties. It will be our objective to invite to serve on this commission a body of persons fully representative of opinion in Northern Ireland."

A week later, Boal and McQuade were the first to resign in protest. Just prior to the final sitting of the House at 5:17pm on 28th March, Captain Cooke, the Minister of State for Finance recited a poem by Rudyard Kipling from 1912: Ulster.

> The dark eleventh hour
> Draws on and sees us sold
> To every evil power
> We fought against of old.
> Rebellion, rapine hate
> Oppression, wrong and greed
> Are loosed to rule our fate,
> By England's act and deed.
>
> The Faith in which we stand,
> The laws we made and guard,
> Our honour, lives, and land
> Are given for reward
> To Murder done by night,
> To Treason taught by day,

    To folly, sloth, and spite,
    And we are thrust away.

    The blood our fathers spilt,
  Our love, our toils, our pains,
    Are counted us for guilt,
    And only bind our chains.
    Before an Empire's eyes
    The traitor claims his price.
    What need of further lies?
    We are the sacrifice.

We asked no more than leave
  To reap where we had sown,
Through good and ill to cleave
  To our own flag and throne.
Now England's shot and steel
  Beneath that flag must show
How loyal hearts should kneel
  To England's oldest foe.

    We know the war prepared
    On every peaceful home,
    We know the hells declared
  For such as serve not Rome --
    The terror, threats, and dread
  In market, hearth, and field --
    We know, when all is said,
    We perish if we yield.

    Believe, we dare not boast,
    Believe, we do not fear --
    We stand to pay the cost
    In all that men hold dear.
  What answer from the North?
  One Law, one Land, one Throne.
    If England drive us forth
    We shall not fall alone!

Conclusion

In seeking to lift the fog from the subject of the 'old Stormont', I attempted to acknowledge that amongst the minority in the state, Parliament acted as a partisan and divisive player.

However, as much as that is true, it is also as important to testify to its strengths in securing parity with the UK welfare state for residents here, for setting in place our current transport infrastructure (for good or ill) and its uncanny ability to extract concessions from the UK Government and from Whitehall using only the argument that 'subvention without intervention' was best for the Union.

The explicit dangers for both the new Parliament and the new state from 1921 are clear to consider in this book – not only the violence or the relationship with Eire but a constant teetering on the edge of bankruptcy. These must be put in context if we are to really understand the mentality of some of Ulster's leaders at that time.

Nationalism, too has questions to answer arising from its performance both inside and outside Parliament. We must ask if, even after the completion of the boundary discussions, official boycotting of the new Parliament was wise, and if removing Catholic influence on the future of education in the early days of the state was ill-advised.

Notwithstanding the ethical grievances Nationalism had with the Northern Ireland state and its apparatus, to leave so many without a voice until effectively after World War Two when the character and practice of the leadership and civil service had long been established, did the minority more harm than good.

Organisationally, the Nationalist Party's abandonment of Belfast after Thomas Campbell took his seat on the bench is a clear indictment of a badly organised band without foresight.

The rivalry in many constituencies between Nationalist and Labour organisations only served to solidify a confident Unionism. Labour's threat to Unionists in Belfast should not be underestimated, yet as a regional force both camps in the minority could not see the bigger picture.

From the 1950's we can start to see the beginning of a splintering of Unionism, despite the painstaking work of Carson and Craig in bygone generations to unify and maintain Unionist unity. Nowhere else can this fracture be seen than in pro and anti-O'Neillism, which should have caused so much embarrassment to a once regimented and disciplined party.

It's failure – personified by Brookeborough, to recognise the change in the nature of politics in the UK mandated it would always have to go through a period of deep reflection.

Towards the end of the 1960's as much as the Civil Rights Movement was a threat not only to the state but to Unionist homogeneity – it was Unionism itself and its fractured nature – led in many ways by B Craig, Boal and Paisley that ultimately, in my opinion to the end of any functioning state.

If the Civil Rights Movement had not been as successful, if the 'security situation' had not manifested itself in the way that it did, Unionism could never again be put back together and it is indeed possible that an impasse between the reformers and the back peddlers could have led to a deadlock in the Parliament and in its apparatus just as we see today.

What struck me during the research for this book was the sad fact that despite our clinging to history in our communities, such lessons on the futility of violence, the need for reconciliation and the very real abyss that we often stood on the precipice of during the early days of the state were overlooked, and perhaps it was and is beneficial to those who still engage in zero-sum politics today that we have forgotten about our past and the past of what should have been a Parliament based on mutual respect.

Constituency	Year								
Antrim	1921	Barbour	O'Neill	Hanna	Crawford	Megaw	Gordon	Devlin	
	1925	McAllister	Henderson	Barbour	O'Neill	Crawford	Hanna	Gordon	
Armagh	1921	Collins	Nugent	Best	Shillington				
	1925	Donnelly	Collins	Shillington	Best				
Belfast E	1921	Dawson Bates	Dixon	Donald	Duff				
	1925	Beattie	Gyle	Dawson Bates	Dixon				
Belfast N	1921	Campbell	McGuffin	Grant	McKeown				
	1925	Kyle	Henderson	Grant	Campbell				
Belfast S	1921	Moles	Pollock	McCullagh	McMordie				
	1925	Babington	Moles	Pollock	Black				
Belfast W	1921	Devlin	Lynn	Twaddell	Moles				
	1925	McMullen	Devlin	Woods	Lynn				
Down	1921	De Valera	O'Neill	Craig	Andrews	Lavery	Mulholland	McBride	McMullan
	1925	De Valera	O'Neill	Craig	Miller	Lavery	Mulholland	McBride	McMullan
Ferm Ty.	1921	Griffith	Milroy	O'Mahony	Harbison	Archdale	Coote	Miller	Cooper
	1925	Donnelly	McHugh	Healy	Harbison	Archdale	Elliott	Miller	Cooper
Derry	1921	MacNeill	Leeke	Anderson	Chichester	Mark			
	1925	Leeke	McGuckin	Anderson	Chichester	Mark			
Queen's	1921	Campbell	Robb	Johnstone	Morrison				
	1925	Campbell	Robb	Johnstone	Morrison				

	1929	1933	1938	1945	1949	1953	1958	1962	1965	1969
Antrim	Minford, H	Minford, H	Minford, H	Minford, H	Minford, H	Minford, N	Minford, N	Minford, N	Minford, N	Minford, N
Borough	Young	Young	Young	Patrick	O'Neill	O'Neill	O'Neill	O'Neill	O'Neill	O'Neill
Bannside										
Carrick	Gordon	Gordon	Gordon	Curran	Curran	Hunter	Hunter	Hunter	Ardill	Dickson
Larkfield										McIvor
Larne	Hanna	Hanna	Hanna	Robinson	Topping	Topping	Topping	Craig	Craig	Craig
Mid Antrim	Crawford	Crawford	Crawford	Patrick	Wilson	Simpson	Simpson	Simpson	Simpson	Simpson
N'abbey										Baillie
N Antrim	Lynn	Lynn	Lynn	Lynn	McCleery	McCleery	O'Neill	O'Neill	O'Neill	O'Neill
S Antrim	Barbour	Barbour	Barbour	Barbour	Barbour	McConnell	McConnell	McConnell	McConnell	Ferguson

	1929	1933	1938	1945	1949	1953	1958	1962	1965	1969
Central Armagh	Shillington	Shillington	Shillington	Dougan	Dougan	Dougan	Hawthorne	Hawthorne	Hawthorne	Whitten
Mid Armagh	Davison	Davison	Davison	Stronge	Stronge	Stronge	Stronge	Stronge	Stronge	Stonge, J
N Armagh	Johnston	Johnston	Johnston	Johnston	McNabb	McNabb	McNabb	McNabb	McNabb	Mitchell
S Armagh	Conmellan	McLogan	Agnew	Conlon	McGleenan	Richardson	Richardson	Richardson	Richardson	O'Hanlon

	1929	1933	1938	1945	1949	1953	1958	1962	1965
Queen's	Robb, JH	Johnstone	Corkey	McSorley	Irwin	Irwin	Irwin	McClure	McClure
Queen's	Corkey	Corkey	Johnstone	Stevenson	Hickey	Kelly	Stewart	Murnaghan	Maconachie
Queen's	McNeill, R	Robb, JH	Mitchell	Calvert	Calvert	Maconachie	Maconachie	Maconachie	Murnaghan
Queen's	Johnstone	McNeill, R	MacDermott	Quin	Lyle	Lloyd-Dodd	Lloyd-Dodd	Stewart	Stewart

233

	1929	1933	1938	1945	1949	1953	1958	1962	1965	1969
Ballynafeigh	Moles	Moles	Thompson	Thompson	Neill	Neill	Neill	Neill	Neill	Neill
Bloomfield	Dixon	Dixon	Dixon	Dixon	Dixon	Dixon, D	Dixon, D	Scott	Scott	Scott
Central	Devlin	Devlin	Campbell	Campbell	Hanna	Hanna	Hanna	Hanna	Brenan	Kennedy
Clifton	H-Thompson	H-Thompson	H-Thompson	H-Thompson	H-Thompson	Porter	Kinahan	Morgan	Morgan	H-Thompson, L
Cromac	Babington	Babington	Sinclair	Sinclair	Sinclair	Morgan	Morgan	Kennedy	Kennedy	Kennedy
Dock	B-Houston	Midgley	Clark	Downey	Cole	Morgan	Oliver	Fitt	Fitt	Fitt
Duncairn	Grant	Grant	Grant	Grant	Hanna	Hanna	Fitzsimmons	Fitzsimmons	Fitzsimmons	Fitzsimmons
Falls	Byrne	Byrne	Byrne	Diamond	Diamond	Diamond	Diamond	Diamond	Diamond	Devlin
Oldpark	Hungerford	Hungerford	Hungerford	Getgood	Morgan	Morgan	Simpson	Simpson	Simpson	Simpson
Pottinger	Beattie	Beattie	Beattie	Beattie	Rodgers	Rodgers	Boyd	Boyd	Boyd	Cardwell
St Anne's	McCormick	McCormick	Warnock	Warnock	Warnock	Warnock	Warnock	Warnock	Warnock	Warnock
Shankill	Henderson	Henderson	Henderson	Henderson	Henderson	Holmes	Holmes	Boal	Boal	Boal
Victoria	Dawson Bates	Dawson Bates	Dawson Bates	Alexander	Alexander	Henderson	Bleakley	Bleakley	Bradford	Bradford
Willowfield	Black	Black	Black	Midgley	Midgley	Midgley	Hinds	Hinds	Hinds	Caldwell
Windsor	Pollock	Pollock	Dowling	Wilson	Wilson	Wilson	Kirk	Kirk	Kirk	Kirk
Woodvale	Nixon	Nixon	Nixon	Nixon	Nixon	Harcourt	Boyd	Boyd	Boyd	McQuade

	1929	1933	1938	1945	1949	1953	1958	1962	1965	1969
Ards	Mulholland	Mulholland	Mulholland	P. Maxwell	May	May	May	Long	Long	Long
Bangor										McConnell
E Down	Gordon	Gordon	Gordon	Gordon	Gordon	Faulkner	Faulkner	Faulkner	Faulkner	Faulkner
Iveagh	Waring	Wilson	Maginness	Maginness	Maginness	Maginness	Maginness	Maginness	Magowan	Magowan
Lagan Valley										Porter
Mid Down	Andrews, JM	Andrews, JM	Andrews, JM	Andrews, JM	Andrews, JM	Andrews, J	Andrews, J	Andrews, J	Kelly	Kelly
Mourne	O'Neill	O'Neill	Panter	McSparran	McSparran	McSparran	O'Reilly	O'Reilly	O'Reilly	O'Reilly
N Down	Craig	Craig	Craig	Bailie	Bailie	Nixon, R	Nixon, R	Nixon, R	Nixon, R	Babington
S Down	Collins, JH	De Valera	Brown	Munroy	Connellan	Connellan	Connellan	Connellan	Connellan	Keogh
W Down	McBride	Fryar	Bailey	Bailey	Bailey	Bailey	Bailey	Little	Dobson	Dobson

	1929	1933	1938	1945	1949	1953	1958	1962	1965	1969
Enniskillen	Archdale	Archdale	Ferguson	Ferguson	Nelson	Nelson	West	West	West	West
Lisnaskea	Brooke	Brooke	Brooke	Brooke	Brooke	Brooke	Brooke	Brooke	Brooke	Brooke, J
S Fermanagh	Healy	Healy	Healy	Healy	Healy	Healy	Healy	Healy	Carron	Carron

	1929	1933	1938	1945	1949	1953	1958	1962	1965	1969
City of Derry	Murphy	Murphy	Murphy	Lowry	McManaway	Jones	Jones	Jones	Jones	Anderson
Foyle	McCarroll	McCarroll	Maxwell	Maxwell	Maxwell	McAteer	McAteer	McAteer	McAteer	Hume
Mid Derry	Leeke	Leeke	Leeke	McAteer	Gormley	Gormley	Gormley	Gormley	Gormley	Cooper
N Derry	Mark	Christie	Moore	Moore	Moore	Moore	Burns	Burns	Burns	Burns
S Derry	Chichester-Clark, JL-C	Parker	Parker	Parker	Parker	Parker	Chichester-Clark, J	Chichester-Clark, J	Chichester-Clark, J	Chichester-Clark, J

	1929	1933	1938	1945	1949	1953	1958	1962	1965	1969
East Tyrone	Stewart	Stewart	Stewart	Stewart	Stewart	Stewart	Stewart	Stewart	Currie	Currie
Mid Tyrone	McAleer	McAleer	McAleer	McGurk	McCullagh	Kelly	Blevins	Gormley, T	Gormley, T	Gormley, T
N Tyrone	Miller	Gamble	Gamble	Lyons	Lyons	Lyons	Lyons	Lyons	Lyons	Fyffe
S Tyrone	Elliott, R	Elliott, R	Elliott, R	McCoy	McCoy	McCoy	McCoy	McCoy	Taylor	Taylor
W Tyrone	Donnelly, A	Donnelly, A	Donnelly, A	Donnelly, A	O'Connor, R	O'Connor, R	O'Connor, R	O'Connor, R	O'Connor, R	O'Connor, R

Endnotes

[1] Walker, Graham 'A History of the Ulster Unionist Party: Protest, Pragmatism and Pessimism' pg. 73
[2] House of Commons, March 31, 1920, vol 127, c1308
[3] Maguire, M 'The civil service and the revolution in Ireland' pg. 106
[4] Maguire, M 'The civil service and the revolution in Ireland' pg108
[5] Ibid, pg. 109
[6] Maguire, M 'The civil service and the revolution in Ireland' pg. 110
[7] Ibid
[8] Kenna, G. B. 'Facts and Figures of the Belfast Pogrom 1920-1922' pg. 18
[9] Ó Murchu, N 'Ethnic politics and labour market closure: shipbuilding and industrial decline in Northern Ireland', Ethnic and Racial Studies, 28:5, p869
[10] Goldstrom J.M et al, 'Irish population, economy and society: Essays in honour of the late K.H Connell' pg. 288
[11] Bureau of Military History, ref BMH.WS0581
[12] Goldstrom J.M et al, 'Irish population, economy and society: Essays in honour of the late K.H Connell' pg. 292
[13] Ibid, pg. 300
[14] Ó Murchu, N 'Ethnic politics and labour market closure: shipbuilding and industrial decline in Northern Ireland', Ethnic and Racial Studies, 28:5, p871
[15] Brewer, J.D and Higgins, I 'Anti-Catholicism in Northern Ireland 1600-1998' Pg. 101
[16] Brewer, J.D and Higgins, I 'Anti-Catholicism in Northern Ireland 1600-1998' Pg. 101
[17] PRONI, CAB/B/60
[18] PRONI, CAB/4/12, NI Cabinet minutes 4 August 1921
[19] Maguire, M 'The civil service and the revolution in Ireland' pg. 112
[20] PRONI, CAB/4/12, NI Cabinet minutes 4 August 1921
[21] PRONI, CAB/4/1, NI Cabinet minutes 15 June 1921
[22] PRONI, CAB/4/19, NI Cabinet minutes 12 September 1921
[23] PRONI, CAB/4/22, NI Cabinet minutes 19 September 1921
[24] PRONI, CAB/4/26/17, NI Cabinet minutes 4 November 1921
[25] PRONI, CAB/4/15/1, NI Cabinet minutes, 23 August 1921
[26] PRONI, PM/11/1, Correspondence in peace negotiations and Articles of Agreement.
[27] O'Brien, J 'Discrimination in Northern Ireland 1920-1939: Myth or Reality?' Pg. 10
[28] PRONI, CAB/4/30, NI Cabinet minutes 26 January 1922

[29] PRONI, PM/11/1, Correspondence in peace negotiations and Articles of Agreement.
[30] Kenna, G.B. 'Facts and Figures of the Belfast Pogrom 1920-22' pg. 122
[31] Documents on Irish Foreign Policy, No. 256 NAI DT S1801A
[32] Norton, Christopher 'Creating Jobs, Manufacturing Unity: Ulster Unionism and Mass Unemployment 1922-1934', Contemporary British History, 15:2, 1-14, pg. 2
[33] PRONI, PM/11/2
[34] Norton, Christopher 'Creating Jobs, Manufacturing Unity: Ulster Unionism and Mass Unemployment 1922-1934', Contemporary British History, 15:2, 1-14, pg. 3
[35] PRONI, PM/11/2
[36] Ó Murchu, N 'Ethnic politics and labour market closure: shipbuilding and industrial decline in Northern Ireland', Ethnic and Racial Studies, 28:5, p872
[37] Donohue, L 'Regulating Northern Ireland: The Special Powers Acts 1922-1972' The Historical Journal, Vol. 41, No. 4 (Dec. 1998), pp. 1089-1120
[38] Bureau of Military Archives, ref MSP34REF318 James Marron
[39] Bureau of Military Archives, ref MSP55889, Mary Egan
[40] PRONI, CAB/4/50/1, NI Cabinet minutes 27 July 1922
[41] Brewer, J.D and Higgins, I 'Anti-Catholicism in Northern Ireland 1600-1998' Pg. 100
[42] PRONI, CAB/4/18, NI Cabinet minutes 9 September 1921
[43] Ibid
[44] Akenson, Donald 'Education and Enmity: The Control of Schooling in Northern Ireland 1920-1950' pg. 1092
[45] PRONI, CAB/4/61, NI Cabinet minutes 15 December 1922
[46] Follis, Bryan A. 'A State Under Siege: The Establishment of Northern Ireland 1920-1925' pg. 138
[47] Ibid, pg. 144
[48] Follis, Bryan A. 'A State Under Siege: the Establishment of Northern Ireland 1920-1925' pg. 150
[49] PRONI, CAB/4/101/15, NI Cabinet minutes 26 February 1924
[50] PRONI, CAB/4/126, NI Cabinet minutes 22 October 1924
[51] Bogdanor, V 'Devolution in the United Kingdom' p 83
[52] Belfast Newsletter, April 27, 1925
[53] CAB/4/154, NI Cabinet minutes 12 November 1925
[54] PRONI, CAB/9/H/5/1
[55] Ibid
[56] Royal Irish Academy Documents on Foreign Policy, MacNeill, E 'Statement to the Executive Council' 21 Nov 1925

[57] Royal Irish Academy Documents on Foreign Policy, Telegram from T.M. Healy to Leopold Amery (London) 25 November 1925
[58] Royal Irish Academy Documents on Foreign Policy, Minutes of a meeting between Stanley Baldwin, Kevin O'Higgins, Patrick McGilligan and John O'Byrne (Secret) (I.A (25) 6) 28 November 1925
[59] Bogdanor, V 'Devolution in the United Kingdom' p 79
[60] PRONI, CAB/4/203, NI Cabinet minutes 1 February 1928
[61] PRONI, GOV/3/6/7, Documents relating to the Laying of the Foundation Stone at Parliament Buildings, 19 May 1928
[62] Walker, Graham 'A History of the Ulster Unionist Party: Protest, Pragmatism and Pessimism: Protest, Pragmatism and Pessimism' pg. 78
[63] PRONI, CAB/4/215, NI Cabinet minutes 31 July 1928
[64] PRONI, CAB/4/218, NI Cabinet minutes 28 September 1928
[65] NAI, TSCH/3/98/6/434 'Briefing for An Taoiseach for a meeting with the British Prime Minister, 19 Dec 1966'
[66] R.J. Lawrence 'The Government of Northern Ireland: public finances and public services 1921-1964' pg. 112
[67] PRONI, CAB/4/262 – Cabinet minutes 4th June 1930
[68] Documents on Irish Foreign Policy, No. 617 NAI DFA 5/3
[69] Secretary of State for the Dominions, 'Mr Thomas to Mr De Valera (No. 69) 23 March 1932' Presented to Parliament 11 April 1932
[70] Belfast Newsletter, 3rd October 1932
[71] Bew, P 'The Unionist State and the Outdoor Relief Riots of 1932' Economic and Social Review, Vol 10, no. 3 April 1979 p262
[72] Belfast Newsletter, Monday November 7, 1932
[73] Norton, Christopher 'Creating Jobs, Manufacturing Unity: Ulster Unionism and Mass Unemployment 1922-1934', Contemporary British History, 15:2, 1-14, pg. 11
[74] Greer, P. E 'Road versus rail: documents on the history of public transport in Northern Ireland 1921-1948' pg. 30
[75] Commission of Inquiry Report on behalf of the National Council for Civil Liberties, 1936, page 41
[76] Northern Ireland Parliament, 26 May 1936
[77] Walker, Graham 'A History of the Ulster Unionist Party: Protest, Pragmatism and Pessimism: Protest, Pragmatism and Pessimism' pg. 88
[78] PRONI, CAB/4/446, NI Cabinet minutes 1 July 1940
[79] PRONI, CAB/4/454, NI Cabinet minutes 25 November 1940
[80] Brewer, J.D and Higgins, I 'Anti-Catholicism in Northern Ireland 1600-1998' Pg. 98
[81] Bardon, J 'A History of Ulster' pg. 591

[82] Walker, Graham 'A History of the Ulster Unionist Party: Protest, Pragmatism and Pessimism: Protest, Pragmatism and Pessimism' pg. 90
[83] 16 December 1941, Northern Ireland House of Commons Hansard
[84] PRONI, CAB/9/Q/9/39
[85] Lynn, Brendan 'Holding the ground: the nationalist party in Northern Ireland, 1945-72' pg. 21
[86] Brewer, J.D and Higgins, I 'Anti-Catholicism in Northern Ireland 1600-1998' Pg. 92
[87] Dáil Eireann, Vol 98 No. 10 col 1184
[88] Lynn, Brendan 'Holding the ground: the nationalist party in Northern Ireland, 1945-72' pg. 22
[89] Lynn, Brendan 'Holding the ground: the nationalist party in Northern Ireland, 1945-72' pg. 64
[90] PRONI, CAB/4/683, NI Cabinet minutes 26 August 1946
[91] R.J. Lawrence 'The Government of Northern Ireland: public finances and public services 1921-1964' pg. 121-22
[92] Lynn, Brendan 'Holding the ground: the nationalist party in Northern Ireland, 1945-72' pg. 45
[93] Donohue, L 'Regulating Northern Ireland: The Special Powers Acts 1922-1972' The Historical Journal, Vol. 41, No. 4 (Dec. 1998), p 1107
[94] Mulholland, M 'Northern Ireland at the Crossroads' pg. 17
[95] Mulholland, M 'Why Did Unionists Discriminate?' in Wichert, S 'From the United Irishmen to twentieth-century unionism: essays in honour of A.T.Q. Stewart' Pg. 14
[96] Walker, Graham 'A History of the Ulster Unionist Party: Protest, Pragmatism and Pessimism: Protest, Pragmatism and Pessimism' pg. 140
[97] Mulholland, M 'Why Did Unionists Discriminate?' in Wichert, S 'From the United Irishmen to twentieth-century unionism: essays in honour of A.T.Q. Stewart' Pg. 11
[98] PRONI, CAB/4/1203 – Cabinet minutes 3rd Oct 1962
[99] Mulholland, M 'Northern Ireland at the Crossroads' pg. 39
[100] Mulholland, M 'Why Did Unionists Discriminate?' in Wichert, S 'From the United Irishmen to twentieth-century unionism: essays in honour of A.T.Q. Stewart' Pg. 2
[101] Northern Ireland Parliament, 7 October 1965
[102] Walker, Graham 'A History of the Ulster Unionist Party: Protest, Pragmatism and Pessimism: Protest, Pragmatism and Pessimism' pg. 149
[103] Mulholland, M 'Northern Ireland at the Crossroads' pg. 30
[104] PRONI, CAB/4/1235
[105] Ibid
[106] PRONI, CAB/4/1271, NI Cabinet minutes 1 July 1964

[107] PRONI, CAB/4/1286 – Cabinet minutes 21st December 1964
[108] Brewer, J.D and Higgins, I 'Anti-Catholicism in Northern Ireland 1600-1998' Pg. 105
[109] Mulholland, M 'Why Did Unionists Discriminate?' in Wichert, S 'From the United Irishmen to twentieth-century unionism: essays in honour of A.T.Q. Stewart' Pg. 9
[110] PRONI, CAB/4/1312, NI Cabinet minutes 6 July 1965
[111] PRONI, CAB/4/1338/2, NI Cabinet minutes 9 August 1966
[112] PRONI, HA/32/2/27
[113] NAI, 2000/5/12
[114] PRONI, CAB 4/1413, NI Cabinet minutes 7 November 1968
[115] PRONI, CAB/4/1414/5, NI Cabinet minutes 14 November 1968
[116] PRONI, CAB/4/1418/11, NI Cabinet minutes 20 November 1968
[117] Bardon, J 'A History of Ulster' pg. 657
[118] PRONI, CAB/4/1425/12, NI Cabinet minutes 6 January 1969
[119] PRONI, CAB/4/1427
[120] PRONI, CAB/4/1427, NI Cabinet minutes 15 January 1969
[121] PRONI, HA/32/2/35, Security – Use of Army
[122] PRONI, HA/32/2/1
[123] Ibid
[124] HMSO, Disturbances in Northern Ireland Report of the Commission appointed by the Governor of Northern Ireland, 16 Aug 1969
[125] Mulholland, M 'Why Did Unionists Discriminate?' in Wichert, S 'From the United Irishmen to twentieth-century unionism: essays in honour of A.T.Q. Stewart' Pg. 3

Portraits of Viscount Craigavon, John Miller Andrews and Sir Henry Wilson which previously hung in Parliament Buildings are currently in storage and are used with the permission of, and following viewings by Mr Jim Allister QC MLA and Mr Sammy Morrison.

Bibliography

Akenson, Donald *'Education and Enmity: The Control of Schooling in Northern Ireland 1920-1950'* Newton Abbot, 1973

Bardon, Jonathan *'A History of Ulster'* Belfast, 1991

Bew, Paul "The Unionist State and the Outdoor Relief Riots of 1932" *Economic and Social Review,* Vol 10, No. 3, April, 1979, pp. 255-265.

Bew, Paul "The Political History of Northern Ireland since Partition: The Prospects for North-South Co-operation" *Proceedings of the British Academy,* 98, 401-418. The British Academy 1999.

Bogdanor, Vernon *'Devolution in the United Kingdom'* Oxford, 1998

Brewer, John D; Higgins, Gareth *'Anti-Catholicism in Northern Ireland, 1600-1998: the mote and the beam'* Belfast, 1998

Cusack, Jim and McDonald, Henry *'UVF, the Endgame'*, Dublin, 2000

Donohue, Laura "Regulating Northern Ireland: The Special Powers Acts 1922-1972" *The Historical Journal* Vol 41, No. 4, Dec 1998 pg. 1089-1120

Follis, Bryan *'A State Under Siege: The Establishment of Northern Ireland 1920-1925'* Oxford, 1995

Greer, P. Eugene *'Road versus rail: documents on the history of public transport in Northern Ireland 1921-1948'* Belfast, 1982

Goldstrom J.M et al *'Irish population, economy and society: Essays in honour of the late K.H Connell'* Oxford, 1982

Kenna, G.B *'Facts and Figures of the Belfast Pogrom 1920-1922,* Dublin, 1922

Maguire, Martin *'The civil service and the revolution in Ireland'* Manchester, 2008

Lawrence, R.J *'The Government of Northern Ireland: public finances and public services 1921-1964'* Oxford, 1965

Lynn, Brendan *'Holding the ground: the Nationalist Party in Northern Ireland'* Ashgate, 1997

Mulholland, M *'Northern at the Crossroads'* Ipswich, 2000

Mulholland, M "Why Did Unionists Discriminate?" In Wichert, S *'From the United Irishmen to twentieth-century unionism: essays in honour of A.T.Q Stewart'* Dublin, 2004

Norton, Christopher *'Creating jobs, manufacturing unity: Ulster unionism and mass unemployment 1922-1934'* in A O'Day and NC Fleming (eds) Ireland and Anglo-Irish Relations Since 1800: Critical Essays, Volume III: From the Treaty to 2006 (Aldershot, Ashgate, 2008)

O'Brien, John *'Discrimination in Northern Ireland 1920-1939: Myth or reality?'* Cambridge, 2010

Ó Murchu, Niall "Ethnic politics and labour market closure: shipbuilding and industrial decline in Northern Ireland" *Ethnic and Racial Studies* Vol 28 2005 pg859-879

Walker, Graham *'A History of the Ulster Unionist Party: Protest, Pragmatism and Pessimism'* Manchester, 2001

Printed in Great Britain
by Amazon